BY THE GRACE OF GOD

BY THE GRACE OF GOD

A True Story of Love, Family, War and Survival From the Congo

by

Suruba Ibumando Georgette Wechsler
with Howell Wechsler

New Horizon Press
Far Hills, NJ

For Susan, Ben & Adam,

Do I have to tell you how much I feel blessed to have you in my life? You know that. Love you lots of love, happiness & JOY!

Love Suruba Wechsler

Feb 22, '99

Requests for permission should be addressed to:
New Horizon Press
P.O. Box 669
Far Hills, NJ 07931

Suruba Ibumando Georgette Wechsler with Howell Wechsler
By the Grace of God: A True Story of Love, Family, War, and Survival from the Congo

Interior Design: Susan Sanderson

Library of Congress Catalog Card Number: 98-66170

ISBN: 0-88282-171-7

New Horizon Press
Manufactured in U.S.A.

2003   2002   2001   2000   1999 / 5   4   3   2   1

CONTENTS

ACKNOWLEDGMENTS

Thank you to my family in Congo and my families in the United States. I hope this story shows how grateful I am for all you have done and continue to do to make my life very special; to my friends for their support, especially the Zaban moms, who were the first audience for this book and who believed so much in me and my work; to my publisher, Joan Dunphy, who gave me the chance to tell my story and who has been a pleasure to work with; to my husband and children for helping so much around the house and putting up with me as I devoted so much time to this project; to Sandra, Bob, and Rocky, who will through this book, I hope, come to appreciate even more how lucky they were to have had my sister as their mother; to Alex and Tatiana, who will through this book, I hope, come to cherish their grandfather and the memory of their mother's sister; and to Howell, my partner in writing and in life, for his devoted, unconditional support and for always finding the right words.

Suruba Wechsler

AUTHOR'S NOTE

These are the actual experiences and personal history of Suruba Ibumando Georgette Wechsler and this book reflects her opinions of the past, present, and future. The personalities, events, actions, and conversations portrayed within the story have been reconstructed from her memory, documents, letters, personal papers, press accounts, and the memories of other participants. In an effort to safeguard the privacy of certain individuals, the author has changed their names and, in some cases, altered otherwise identifying characteristics. Events involving the characters happened as described; only minor details have been changed.

PROLOGUE

The taxi driver slammed on his brakes at the first loud boom. Josée and I jolted forward toward the front of the car. The driver stuck his head out of the window to see and hear as much as possible, to confirm that he had indeed heard what he thought he had heard. Josée and I just looked at each other. We needed no confirmation, we knew what the sound was and we knew what it meant.

It was thirty years earlier that we had first heard the roar of cannons and the *ratatata* of automatic gunfire. Josée had tightly held the hand of her mischievous five-year-old sister, as we raced through a town suddenly engulfed in civil war. With gunfire echoing on all sides, we saw what those loud noises led to: corpses lying still under the equatorial sun, with gaping holes in their bodies and hordes of flies feasting on the remains; the moaning, agonizing wounded, crying out for help, splashing the pools of blood by their sides; the look of fear on the face of the man sprawled motionless under the tree and the realization that this was a familiar face, the face of a family friend, a face I would never see again; my brave Papa waving from the riverbank just before the sniper's bullet sent him flying into the water; the endless marching, with next to nothing to eat, with no shelter to protect us from the sun and the rain, with the only thought in mind being to get away from those noises, to find a place where we could be safe.

A series of booms, each louder than the first one, pushed the taxi driver to decisiveness. "I'm sorry, ladies. There's shooting going on downtown. We can't go any further."

Josée, ever the older sister, took charge. She quickly gave the driver the address of a friend who lived in the direction from which we had just come. How could she do that? I thought. How could we stop and turn around? We needed to drive forward through the downtown area, shooting or no shooting. That was the only way to get to the house where Josée's three children and my twenty-one-month-old son awaited us. I had to get to my baby, I had to see that he was safe, I had to do all I could to protect him, just as Papa had done all he could to protect us. We were the grown-ups this time; we were the ones who needed to risk all to save our children. I would not let my boy live through what I had lived through, I would have to find some way to get him out of danger. This wasn't even his country, this wasn't his war. He needed to be home, safe with his American father, far from this madness.

Josée sensed my distress and grabbed my hand. "The children will be fine," she said softly. "There won't be any fighting so far from downtown. We need to avoid the fighting so we can get safely to them."

She was right, of course. We had learned a lot about surviving, and it was time to apply those lessons. So, after arriving at Josée's friend's house, we spent the next few hours crouched on the floor, down low to avoid any bullets that might crash through the windows. One of the keys to survival was having the patience to wait out the fighting. The neighborhood was calm, and we grew optimistic that perhaps this wouldn't be the start of the Big One, the Great Rebellion. Not that we weren't looking forward to the results of the Great Rebellion: twenty-six years of hopelessly corrupt tyranny were more than any people should endure. But we wanted the change to come without the bloodshed, the terror that had convulsed our nation in the early 1960s.

As the hours passed and we were spared, I became calmer. I smiled as I realized how near we were to the American Consulate. They knew we were in town, they would help my baby and me get out of the country.

Then I looked at Josée, who had always been for me big sister, role model, best friend, and the closest thing I ever had to a mother. She had no way out, no way out of the country, no way out of the impending war, and, worst of all, no way out of the nightmare that threatened to take her from us much too soon. At the sight of tears in my eyes, Josée leaned toward me with a comforting smile. She must have thought I was still anxious about my baby.

"Just a couple more days," she said cheerfully, "and you'll be back in New York waving at that Statue of Liberty." She was trying her best to give me hope.

Then I remembered that one of the main reasons I had taken the long voyage back to the land of my birth was to give her hope. I smiled back at her and reminded myself that there was always reason to hope. It was, after all, only by the grace of God that we had survived the wars that occurred during our childhood. Maybe there were a few more miracles left for us.

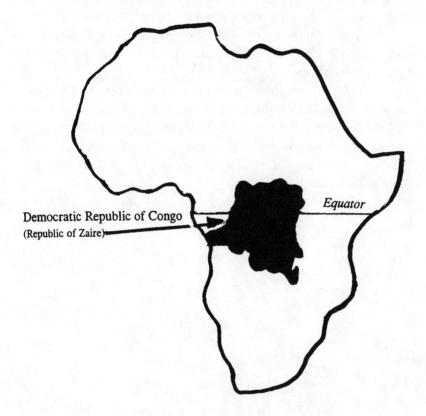

Congo is located in the very center, the heart, of Africa.

CHAPTER 1

A MATCH MADE IN PRISON

The story begins in early 1952 in the city of Albertville in the province of Katanga in the country known to the world as the Belgian Congo, located right in the center, the heart of Africa. Today, the city is called Kalemie. The province was called, for a lost generation, Shaba, but it is now known once again as Katanga. The country became the Democratic Republic of Congo and then, for that same lost generation, the Republic of Zaire. It is now once again the Democratic Republic of Congo.

Names come and names go, but the character of a good person remains constant.

She was the most unusual prisoner he had ever seen. As deputy warden at Albertville's central prison, Corporal Suruba Benoit had seen Congolese imprisoned for all kinds of reasons: theft, murder, fraud, drunkenness, paganism. But this was the first time he had seen a woman imprisoned because she insisted on getting a divorce from a violently abusive husband. It was painful, having to help enforce these obscene colonial laws.

Benoit's father, Mava Mazambula Andingba Suruba, was the sultan, or chief, of the village of Kopa in *Congo Oriental* [Eastern Congo] province. Sultan Mava Mazambula was born near the turn of the century, when the great European powers were letting King Leopold of Belgium rule the Congo as his own private dominion. It wasn't until 1908, after numerous reports of the countless atrocities and brutal exploitation of the land's immense natural resources committed by Leopold's henchmen, that the Belgian government stepped in and made the Congo an official, government-managed colony.

Sultan Mava Mazambula had reason to distrust and fear the white men who ruled his land. But he accepted their system and wanted to succeed as best he could within it. The key to success, he understood clearly, was getting the white man's education for his children. His first son, Benoit, was extremely intelligent, and the local missionaries, ever anxious to co-opt indigenous authorities, encouraged the Sultan to send Benoit to the Marist seminary in Paulis (now Isiro). This was a great honor, as there weren't many Congolese priests at the time and being a priest was about as powerful as a Congolese could get in the rigidly paternalistic Belgian colonial system. Unlike the British and French, the Belgian colonialists did not try to create a sympathetic African elite by allowing bright students to study at the university level; indeed, they made it next to impossible for most Congolese to go past even the primary school level.

Benoit was delighted by the chance to continue his studies at the seminary. He looked forward to a priest's life of comfort and prestige, and he was anxious to serve the God of the Catholic Church and His Son, Jesus Christ. He knew that the missionaries had done many good things in Congo, such as ending the terrible local custom of burying alive a sultan's youngest wife as part of a sultan's funeral to help take care of him in the afterlife.

In the seminary, however, Benoit found one discrepancy after another between the teachings of the Church and the reality of how the Belgian priests actually dealt with the Congolese people. They promised the "natives" wonders of wonders to come in the afterlife—but did little to help the people have an easier time in this life. They talked of one universal Church for all mankind—while living in separate rectories, apart from the Congolese priests. They preached about the "savage" Congolese customs that had to be abandoned—while helping the government torture people for maintaining customs that promoted social and environmental harmony and justice. Benoit himself had seen people flogged to death for following their traditions by worshiping their ancestors. All this, in the name of Jesus Christ our Savior.

Benoit was a tolerant young man with great patience. But somehow, somewhere he had developed an abiding hatred for hypocrisy. And so, after completing all the required studies, he gave up the great power of a life in the priesthood. The Belgian authorities did not take kindly to the idea of a sultan's son abandoning the priesthood. As punishment, he was drafted into the Congolese army and ordered to serve in the faraway land of Katanga, where the people spoke languages he couldn't understand and had customs he couldn't recognize. Albertville was about six hundred miles away from his home village, but it might as well have been ten thousand. He had no possibility of speaking with his parents; the telephone and telegraph systems were only for the use of the colonial officials and priests. Letters took months to get to his village. Any leaves of duty that he might have had didn't allow him enough time to get home for a visit and back in time to resume his duty. So, Suruba Benoit became a stranger in a strange land. He would never return home to see his family.

By 1952, he was a twenty-six-year-old corporal who had been working in the Albertville prison for over a year. The prisoner who changed his life, the one jailed for demanding a divorce, was twenty-seven-year-old Mtono Thérèse. With her in prison was her baby daughter Charlotte, only a few months old.

Thérèse's father, Mtono Augustin, was the grandson of *Capitaine* Joubert, a French sailor who came in the late 19th century to help the missionaries bring "civilization" and Catholicism to the natives of the Congo. Joubert settled in northeastern Katanga and married a sultan's daughter, with whom he had twelve children. Both of Thérèse's parents were literate, educated people at a time when most of the population was kept illiterate and uneducated. Mtono Augustin was a nurse, and his wife, Marguerite, was a teacher. Naturally, they wanted their children to marry only literate people. The Congolese had a term for people who could read, who might have finished primary school, who had white-collar jobs. They called their new elite *les évolués*, the evolved ones. They were limited in number, *les évolués*. After all, the Belgians had no plans for ever letting the Congolese govern themselves. The natives would be kept in their place, and their place was meant to be forever inferior.

Thérèse's husband, Kalundi Albert, was surely an *évolué:* he came from an educated family and worked as an administrative clerk in the largest city of Katanga, Elisabethville (also known at the time as E'ville and now known as Lubumbashi). Following the custom of the times, the marriage was arranged by the parents; the bride and groom didn't even meet each other until just before the wedding.

Thérèse was impressed by Albert's intelligence, and, gradually, she grew to care for him. But her world started to fall apart after the couple had their second child. Albert began to drink a little too much a little too often, and with the drinking came verbal abuse of his wife. When Thérèse asked him to drink less, the verbal abuse became physical: he began to beat her on a regular basis. Thérèse, whose father had never once struck his wife, complained to Albert's family and to her own relatives in E'ville. But it was to no avail.

"That's how men are. You have to be patient," she was told every time.

After Albert's company transferred him to Albertville, the abuse continued. Thérèse was a devout Catholic, but, after suffering a broken nose and an assortment of scars and bruises, she asked Albert for a divorce. His response was to laugh, for he had no intention of letting her go. She was his wife, and he could do with her whatever he pleased. He knew that the Belgian authorities, influenced by the Catholic prohibition of divorce, made it next to impossible for a woman to end her marriage.

Pregnant with her fourth child, Thérèse could not endure her unhappiness any longer. She took her case to court, where she was told to think it over until the baby was born. When the baby was a few months old, she went back to court and insisted again on getting a divorce. The court told Thérèse that divorce was a criminal act, and she'd have to go to prison to get one. She called their bluff, and they sentenced her to three months behind bars.

She was serving her time in the Albertville prison, when Corporal Suruba Benoit took an interest in her. Despite the scars and bruises on her face, she was still a very beautiful woman. He couldn't understand how any man could treat a woman as Albert had treated Thérèse. Benoit went out of his way to visit her every day. Thérèse had entered prison with no interest left in men, but Benoit won her over by remembering, at every visit, to bring something special for the baby. It didn't hurt, of course, that he was a very attractive man. He stood about five feet, nine inches tall, with a lean, well-toned body. His stomach was flat, and his biceps bulged with power. His face was smooth, almost boyish, and his features quite handsome. He walked with great confidence and authority, just what one would expect of a sultan's son. For the first time in her life, Thérèse was in love.

After three months, Thérèse was liberated from prison and her marriage. Her freedom from Albert, however, came at a heavy price: under the patrilineal system installed by the Belgians, Albert got custody of their three older children. Thérèse lived with an uncle in Albertville and got a job as a teacher at a community center, where she soon became assistant director.

Benoit visited her regularly, and, no longer bound by military restrictions on contact between prison staff and inmates, he was free to declare his love. When Benoit proposed marriage, Thérèse readily accepted. The Church would not marry a divorcée; so they had a civil ceremony. Soon after, Benoit completed the final year he was required to serve in the army. Now preoccupied with supporting a family, Benoit decided not to enlist for another tour of duty. There was no hope of a better life in the army, no matter how bright and experienced you were. Only Belgians got promoted to leadership positions, that was black and white in the colonial army code. In the private sector, segregation between blacks and whites was the rule, but there were still opportunities for a black man to make a good living. And you could work for companies headed by other Europeans, such as Portuguese, Greeks, or Frenchmen, whose bigotry seemed less rigid than that of the Belgians.

Benoit got a job as an accountant for INTERFINA, a large trading company, in the town of Kongolo, about 150 miles west of Albertville and 450 miles north of E'ville. Kongolo was the administrative center of north central Katanga, with a population of about 15,000 Congolese and 300 expatriates, mostly Belgians, with some Greeks, Arabs, and Pakistanis. Like all Congolese cities, it was divided into a downtown area, where the major stores and businesses were located and where all the white businessmen and a handful of wealthy Congolese lived, and the neighborhoods of simple clay brick houses, most with straw roofs, where the overwhelming majority of the Congolese lived. The Kongolo area was well-known for its production of corn and fish. Two rivers bounded the city: the Kangoy, a minor tributary, fed into the much larger Lualaba, which about 400 miles downstream became the mighty Congo River that flowed through much of the country all the way to the Atlantic Ocean. River travel between Kongolo and the downstream ports, however, was impossible; about thirty miles north of Kongolo, the Lualaba became unnavigable due to a series of thunderous rapids and gorges that had come to be known as *Les Portes d'Enfer* [The Gates of Hell].

It was in Kongolo that Benoit and Thérèse happily started their life together as husband and wife. A few months later, on March 24, 1953, a hefty baby girl weighing more than ten pounds was born at Kongolo's General Hospital. Her name was Marie-Joséphine Kanero, and they came to call her Josée. Almost three years later at the same hospital, on January 18, 1956, I came into the world.

CHAPTER 2

THE LION SLAYER

It was raining hard one Sunday in early 1960 soon after my fourth birthday. Six-year-old Josée and I were home alone with Papa. It was over a year since the divorce, when Maman left us.

Josée and I loved the rain. We would play in the rainwater by the patio sometimes in our underwear and sometimes just in our birth suits. But that day, small rocks were pinging to the ground. Papa's voice was unaccustomly stern.

"No playing outside today," he said, strongly emphasizing the "No" and looking straight at me. "It's very dangerous. You see those ice balls falling? Well, they can hurt you real bad."

"Papa, what if we just pick up the little ice balls on the patio, please," pleaded Josée with her most angelic voice. "Geolo and I like them, please!" Josée had trouble pronouncing my name, so she settled on calling me "Geolo."

"All right," said Papa, "but not beyond the patio. Do you hear me, Georgette?" I nodded yes.

Josée and I each grabbed a cup, and iceballs hunting we went. Josée, of course, was bigger, stronger, and quicker than I, so she soon had a lot more iceballs. I spied a bunch of big ones just a little bit beyond the patio, then turned around to see if Papa was looking. The coast was clear. I dropped my cup and took a step beyond the patio, then another step, then a few more. The rain came down hard on me once I was beyond the partial shelter of the walls of our house. But I didn't mind, I was getting some of the best ice balls anyone could get. I stuffed the ones I couldn't hold into my pockets. My clothes were soaked, but I was so happy I began to do a little dance. I giggled, jumped in the air, turned to show off my prize finds to Josée—and saw Papa, standing on the patio staring at me ever-so-sternly. He beckoned me with one finger and I sheepishly went back to the house.

"What am I going to do with you, Georgette, what am I ever going to do with you?" Papa said, as he helped me change my clothes. "One day I might just have to sell you to my friends, the pygmies."

I checked to see if Papa was serious, but he had that loving smile on his face, so I knew I was safe for another day, at least. Not only was I out of danger, but it was my favorite time of day—lunch time. Papa took great pleasure in cooking for us on Sundays.

"I know you two like rice very much, that's why today I made a special dish of rice and guess what?"

Josée and I tried to guess. "Is it rice with goat meat? Cow meat? Sheep meat? Peanut sauce?"

"Noooo. I'm making you rice with *sombe* [cassava leaves] just the way Maman used to make it. So, what do you say?"

"Yippee," Josée and I shouted in unison. It had been a long time since we had had *sombe* cooked that way.

"Josée and I will have our lunch on the floor with you, Georgette," said Papa.

What a wonderful day! Papa didn't let me sit at the table with him and Josée, because I never sat still and usually wound up falling off my chair or spilling all my food. But that day they joined me on the floor. Of course, I went and ruined it with my non-stop fidgeting: before lunch had ended, I managed to knock over the bowl of *sombe*, spilling all its contents onto Josée's lap. By the time Josée changed her dress and Papa finished scolding me, the rain had stopped, and Josée and I flew outside to play with our friends.

We played jump rope, pattycake, and over and over again, we played *kange*. *Kange* begins when the captains of each of two teams choose their team's sign—either arms crossed or arms straight out. The two teams line up facing each other. Everyone sings the *kange* song, then the first two players start clapping hands and jumping up and down. At a certain point in the song, the players kick a leg out. If they kick out legs on the same side, the arms-straight-out team wins the round. If they kick out opposite legs, the team with arms crossed wins. The losers of each round are eliminated from the game, and a team loses when all its players are out.

We were almost always outside playing, even at night. On dark nights or rainy days, we'd play inside or dance to music from the radio or Papa's wind-up phonograph. The radio and phonograph were luxury items in Kongolo, very few people had such treasures. Of course, even we didn't have a television. In fact, nobody in town had television. No video games, no dolls that cry, no battery-powered toy trucks to control. Oh, but what entertainment we did have—children, lots of creative, imaginative, fun-loving children with whom we could play at just about any time. And when the other children had to go inside their homes, we always had each other: I had my big sister Josée, and she had her most devoted copycat.

Play time finally ended that Sunday when Papa called us home for bathtime. He filled our "tub"—an empty barrel cut in half—and, after hearing a great deal of begging and pleading, he gave us some time to play with dolls before washing us. While we ate a light supper, Papa saw that I was a little troubled and asked what was bothering me.

"Papa, Henri was making fun of us. He said that we must be pygmies, because we go see your pygmy friends."

Papa laughed. "We're not pygmies, Georgette. But you tell Henri that if we were pygmies, that would be just fine. Pygmies are people just like the rest of us. It's wrong to treat them badly just because they're smaller than us and look a little different. If they're here, it's because God wants them here. Do you understand, Georgette?"

"Yes, Papa," and my worries vanished just like that.

After supper, we headed for bed and story time. "Now what story do you want to hear tonight?" Papa asked, though he must have known what our answer would be.

"The lion story, tell us the lion story," we both responded.

"Oh no. I've told you that so many times."

"Please, Papa. The lion story, we want the lion story," we cried out, as if we had never heard it before, as if we hadn't heard it every night that week.

"Alright, alright," Papa said with a grin. "I'll tell you the lion story—just one more time. But I want you under the blanket and ready for sleep as soon as I finish." We instantly complied with his command, and Papa began the tale.

It was a true story from when Papa was in the army. Some villagers in the town of Baudouinville (now Moba) had been killed by lions while working in their fields. Papa was sent to investigate the area, along with two other soldiers. Hours passed, and there was no sight of a lion. When the sun was starting to set, Papa went off for one last patrol around the area. As he walked, he suddenly heard a roar—and it was coming from somewhere close! He thought of climbing up a tree, but there wasn't one nearby. He called out loudly for the other soldiers, but they didn't answer. They weren't that far away, they should have heard him. Papa realized then that his helpers might have run away when they heard the lion's roars. He stood by the path and faced the direction from which the roars had originated.

With his rifle ready, he watched a furry golden head move lazily in his direction. Papa called out again for his helpers but again there was no answer. He knew he was alone, it was all up to him to stop the man-eating lion. The lion was now near Papa. It lifted its head and stared in Papa's direction, then started to accelerate its pace. It was racing right at Papa! Papa knew that he no longer had time to hide, he either was going to kill the lion or be killed by it. Papa raised his rifle, closed one eye, and aimed for the lion's head. When the lion got so close he could smell its breath, just when it seemed ready to pounce, Papa pulled the trigger. Down went the lion! Hooray for Papa! And where were the other soldiers? They were up in a tree the whole time, too scared to come down and help Papa. When they did come down, they told Papa that they thought the lion had eaten him! As we closed our eyes to sleep on that Sunday night—and every night—Josée and I thanked God that they were wrong.

Only a few hazy memories remain from the first few years of my life, when Maman lived with us, though it's hard to say which ones are actual remembrances and which have been imprinted in my mind by stories told again and again over the years by family members. I remember her taking us to church every Sunday—that was very important to her. Papa would always stay home.

I also remember how Maman saved my life one afternoon. Josée was playing across the street with our Arab friends, while I had to stay with Maman in our yard. I could hear Josée and the others shouting and giggling. I could picture them under the shade of the acacia tree near the concrete fence entrance. That was where we often played while Maman and her friends sat and chatted on the porch. If I could only get to the compound entrance and push open the door, I would get to play with the others. One big problem: a street in the middle. Many times Papa had told us not to cross it without an adult, but my legs were irresistibly taking me in that direction.

When Maman was concentrating on her sewing, I slipped out of our compound and into the street. In the middle of the street, I looked to my right and saw a car that was getting bigger and bigger. I stopped and stared at it. Was it Papa coming home? It sure looked like Papa's car, a black and white Impala whose rear moved up and down just like a duck's tail.

The big car started honking, but I was glued to the ground. People were screaming, but I just couldn't move. Then, suddenly, two hands whisked me around and lifted me up and off the road. It was Maman! She held me tight and apologized to the driver, who had screeched to a stop. The clothes she had been sewing were scattered on the ground as she had tossed them aside to rush to my rescue.

After that incident, Maman tied me to a long rope whenever she was sewing or busy with something and Josée wasn't there to keep an eye on me. One end of the rope was tied to my waist and the other end to the papaya tree in our yard. The cord was long enough to take me up to the acacia tree in front of our compound yet short enough to keep me from the street. Josée said that I looked like a dog on a leash.

Most of all, I remember the day Maman came home after being away for a long time—and I didn't even know who she was. First, Maman left for a few weeks to go to Albertville, where her ex-husband had gone to court to reclaim their youngest daughter, Charlotte, who had been living with us; the court ruled that she was old enough to go live with her father. That seemed kind of funny because Maman's other children weren't even staying with their father; they were with their paternal aunts and uncles. Albert's drinking problems had never stopped. It must have hurt Maman so much to give up her child, and to see her other children who had been taken away from her for no good reason. When Maman came back from that trip, something changed between her and Papa. Soon after, she left again, but this time she stayed away for a couple of months. Josée kept on asking Papa when Maman would be back. I also used to ask in the beginning, but then I started to forget about her.

A while later, Papa told us that Maman would probably not come back to live with us. Josée was furious at Papa. He tried to explain that sometimes things don't work out between a man and a woman and they have to go their own ways, but Josée didn't want to listen.

More months went by and then, one day, like in a dream, I saw Josée jumping up and down in front of a car. There was a very beautiful lady inside.

"Maman, Maman is back, Maman is back. I knew you'd come back!" Josée shouted. She was so excited she didn't realize that she was holding the car door shut on the side in which the lady was sitting.

"Watch out, Josée! Let me open the door," the lady said. Josée finally moved to the side and let her out.

"Josée, come here! Where is Georgette?"

She lifted up Josée, who wrapped her arms around the lady's neck. The lady was now apparently searching with her eyes for me. How come she knew my name, I asked myself, and when did Josée meet this lady? She seemed very nice and beautiful. Who was she? Her voice, even her face reminded me of somebody.

"Geolo, Maman is back!" Josée shouted. "Maman is here!" Then the lady headed in my direction.

"Georgette, don't you remember me any more?" the lady asked, looking straight in my eyes.

She had tears in her eyes as she realized that I took her for a stranger. Suddenly, it started to sink in. This beautiful lady was our mother whom Josée was always talking about. She was back. Where had she been? She put Josée down and picked me up.

Josée said that Maman and Papa were going to try to be married again. Maman stayed with us for about a month. Then one morning we woke up and she was gone. Papa told us that Maman had left for good. They had decided to get a divorce instead of turning into enemies. She would write to us all the time, he assured us. And sometimes, he said, she would come to visit. Ten years passed before I would see her again.

One day, Papa told Josée and me that we would have another mother, Mama Apoline. Many years later I learned that Papa had become friendly with Mama Apoline before Maman left and realized that she was one reason why Maman left. Mama Apoline started visiting us every day; she was very friendly, even though Josée was not so friendly to her.

"Why are you here?" Josée would taunt her. "You know our mother went to Albertville. She will be back, you know. Papa says you'll be our mother. I know you are not our mother. Our mother's name is Thérèse, Mtono Thérèse. We really don't need another!"

Mama Apoline came to live with us for good in 1960 when I was four years old. Along with her came her daughter Marie, who was a couple of months younger than me, and our baby brother Benjamin, who Mama Apoline and Papa had had in late 1959. Mama Apoline also had two other sons, Jean-Paul N'Kongolo, who was a couple of months older than Josée, and Gilbert, who was in his early teens. Her two sons lived with her mother, Colette, on *Avenue Kindu* on the other side of town. We called her *kambo* [grandma].

Although Josée longed for our own Maman to return home, we were happy to have a big family. We loved holding our baby brother and teaching him how to crawl and walk. With Marie and N'Kongolo we had two more partners in play. Marie was the sweetest little girl in the world—until she lost her temper. She had the unpleasant habit of sinking her teeth into anyone who made her angry. N'Kongolo, on the other hand, was a happy-go-lucky boy who would only lose his cool when Mama Apoline or *kambo* insisted that he take a bath. As for Gilbert, he liked to think that he was a grown-up, so he didn't pay much attention to us little kids. When it rained and he had to be inside with us, he would tell us scary ghost stories. Sometimes, he told us about the things that men and women do when they close the bedroom door and take their clothes off.

Perhaps our favorite addition to the family was *kambo* Colette, Mama Apoline's mother. She obviously had a soft spot in her heart for girls, and she was delighted to have two ready-made granddaughters.

"I'm not your real *kambo*," she would say, "but I love you just like my own." She seemed so happy when she showed Josée, Marie, and me how to cook and clean and make raffia baskets.

We lived in Kangoy Neighborhood, on *Avenue des Fonds d'Avance,* near the city limits: three houses down, the street became just a little dirt path leading to wells and fields of crops. Our house had a roof made of straw, walls made of earthen bricks, a smooth concrete floor, and a kitchen with a separate entrance. The toilet was in an out-house that also doubled as a shower. We had running water but no electricity.

It was a very modest house considering my father's social sta-tus in the town of Kongolo. A few months after I was born, Papa left INTERFINA for an even better job as accountant-manager for TRANGEN, an import-export company owned by Greeks. Papa's jobs were usually held by Belgians or some other white expatriates. Because of that, and also the fact that he came from another province, local people very often referred to him as *muzungu* [white man] or *colon* [colonist], names given to Belgians in the Congo. Papa didn't appreciate those nicknames; he didn't like to be seen as an outsider. Little did he know that being seen as an outsider would soon put his life in mortal danger.

When TRANGEN's owner, Constantinides Papadopoulous, moved to Albertville in late 1960, he appointed Papa as head of TRAN-GEN's Kongolo Division.

"*Monsieur* Constantinides has asked me to move into his two story house downtown," Papa told us with great pride. "He wants me to be near the center of business activities."

Josée and I were thrilled to go live in a two-story building. Why, it was the tallest building in town! Mama Apoline couldn't believe her good fortune. Not only had she married a *kalani* [a well-educated man with a good job], but she was also going to live in a lux-urious home! She couldn't believe that *Monsieur* Benoit would leave his beautiful wife for her. But he did, though Apoline was still troubled by the ongoing correspondence between Benoit and Thérèse. Apoline must have known that, even though Benoit and Thérèse were sepa-rated, there was still something between them. And Josée worked hard to make sure she never forgot it.

One night, when I was five, Josée and I overheard Mama

Apoline arguing with Papa. The next morning, after Papa had left for work, Josée and I went after Mama Apoline.

"We heard you quarreling with Papa last night. Why were you fighting?" Josée asked. "Are you getting a divorce?"

"No," said Mama Apoline patiently. "Sometimes people have arguments, that's all."

"Are you going back to *kambo* on *Avenue Kindu*?" I asked her. "No."

"Why not?" asked Josée, "Why don't you want to go back to your home?"

"No, my home is now here. That's why I stay here."

"What if Papa tells you to go back to your parents, will you go then?" asked Josée.

"No, I'll stay right here."

"What if Papa breaks the house?" I asked.

"I'll still stay," Mama Apoline replied calmly.

"Why don't you want to go back to your parents?" Josée asked.

"Well, your father is now my parents. That's why I'll stay."

"You know what?" Josée said, pulling out her trump card. "One day, Maman will come back!"

Josée still remembered Maman vividly. Papa showed her all the letters that Maman wrote him. There were hazy flashes of her in my memory. But I didn't really understand how we could have one mother here and then another in some other place. Mama Apoline was our mother. The other mother that Josée and Papa talked about sounded to me like a fairy tale character from a faraway land.

Years later, when I took catechism classes for my first communion, I discovered that, to have us baptized, Maman had put down the name of Albert Kalundi, her ex-husband, as our father. Only her first marriage to Albert Kalundi was recognized as being valid by the Catholic Church. Therefore, her marriage to Papa was, according to the Church, "concubinage." Josée and I were considered by the Church to be children born out of wedlock. Bastards!

I remember angrily crossing out the name of Albert Kalundi in my baptism booklet. "Wrong, Father," I said to the priest, "As you all know very well, my father is *Monsieur* Benoit, Suruba Benoit. Please change it in your records." Josée, who had had her communion years before, wasn't pleased either. We asked the priest to cancel our baptisms.

"A baptism is still valid. We can't cancel it," said the exasperated priest. Josée and I then asked Papa how he could have let them list Albert Kalundi as our father.

"It meant a lot to your mother that you get baptized. She insisted you two get baptized. There's nothing else to it," Papa said. "You know who your father is, don't you? Don't you let that trouble you."

"Is that why you don't go to church, Papa?" asked Josée.

"No, it's not really that. It's many other things. But I want you to go. I did when I was younger. It will help you later in your lives."

"Does Father Michel get angry at you for not going to church?" I asked. Father Michel Vanduffel, a Belgian priest, was a good friend who often came to visit Papa at home.

"Why do you bother your Papa with so many questions?" Mama Apoline interrupted.

"It's okay," Papa cut her off with no hesitation. "How else are they going to learn?"

"But they have to learn not to bother you with every little thought that comes into their heads. They owe you more respect than that," Mama Apoline said with great certainty.

Papa just smiled at her. He turned toward me and said softly, "Father Michel isn't very happy about me not going to mass, but he is very happy that I send you girls to church."

Mama Apoline shook her head and walked away. Poor Mama Apoline. She never understood where Papa was taking us with all those questions and answers. But he did. Though we were children—girls at that—and born in a country where females were valued more for the dowry they would bring in, Papa had a vision for us and he was beginning to shape it.

CHAPTER 3

FREEDOM

"Lipanda!
Uhuru!"

All over Kongolo people were shouting those two magical words. *Lipanda* was our local patois' transformation of the French: *l'indépendence. Uhuru* was our own precious kiSwahili word for *la liberté*–freedom. Those who weren't shouting *lipanda* and *uhuru* were making the joyful sound of *bikelekele* [a noise made by flipping the tongue quickly up and down while moving one or two hands over the mouth]. It was bigger than Christmas and New Year's, bigger than the biggest party I had ever seen.

It was June 30, 1960. Congo had become an independent nation, free from Belgian colonial rule. The Congolese people had gained the freedom to guide their own destiny. Sort of. Despite independence, Belgians were left in charge of the military, the mines, the plantations, and just about everything else that mattered. That might have worked out, if they hadn't started rubbing it in. Just a few days after independence, the Belgian commander of the army laid out the facts of life as he saw it to his Congolese subordinates: at a staff meeting, he wrote on a blackboard, "Before independence = After independence."

The Congolese soldiers mutinied against their arrogant Belgian officers. Against the wishes of the Congolese government, Belgium then sent troops into the newly independent nation to end the soldiers' mutiny. Our first Prime Minister, Patrice Lumumba, tried to resolve the crisis by appointing his uncle, Victor Lundula, commander in chief of the army. To the key position of army chief of staff, Lumumba appointed a friend of his, a young Congolese named Joseph Desiré Mobutu.

Everything soon spiraled out of control for the new nation. And nowhere was it more out of control than in my home region of Katanga. The most powerful political party in Katanga, the *Confédération des Associations Tribales du Katanga* (Confederation of Tribal Associations of Katanga or *CONAKAT)*, was greatly influenced by Belgians who were trying to maintain their control over Katanga's immense mineral wealth. Just eleven days after independence, *CONAKAT*'s leader, Moïse Tshombe, declared Katanga independent from the rest of the nation. Tshombe had strong support from Belgian settlers and mercenaries, as well as many Katangese. Fighting broke out in the large cities, but it all seemed far away from our life in Kongolo. Papa said it would all be settled long before any violence spread to a small town like Kongolo, so far from the center of power and wealth.

Nothing really seemed to change much in our lives those first few months after independence. I was much more pre-occupied with my own, very personal Congo crisis than I was with the national turmoil that had become the number one news story throughout the world. How could fighting in far-away cities compete for my attention with the daily terror I faced as I began my academic career in the preschool class at the Kangoy Parish school. Her name was Sister Emilie.

Like almost all the schools in the Belgian Congo, ours was run by the Church, and most of the teachers were priests and nuns; some were white and others, like Sister Emilie, were Congolese. I had been so excited to start school, but Sister Emilie demanded full obedience and complete submission—alien concepts for me. I got in trouble from day one. After having us recite Hail Mary and Our Father, Sister Emilie began laying down her laws: "After you sit down, you must cross your hands on your desks at all times and look toward the blackboard." She continued by reciting an endless string of rules and warned that we must strictly obey each and every one. Or else. Nobody was allowed to move unless Sister Emilie called out his or her name. Nobody was allowed to ask questions. Students could raise their hands only to answer her questions.

Was she serious? How could I just cross my hands and not do anything at all? How could I not ask questions? Papa let us ask questions all the time.That's how we learn, he always told us. I couldn't understand why I had to follow all these crazy rules. But since everyone else was sitting still, I tried to do the same.

Our first lesson was "reading": Sister Emilie read a French children's book to us and we had to memorize and chant back to her what she had read. After we finished the story, she explained it to us in kiSwahili. Somehow this failed to hold my attention. Soon my eyes went to work. I spied the ink well on my desk, and, before I could remind myself of the "no move" rule, my hands got hold of it.

Suddenly, I heard Sister Emilie shriek, "Georgette, what do you think you're doing?" Her voice startled me and I dropped the ink well, spilling its contents over the desk and onto my white shirt. Everyone in class looked at me with pitiful eyes, all imagining the dreadful punishment to which I would be subjected.

"What did I just tell you about moving and fussing with your things? You see now why I warn you? Look at yourself," she scolded. "You come here this very minute and get on your knees at the pedestal. Just remember, the next time you try anything, you'll first get the ruler, then the pedestal."

I sat on my knees, facing the blackboard, for what seemed like eternity. Shifting my weight from one knee to the other didn't help; the concrete pedestal hurt worse than any of Papa's spankings.

The next day, I tried to follow the rules, but it was no use. It seemed that I couldn't stay out of trouble. I moved too much, I distracted, I hindered her teaching, Sister Emilie said. I had to be punished to learn my lesson. This time I got the dreaded ruler, five smacks across my fingers on each hand. Oh, did that hurt! Worst of all, my fingers were still sore and numb, but she insisted that I keep up with the others in the drawing exercises.

This scenario repeated itself almost every day, but I didn't get any sympathy at home. Papa and Mama Apoline believed the teacher was always right; they said I had to get used to following rules from other people who take my parents' place. I tried to explain that Sister Emilie wasn't fair, that her punishments didn't fit my crimes. I was a bit of an expert on punishment. I was often punished at home—more than any of my siblings—but not for moving a little or just trying to do something. When Papa punished me, I deserved it, I really deserved it.

I began to plot an escape from the ruler. "What if I just don't go into the classroom?" I asked Josée.

"Papa won't let you. You'll get a bad spanking. Don't you try that."

I certainly didn't want a spanking, and I didn't want to upset Papa. But one day, as soon as the bell rang telling us to enter our classrooms for the first period, the image of the ruler became so vivid in my mind and on my fingertips that I decided I had to run away to find the nearest hiding place.

Now where could I go? To the right of the school yard was the church. I couldn't go there, I'd be easily spotted and brought back to school. To the left was a cemetery. Bingo! Now that was a good hiding place. I ran like a gazelle. Before the lines were formed in front of the classrooms, I was already in the graveyard. I turned around to see if anyone was behind me. No one in sight! I looked around in search of a good spot to claim for myself. There were many rectangular-shaped mounds all around. Some were cemented, and all had crosses. Many were in the sun. Then, *voilà*, I spied a perfect spot to my right—a concrete, rectangular mound under a palm tree shade. Just perfect!

And it was there that I spent my next three school days. I passed the time sharpening my crayons, staring at the clouds above and flowers below, nibbling on the snack Mama Apoline prepared for me each day, and collecting greasy palm nuts that I eagerly devoured. During recess I would race back to school to join the other students playing in the courtyard. As soon as recess ended, I'd race back to my cemetery hiding spot. And nobody ever caught me.

The weather was beautiful each day, and, since it was the dry season, I had no need for shelter. Although Kongolo is less than six degrees away from the Equator, the climate is fairly temperate. There's a rainy season when the temperatures range from highs in the upper 80s (Fahrenheit) to lows in the 60s, and a dry season, when it tends to be about five to ten degrees cooler. It rains a couple of times a week during the rainy season, compared to just a couple of times a month in the dry season.

On my third day of hooky playing, the school sent a report to Papa about my absences. After giving me a good spanking and a long lecture, Papa asked where I had spent the time when I wasn't in school. Without hesitating, I told him about my hiding place. Papa's eyebrows shot up and down.

"Explain to me what you fear so much with your teacher that pushes you to hide in the cemetery. You know that's not a place for you to go and hang around. Do you understand what a cemetery is?"

"Sure, it's a home for people who don't breathe, speak, or walk any more."

"And you needn't disturb them."

"So far, I haven't been disturbing them. I don't make any noise, except for whistling, and maybe singing. But that's not really noise."

Biriki, the company chauffeur who drove us to school every day because it was too far to walk, muffled a laugh, but Papa somehow managed to stay stern.

"You go back in that classroom starting tomorrow, period. Your teacher has good reasons to punish you. Do you hear me?"

The next day, Biriki didn't leave until he saw me going into the classroom. I forced myself to stay in line and somehow found the strength to resist the urge to run away. In the classroom, I tried hard to follow the rules, and the first three days went by without incident. But I just couldn't keep it up, my body wasn't made to be so still, my mind wasn't made to be so passive. Soon enough, Sister Emilie found fault with my fidgeting, and the good old ruler found its way back to my knuckles.

Sometimes I think my entire academic career was saved by the chain of events that began the next day. When the bell rang to start the first period, I turned and looked back in Biriki's direction. He was there by the car waiting to see that I went inside the classroom as he had been doing ever since Papa got the report about my absences. Biriki or no Biriki, my feet took me away from my classroom of torture to my haven of safety. This caught Biriki off guard and gave me a head start. But when I turned around, Biriki was running after me! I ran like a cheetah into the graveyard, past my usual hiding spot, and dove for cover behind a large stone with bushy grass all around it. Peeking out from behind the stone, I saw Biriki at the entrance, out of breath, gasping for air. He hesitated, then took a few steps into the grounds, and looked around. All was quiet, not even a cricket could be heard chirping.

Biriki must have known that I was in there, somewhere. Suddenly, he shouted, "I know where you are. I'm going to get you!"

How could he know where I was? He was looking away from me when he shouted. Still, I lied flat on the ground and closed my eyes, expecting his two large hands to lift me up at any moment. After what seemed like hours, I heard Biriki's footsteps going away. I looked up just in time to see him exiting the graveyard.

My excitement about escaping arrest soon dwindled and, after awhile, all I could think about was food. Unfortunately, there was nothing to eat in my bag because Papa had started having Josée carry my snack—another strategy for making sure I went into my classroom. I ate some ripe palm nuts, but that just made me as thirsty as I was hungry. I decided to head slowly to the school, where I would wait in the courtyard until the bell rang.

Some of the children at school brought *beignets* [fried, round sweet dough], toasted cassava, roasted peanuts, and other snacks for sale during the break. They would leave their merchandise up on the concrete counter on the side of the classroom building. When I saw all that food, I got even hungrier. The smell of *beignets* and toasted cassava became irresistible. I decided I would tide myself over with a couple of peanuts. Nothing wrong with that, because peanut vendors always let their clients taste a couple of peanuts before buying. I tasted one, two, then three peanuts. Back and forth to the peanut bowl I went until, finally, I just sat down with the bowl on my lap and devoured peanut after peanut.

Suddenly, I heard the voice of a woman passing by the school. "Why aren't you in your classroom? You're eating up all your mother's peanuts for sale!"

If only she knew the truth! "Oh, *Mungu wa Ibrahim, Isaac na Yacobu* [God of Abraham, Isaac, and Jacob]," I said to myself. "There are only a few left! What am I going to do? I don't have any money to pay for it."

No sooner had I put the peanut bowl back than the bell rang. I ran around the building and went straight to Josée, who realized something was wrong when I showed no interest in my snack.

"Why aren't you hungry? You didn't go into your classroom, did you?"

Before I could explain what had happened, we heard a girl shriek, "Somebody took my peanuts. What am I going to do? My mother will kill me. Please, give me back my peanuts," the girl said in between sobs. The more she cried, the sadder and gloomier I got.

Josée put two and two together and figured out that I was the peanut culprit.

"I was very hungry," I confessed to her. "I wanted to taste only a few."

"You are in big trouble, much bigger trouble now. Not only you didn't go to your classroom, but you also stole somebody's peanuts." I pleaded with her not to tell Papa, but she said that what I did was wrong and Papa needed to know about it.

When the bell rang, I didn't have the guts to face the ruler, under any circumstances. So, I escaped to my hiding spot for a long nap. I slept through the dismissal bell and, by the time I got back to school, Josée and Biriki were already gone. I started running home, but then slowed down when I realized the big trouble I faced there.

I walked home very slowly, stopping to look at the goods in all the shop windows and taking a dip in a stream to cool off. When I saw the huge orange sun starting to set, I put my shoes on and ran all the way to a square that could be seen from the second floor balcony of our house. To avoid detection I walked close to the edge of the avenue, under the tree branches. My plan was to hide in the garage on the first floor until it was dark and then sneak upstairs to our room.

Suddenly, I heard an excited voice shouting, "There's Geolo under the trees. There she is!" It was Gilbert from the balcony. I ran to the opposite side of the street, but halfway across, I smashed head-on into a speeding bicycle. Tossed to the ground, I found myself lying beside the bicycle rider, a woman who had been thrown from her seat by the force of the collision. The lady pulled herself up and shouted, "Don't you look where you're going?"

I sat up and looked at her but couldn't say a word. I was much too numb to speak. Of course, my audience up there on the balcony hadn't missed any bit of what had happened. Soon Papa was there, with Gilbert and Josée directly behind him.

After he examined me and assured himself I wasn't hurt, Papa went to speak with the bicycle lady. I heard him apologize, but as soon as the lady realized that *Monsieur* Benoit was my father, her anger disappeared, and she said, "I'm so sorry I hit her." I had a few scratches and bruises, nothing serious at all. But what a great excuse to attract sympathy and diminish my inevitable punishment. I began to loudly wail. They saw it happen, didn't they? I was knocked down.

"J'ai mal" [I'm hurting], I sniffled through my sobs.

Papa carried me home, where Mama Apoline helped me wash myself, and Papa put some ointment on my scratches. I was then sentenced to spend the rest of the evening—without supper—in the *cachot* [prison], which was really a storage room next to the garage. I managed to make my imprisonment profitable by swiping some tangerines and chocolate from Papa's boxes. When Papa came down to liberate me at bedtime, he found me fast asleep, lying in my underpants atop my robe, with tangerine peels and chocolate wrappers sprawled around me.

"I see you helped yourself to some food," Papa said in a tired voice. I gave a big yawn and a nice stretch.

"Come on, you need to go to the bathroom and then off to bed," Papa said, while giving me a gentle push.

I didn't need to be told twice. I picked up my robe and quickly exited the *cachot* ahead of Papa. Upstairs, everyone looked at the hooky player with scorn. Comments were made, but I was so sleepy I couldn't make sense of it. To the bathroom I went, and then off to bed.

Papa must have realized that night that I was just not cut out for Sister Emilie's class. The next day he took us to school and met with Sister Elisabeth, the principal. After their conference, I found out, to my surprise and delight, that I was being transferred to Mademoiselle Zenobita's class. She was one of the few teachers who was not a nun. She had been Josée's teacher the previous year, and Josée loved her.

In Mademoiselle Zenobita's class, school became non-stop adventure and excitement. I hung on to every word she said. We asked her questions all the time, and we never got scolded for it. She loved to laugh and to make us laugh. I learned so much from Zenobita, but most of all, I learned to love learning. And every time I saw Sister Emilie at school, I'd mime the joyful clicking sound of the *bikelekele* and shout silently to myself: *Lipanda! Uhuru!*

CHAPTER 4

THE HORROR

Over the next few weeks, the fighting between Katangese rebels and central government soldiers crept closer and closer to Kongolo. At school, classes were frequently canceled for security reasons. The city imposed a 6:00 P.M. curfew. Some of Papa's friends moved to the other side of the Lualaba River to remote villages inhabited by the baHemba, the majority tribe in the Kongolo area. But Papa's work was still going well, and he remained optimistic that the troubles wouldn't reach Kongolo.

"The curfew is just a precaution to scare off the troublemakers who'd love to use the secession as an excuse to steal. Things will calm down throughout the country long before any trouble arrives at a little town like Kongolo," Papa said over and over. Then one day six o'clock arrived, and Papa wasn't home.

Mama Apoline walked to and from the compound entrance. She seemed nervous.

"Where is he?" she asked no one in particular. "Doesn't he know that the police are arresting people and making them disappear?

I told him the town isn't safe, but he didn't want to listen." She then looked at us children and said, "He'll be here. Don't worry. Go play."

Marie and I had been playing all along. I didn't think for one second that anything could go wrong with Papa. Who would dare try to do something bad to *Monsieur* Benoit? Around seven o'clock, Papa suddenly appeared, walking furtively, practically clinging to the trees around our yard. As he entered our compound, he looked directly at us, put his index finger over his mouth, and dashed into the house. When he came out, he was wearing a dark, short-sleeve shirt instead of the long-sleeve white shirt he had been wearing all day.

Seconds after he sat down in the yard, a team of three *gendarmes* [police officers] entered shouting, "Where is he?"

Papa stood up, and very calmly asked, "Who is where? What are you looking for?" Then he turned to Mama Apoline and said, "Apoline, take the children inside the house." Mama Apoline, frozen with fear, didn't move.

One of the policemen stepped threateningly close to Papa. "You know what we're talking about. A man wearing a white shirt and dark pants has disappeared around your compound. We're sure he came in this compound. Now where is he?"

"How should I know? I've been sitting here, and I haven't seen any other man but me," Papa replied in his not-so-good kiSwahili. "Search my house, if you feel it's necessary."

They marched around the house and all over the compound. Suddenly, one of them told the others to stop and went to where Papa was standing. I started to get scared. Maybe they really wanted to take Papa away. Who were these bad men, and why were they bothering us?

"Are you Suruba Benoit?" the man asked. When Papa said yes, the man smiled. "Don't you remember me, *Monsieur* Benoit? You helped my big brother Amédeo get his job with INTERFINA. He speaks highly of you."

Papa sighed as he smiled back. "Of course. I'm delighted to see you. Say hello to Amédeo. He's a good man."

Amédeo's little brother then called off the investigation. "I know this man very well; he can be trusted. Let's go now." On their way out, they apologized for disturbing us.

As soon as they left, Josée asked, "Papa, why didn't you tell them that you were wearing a white shirt when you came in? Then they wouldn't have stayed here that long."

"Well, if I had done that," Papa said with a great big smile, "they would have thought that I was a bad guy and they would have taken me away and put me in prison. Sometimes, it's important to be quiet so you can stay out of trouble."

Papa told us that, sadly, in E'ville there had been a massacre of women and children. In Léopoldville, Prime Minister Lumumba had been arrested by the military and other politicians. It wasn't clear any more who was in charge of the country. But Papa kept on saying that things would be all right. After all, it couldn't get much worse than this.

It was the morning of our big day in early 1961. We were all going to live in a really big city. Papa's company, TRANGEN, was opening a new branch in E'ville, the biggest city in Katanga, and Papa was named branch manager. Papa had *Air Congo* plane tickets to E'ville for all of us.

Papa told us that E'ville had lots of street lights, lots of stores, and theaters where they showed movies every day. Now, I really looked forward to that. There was no movie theater in Kongolo. Occasionally, movies were shown in open air off the wall of a downtown building or at the parish. *Charlot* [Charlie Chaplin] movies were the biggest hits.

Our flight was scheduled for early in the afternoon. The plan was to have lunch at home and then Biriki would take us to the airport an hour before departure time. Papa, Mama Apoline with Benjamin on her lap, Josée, and I sat at the table just before noon and started to eat. Suddenly, we heard shouting. We looked outside and saw people running in different directions on the street. *Ba* [honorary father] Bertrand, the company cook, said goodbye to us and left in a hurry. Papa's successor then dropped by to wish us *bon voyage.*

"There's something strange going on in town," he told Papa. "I heard that the Katangese soldiers are coming into Kongolo today. Of course, it could be just another rumor like all the others we've heard for the past few weeks. But if the Katangese soldiers do come," he added just before leaving, "there's probably going to be a confrontation at the airport."

The shouting outside continued. Then we heard another noise, a peculiar, frightening, thunder-like noise. Everyone stared at each other alarmed. What was going on in the city? Could what Papa's colleague said be true? Had the fighting reached Kongolo after all? While Papa and Mama Apoline engaged in a serious conversation, everyone at the table stopped eating. Well, everyone except the one person who was always hungry. Nothing could spoil my appetite.

Suddenly, we heard louder shouting and more of those thunder-like noises that seemed to be getting closer and closer. They were obviously coming from the direction of the airport, the very airport we were supposed to go to in less than an hour. Papa looked up, his face serious, and said, "The big noises are coming from cannons." He went to the window and looked down on *Avenue Commerciale*. There was no other way to find out what was happening: there were no radio or television stations in Kongolo, and we didn't have a telephone. Papa spun around and motioned to Mama Apoline.

"Things are not looking good at all, Apoline. Get the children ready for when Biriki gets here. Is everyone finished yet?" Then he turned in my direction and saw that I was still eating. "What? Georgette, aren't you full yet? That will be enough for now."

I stopped eating, unwillingly. *Ba* Bertrand was surely the best cook ever! What a waste that I couldn't finish the feast he had made for us. I looked at Josée and saw that her face was scrunched up and she was almost crying. I didn't really understand what could upset her so much, but I started to worry about how everyone was acting.

During the next hour, Papa got more and more worried. "What if Biriki doesn't show up?" he asked no one in particular as he continued to peer out the window. We all joined him. Downtown was getting deserted and strangely quiet. Wounded people, some with blood staining their shirts, others with red stained cloths wound around their heads, were running from the direction of the airport, government soldiers as well as civilians. When would we take our plane to the big city? I started to get scared, just like Josée.

"Oh, thank God, there's Biriki!" Papa pointed. "Let's get downstairs. No time to waste." We rushed downstairs and saw Biriki driving the truck toward us. But he didn't slow down when he got near the house.

"Biriki!" Papa shouted as the truck sped past the house. Biriki yelled back something at Papa, waved, and kept going at full speed. Papa didn't believe his eyes. His most trusted employee had just let him down when he most needed him. Without saying a word, Papa took us back upstairs. "We must stay put for now while I think," he said.

The plane didn't land that day at the airport. The shooting between the central government soldiers and the Katangese soldiers with their white mercenary allies had started well before the scheduled time of arrival. Many white businessmen had crossed the Lualaba River earlier in the day. Somehow they had learned ahead of time that there would be serious trouble in Kongolo and that the plane would land on the other side of the river. But nobody had warned Papa. Our last hope had been to drive with Biriki to the other side of the river to catch that plane, and it was gone.

Finally, Papa looked around and called to Mama Apoline, "The only thing to do is to go into hiding in the forest. But, first, we have to get out of the business district safely." Besides the shooting, there was also widespread looting going on. Papa huddled us together and laid out the plan.

"We have to get out of here fast. We're going to have to separate. The soldiers on both sides will see me as a possible enemy. They won't bother a woman alone with small children. You all must get to our house in Kangoy neighborhood, and I'll follow you there."

Josée started to sob out loud. Papa squeezed her hand and smiled.

"Don't worry, Maman, I'll meet you there. None of these pretend soldiers are going to stop your Papa. I'm a real soldier, remember." He managed to get a weak smile out of her, but I could tell that she was still scared.

Our dream about flying to the big city had vanished. The countryside was our next destination—if we could get there. Mama Apoline with Benjamin wrapped on her back, Josée, and I said goodbye to Papa and headed downstairs. Once on the street, Mama Apoline told us to wait for her while she went back upstairs to ask Papa something. As Josée and I stood outside our house waiting for her, two soldiers, one bleeding and badly wounded and supported by the other, passed by, obviously running away from the airport. Josée started sobbing again.

The soldier holding the wounded one stopped, lifted his gun with one hand, then set it down. He looked at us in disbelief: two well-dressed little girls standing in the middle of the war zone all alone.

"What are you hanging around here for? Where are your parents?"

We didn't respond, and they kept on going. Josée couldn't seem to stop crying. Seeing those two soldiers and hearing the way they talked to us made me lose my control. I grabbed hold of Josée's hand and started to cry for the first time.

Thoughts raced through my little head. *Where was Mama Apoline? Why didn't Biriki stop? We could have been on the plane already. I had been looking forward so much to that trip. For Josée and me, it would have been our first plane trip. We wanted to know how it felt to be up there in the sky, looking down below. Who was fighting anyway? Why should we run away and miss our trip just because soldiers were fighting? Couldn't they just choose another spot where they could fight to their heart's content and leave the airport alone? And how long were they going to be fighting? A day? Two days? Would we make our trip as soon as they were finished?*

Mama Apoline arrived, interrupting my thoughts. "Don't cry, girls. We'll be there, away from the fighting in no time. Papa said to tell you that when we get to the house in Kangoy, he'll cook *sombe* for all of us. Now let's go."

As we walked quickly over the streets of Kongolo, Josée and I were too terrified to cry; the last thing we wanted to do was to draw any attention to ourselves. Lying along the streets were scores of dead and dying people. The road we took went past a prison in front of which we saw Katangese soldiers standing guard and many bodies of dead people lying on the ground. I could not help staring. The bodies seemed to be lying in every position one could possibly imagine. Some were lying face down, others face up, others on their sides. Some were curled up like a baby next to his mama. Groups of flies buzzed all over the bodies. Some bodies were missing hands, feet, ears. One had no head. I held Josée's hand tighter and tighter. I didn't quite grasp the reality that all these bodies had been living persons. I wondered if they were going to wake up like dead bodies did in the scary stories that Gilbert told us. I hoped so, because this was starting to get frightening. Then I started to wonder if the bodies would start chasing after us if they woke up. Maybe it was better they didn't wake up.

The soldiers were stopping every adult male passing by asking for identification papers. If they looked suspicious or if they came from another province, they were shot and killed. Especially at risk were those from *Congo Oriental,* Papa's home region, where Lumumba and the central government were very popular. If Papa was stopped, he would have little chance to make it through. He knew that full well; that was why he did not want us to be with him on the street.

Mama Apoline, Josée and I held hands as we went past the prison. In front, we saw two bodies lying apart near a mango tree. One of the bodies looked very familiar.

"Mama, look, isn't that *ba* Zamu?" asked Josée, as she pulled me toward the tree. *Ba* Zamu was TRANGEN's security guard.

"Come back here, don't look at it. Don't look at it," Mama Apoline shouted at us. "We have to keep on going. Come on."

Silent now, somehow despite our fear, we pressed on. Finally, we reached our house in Kangoy. "Mama Apoline," I asked, "was it really *ba* Zamu under the tree?"

"Yes, dear, that was him. Dear Lord, it looked like they beat him to death. His bundle that he usually takes to work was right there next to him. Dear Lord, was he going to work on a day like this? May his soul rest in peace."

Josée clapped her hand over her mouth terror stricken. Although I sensed her fear, I was not able to grasp the finality and true horror of the situation. Instead, I thought about how Josée and I always said hello to *ba* Zamu when he came to work, and how he used to tell us stories from his tribe, the baYazi, while making coffee on a small charcoal grill in front of our house. Did this mean we would never see him again?

I found out later that right after saying goodbye to his wife and children, Papa changed his suit for a casual, sports outfit. He then loaded his two guns, an automatic and a *mauser* shotgun, and put air in his bicycle tires. He waited almost an hour before leaving, to give Apoline and the children time to get to the house in Kangoy. He knew that if he met them on the road, the children would come or call out to him; if any of the soldiers suspected that he was hostile to their cause, they might go after his family as well. He couldn't take such a risk, so he waited until he was sure that his wife and children had had enough time to get to their destination. With one gun over his shoulder and the other held across the front of the bicycle, he looked up and down the road to check for fighting before heading out.

He rode at a steady pace, not too slow, not too fast. His eyes and ears took in all the sights and sounds on the streets of Kongolo;

he was primed to put his guns to use at the first sign of trouble. As Papa passed corpse after corpse on the street, he began to lose faith in the promise that he had made to Josée. His chances of making it to Kangoy neighborhood did not look good. The casualties on the street indicated that either there was still fighting going on ahead of him or one side had taken control of the prison. Either side, Papa figured, would probably shoot at the sight of a passing man. And what if they didn't shoot, if they just arrested him? Papa knew that if the Katangese were in control, chances were that a prisoner from Eastern Congo would never leave the prison alive.

He got within a few blocks of the prison without running into any fighting. Then, from a couple of blocks away, he saw bodies lying by the side of the road across the street from the prison. He couldn't tell whether the dead were soldiers or civilians. Two soldiers were standing by the street just in front of the prison looking in his direction. He kept on riding at the same steady pace. The two soldiers turned toward the prison; they seemed to be saying something to other soldiers who were out of Papa's view. As he got closer, he saw the soldiers were not wearing the uniforms of the central government forces. The Katangese rebels had taken the prison. There was nothing he could do now to change the inscription next to "Place of Birth" on his identification card or the heavy accent with which he spoke kiSwahili. There was nowhere to hide. All he could do was pedal forward and shift his weight ever-so-slightly to get ready to pull up his rifle and shoot.

The two soldiers by the street did not move. As Papa's bicycle approached the prison, they stared straight at him. He, in turn, looked straight in their eyes as he kept on pedaling at that same steady pace. Papa looked beyond them toward the group of about six soldiers at the prison entrance. He spotted the highest ranking soldier by his epaulets and looked intensely at him for a few seconds as he kept on pedaling. He passed the prison, and still the soldiers hadn't said a word. No commands to stop, no gestures, not a single rifle raised.

"Perhaps they don't want to take any chances with my guns," Papa thought. "It's a lot easier just to shoot a man in the back once he's passed them."

Papa picked up his pace slightly as he pulled away from the prison. He expected to hear a command to shoot from the officer, but his ears didn't pick up any sounds. He expected to feel the jolt of a bullet in his back, but it didn't come. He fought the temptation to look back and kept on pedaling ahead. Finally, he heard noise behind him. Voices, the voices of the soldiers. But they weren't shouting, they appeared to have resumed their conversation. They were talking to each other. They had nothing to say to the man passing by on a bicycle with two rifles. When Papa was a couple of blocks away from the prison, he turned his head and looked back. They weren't following him! He shook with relief and started pedaling faster.

"With all those bodies lying around, how have I gotten through?" he asked himself. He had no answer, no way to explain his escape. Did he just luck out and run into a peaceful bunch of soldiers who felt no need to disturb a passing civilian? Not likely. Maybe they'd just done enough killing for the time being. Maybe they had run out of ammunition. Maybe he just wasn't meant to die at this time and in this place.

CHAPTER 5

HIDE AND SEEK

Having miraculously passed the gauntlet by the prison, Papa raced through the streets leading toward Kangoy at breakneck speed. But, halfway to our house, he screeched to a halt as he arrived at the home of one of his best friends, Alingite Jean-Pierre. Like Papa, Alingite was a native of Eastern Congo who had come to Katanga as a soldier and stayed to go into business as a civilian. Alingite was like a brother to Papa and an uncle to us. As anxious as Papa was to see that we had arrived safely in Kangoy, he could not pass up the opportunity to check on his friend, who, like Papa, was in great danger due to his region of origin.

There was no sign of life coming from Alingite's house, but Papa needed to be sure. He tried to open the front door, but it was locked shut.

"Alingite," he called out in a loud whisper. "It's Benoit. We need to get out of here. It's too dangerous to stay."

There was no response, but Papa's soldier's intuition told him that there was somebody inside. He tapped on the door to the beat of an old song that he and Alingite liked to sing after having a few beers.

Five seconds passed and, then, quickly, the door opened. Papa rushed inside and greeted his friend with a handshake and a nervous smile.

"I thought you were already in E'ville. What are you still doing here?" Alingite asked.

"The fighting broke out at the airport before the flight arrived. I sent Apoline and the children ahead to Kangoy, and I'm headed there now to meet them. Why are you still here? You know they'll be out to get us."

"I was downtown when the fighting started. By the time I got back here, the fighting caught up with me. I heard shooting on all sides. It seemed safer just to stay put."

"Did everyone else get away?"

"I think the others are in the countryside by now. Only Monique stayed behind to wait for me. She's in the other room."

While Alingite stayed by the door with his back against the wall, peeking out the corner of the window, Papa went to the other room to see Alingite's younger sister. He had always been fond of Monique, a single woman in her early twenties. He never understood why she hadn't married yet: though she wasn't a beauty, she had a kind heart, worked hard around the house, and loved being around children. She always took good care of Josée and me whenever Papa left us with her. Papa found Monique sitting on a stool in a corner of the room, eyes closed and lips moving. She seemed to be praying. When she opened her eyes and saw him, she greeted him warmly.

"We're going to leave for the countryside now," Papa said matter-of-factly. "So let's get ready to go. And don't you worry, Monique. We're going to be all right."

While Monique prepared to leave, Papa returned to Alingite in the other room and asked, "Is she all right?"

"She's pretty terrified," Alingite said, not leaving for a moment his position against the wall. "The sounds of the cannons are driving her crazy. Doesn't take much to scare Monique. She's scared of mice, she's scared of the dark. She acts like a little girl sometimes. Now she's got something to really scare her."

"We need to get out of here now. It's too close to the prison. Why don't you come with me to my house?"

Alingite agreed and finally abandoned his position by the door to get his bicycle. Monique sat on the back of Papa's bike, and they left, riding as fast as they could. Everywhere, along the road, they saw signs of trouble, including dozens of vandalized homes. It took them about twenty minutes to get to our house in Kangoy neighborhood.

When he saw that the door was closed, Papa's heart started pounding, as he feared the worst. He knocked on the door and called out, "Apoline, are you in there? It's me! I'm with Alingite and Monique."

Mama Apoline opened the door, and the family was reunited. Josée and I raced to Papa's side, each of us clinging to a leg. He pulled us into the house and lifted us onto a table.

"I'm afraid I'll have to make that *sombe* some other time, Josée," Papa said, while patting her head. "We have to get out of here soon." Papa then whispered to Alingite, and the two of them pulled the front door about a third of the way open and all the windows wide open.

For heaven's sake, why are they doing that? I asked myself as I looked toward Josée with fear. *He's going to give up our hiding place!* However, I kept my mouth shut. I didn't understand it, but even I realized that this was one time when we shouldn't ask any questions.

Papa and Mama Apoline went to their room to pack some things. Monique took Josée, Benjamin, and me to the children's bedroom and tried to keep us quiet. Alingite, ever vigilant, kept an eye on the street from our living room window. A few minutes passed, then we heard Alingite call out in a whisper, "Benoit." Papa dashed out of his room to Alingite's side.

"There's a soldier in the house across the street. He's cutting the electrical wiring," Alingite whispered just loud enough for us to hear.

Papa grabbed one of his guns and positioned himself under the window. Peering outside, he saw the soldier across the street, but couldn't tell if it was a central government or Katangese soldier. The rifle on the soldier's shoulder, however, was clearly visible. And it was quite clear that the soldier was indeed vandalizing our neighbor's house.

"I have to scare him away," Papa whispered to Alingite. He looked around, got his gun ready, and aimed it at the trees across the street. Before pulling the trigger, he took another look across the street. What he saw made him lower his rifle, sit on the floor, and sigh before turning toward Alingite.

"He's not alone. There are at least two or three more inside the house. Who knows how many more are in the area."

Upon hearing this, Mama Apoline walked over to close the windows, but Papa jumped up and stopped her.

"If the soldiers see a house with the door and windows open," he whispered, "chances are they'll assume it's already been broken into and that there's nothing left to steal inside."

Papa made sure that we all lied down on the floor in our bedroom, while he and Alingite stood guard at the window. Josée kept her eyes closed the whole time, but mine stayed open; I didn't want to miss a thing when those soldiers entered our house and Papa shot them all down.

But they didn't try to enter our house and, after a long stretch of silence, Alingite reported that the soldiers across the street had moved on. Papa went outside to inspect the situation. When he came back, he said, "We have to leave right away."

"Can you hear gun shots?" Alingite asked. "It sounds like the shooting has started again."

"Yes, it sounds like it has," Papa said. "There's no time to waste. We have to get to the countryside now."

Papa took his small suitcase filled with documents and another one stuffed with towels and blankets. He held Josée's hand, Mama Apoline wrapped Benjamin on her back, and I held *ma* Monique's hand.

"Papa, where are we going? Are we coming back today?" Josée asked.

Papa explained that there was a bad thing going on, a war. "Sometimes, people who are not soldiers, like us, can get hurt, too, if we stay close to the fighting area. That's why we need to be far away from here for now."

"What are they fighting for?" Josée asked.

"Well, people from different parts of the country are not getting along well now that we're independent. They don't realize that we're all brothers and sisters, and we need to stick together." It didn't make much sense to me; I thought big people didn't fight, only us kids.

We took *Avenue des Fonds d'Avance* moving away from town and crossed the Kangoy River at a point at which the river was about twenty feet wide and three feet deep. On the other side, we passed many fields of cassava, corn, and other vegetables. We moved fast and kept quiet, with only the adults exchanging whispers now and then. We didn't see anyone else on the roads. When we stopped for a moment to catch our breath, Papa pulled Josée and me aside.

"This is just like one of your games of hide-and-seek. We're hiding, and the soldiers are seeking us. Now it's very important that we play very well and not get discovered. Okay?"

Game? Did he say game? I was all for that! Somehow, despite the terrible things we had seen that day, I felt excited about playing a game with grown-ups.

Don't worry, Papa. Josée and I will be really good at this game, I said to myself. We won't let those soldiers find us.

We left the path and went further into the countryside, over dirt trails and through farmer's fields, marching single file for about two hours until we stopped at a giant acacia tree. Papa climbed up the tree to get an aerial view of our neighborhood in Kangoy. Things looked calm, but Papa and Alingite decided we had better stay in the woods for the night. A little bit later, as the sun was setting, we heard once more the *ratatata* of automatic weapons and a whole series of explosions. Papa climbed the tree again. What he saw didn't look good at all. Some kind of smoke was rising to the sky from Kongolo. He couldn't see much as it was getting darker, but he believed that much of our neighborhood in Kangoy was in flames.

"I don't think we will find our house standing anymore," we overheard Papa saying to Mama Apoline.

The container of drinking water that we had brought was almost empty, so Papa and Alingite went off to look for a well.

"We won't be very long. Just try to keep the children quiet," Papa said to Mama Apoline as he picked up the container.

It was already dark by the time Papa and Alingite left along the same path we had taken to get there. Meanwhile, Mama Apoline and *ma* Monique arranged a place for us to sleep near the tree. Josée and I helped collect some leaves and straw to use for our "mattress," and Mama Apoline gave us each one large towel to use as a cover. Mama Apoline and *ma* Monique would cover themselves with *pagnes,* the long cloth wraps that Congolese women wear around the lower half of their bodies. Mama Apoline and *ma* Monique lay down, each on one end of the "bed," while I slept between *ma* Monique and Josée.

As Josée and I drifted off to sleep, we heard the two women talking about the war and the many dead people we had seen that day.

"Dear God, how could this be happening," *ma* Monique said. "Blood everywhere. Poor children, they have to witness all this. It's awful, just awful. The poor children." She kept on repeating, "The poor children, the poor children."

Suddenly, I heard, *"Swish, swish, swish,"* coming from the direction opposite from where Papa and *ba* Alingite had gone. Mama Apoline looked that way and saw shadows of people moving toward us.

"*Baba* Josée [Father of Josée], we're dying! *Baba* Josée, we're dying!" Mama Apoline screamed. "Wake up, children, they're coming after us. Fast!"

She picked up Benjamin, and we started to run away from the shadows. One of the shadow people raced to our "bed," and we saw that Josée was not with us, she was still lying in the "bed," sound asleep.

"Josée, hurry. Wake up and come here," Mama Apoline shouted.

"*Shhhhh*, Apoline. It's us. Stop shouting, please. It's us." The voice coming from the shadows belonged to Papa. Mama Apoline realized then that the "shadow people" were Papa and Alingite.

"Why didn't you tell us that you'd return from a different direction?" she shouted at Papa. "You scared the hell out of us."

Papa didn't respond but immediately woke up Josée. "Josée, you can't sleep as soundly as if you were at home. You must be alert all the time not to be caught. We must be ready all the time and stay together."

Papa and *ba* Alingite took turns staying up and being on the lookout, while we tried to sleep. It was the first time in my life I slept outdoors, and it was the least comfortable bed I had ever slept in. Still, I fell asleep in no time. I hadn't realized how very tired I was.

In the middle of the night, I suddenly woke up freezing. The towel I had been using as a blanket was gone. I assumed that Josée had taken my cover, but when I turned to her she had only her towel. I sat up and rubbed my eyes. I looked to my left and was shocked to see that *ma* Monique had taken my towel! Why had she, a grown-up woman, taken my cover away? I slowly pulled it back, covered myself, and went back to sleep. A little bit later, Josée started pulling on my cover.

"Geolo, give me back my towel," she whispered as she jabbed my ribs.

"I don't have it."

"So, where's my towel?"

I turned to my left, and, sure enough, Josée's towel was on top of the *pagne* that covered *ma* Monique. I pulled it off her, passed it to Josée, and went back to sleep. But every time we fell asleep, Monique would pull our covers off again. In the morning we told Papa about it. He said that she probably didn't realize what she was doing.

"How could that be? She did it many times," Josée said angrily.

"Don't be angry with her," Papa said. "You know she loves you two very much, don't you? I'll speak with her."

When we told Mama Apoline about it, she shook her head and muttered, "Great, she's cracking up. Your father knows it but he insists that she come with us. With her hanging around, we'll be arrested or even worse!"

That morning things looked calm from the tree top: there were no new fires and no sounds of guns. It seemed like the worst was over. The adults had a long discussion about whether it was safe to go back to Kongolo. Alingite was anxious to get back to town to find out what had happened to other members of his family, while Mama Apoline was anxious to track down *kambo* and her three children on *Avenue Kindu*. Papa then decided that we should head back toward Kongolo and see if we could pick up some reliable information along the way. This time on the road we ran into many people; most, including some friends of Papa, were returning to town. They convinced Papa that it was safe to return, even though it appeared that the Katangese rebels had taken control of the town.

"Well, *Monsieur* Benoit," his friends told Papa, "you really are Katangese. You've been working with the local people for so long that you won't have any problems back in Kongolo."

Unlike some of his friends from Eastern Congo who were active supporters of Prime Minister Lumumba's political party, Papa had no involvement in politics. He just wanted the government to work with all the people regardless of their tribes. Papa was understandably apprehensive about the secession movement; it was hard for him to accept the idea of Katanga as a country independent of Congo. But Papa felt strongly that Kongolo was where he belonged. And though he feared our house might be destroyed, he decided to take us back home.

When we got near the Kangoy River, we heard a group of men shouting: "People, you have to come back into the city. The town is calm and safe now. The new government is in place." They went on and on, until I heard them finally say, "Anyone who does not get back into town within two days will have to answer to the government. All

Katangese have to work hand in hand." Trouble was, Papa wasn't Katangese! Would he be safe going back?

When we got to our house in Kangoy neighborhood, we found Papa's worst fears confirmed: Everything was gone. The straw roof had been torched, and all that hadn't been taken away had turned into ashes.

"Where are we going to stay? Who did this to our house?" Josée asked.

Mama Apoline just shook her head, and Papa looked around without saying a word. He had an air of complete detachment, as if everything gone with the house had never belonged to him. He didn't curse or kick the walls. For a few moments, as he stared at the roof, he seemed to be lost in thought. Then he snapped out of it and began discussing with Mama Apoline his plans for sheltering and feeding us.

Mama Apoline still had hopes of finding most of her clothes. A few days before our scheduled trip to E'ville, she had dropped them off at her mother's house for storage. For Josée, Benjamin and me, what we were wearing was all we had left. Our suitcases in the TRANGEN house downtown were no doubt lost forever.

"Papa, are we going to find out who stole our things?" I asked.

"No," he said, gently touching my head, while shaking his own.

We moved into the house behind our compound. The owners had fled into the countryside. There were only two rooms, plus a kitchen, but its tin roof was still intact. Papa and Mama Apoline picked food from nearby fields to feed us; that was how everyone who had come back to Kongolo survived in the days after the fighting.

The day after our return Alingite came by and asked if we had seen Monique.

"I can't find her anywhere. When we got into town, she told me she needed to go to the bathroom. She told me to go on and that she would meet me at home. I haven't seen her since. I thought maybe she decided to go back to the countryside. I was on my way there when I saw Josée and Georgette playing in the yard."

Papa promised that if we saw Monique, we would make sure she stayed put. Alingite said that he was planning to leave Kongolo and join his family near the town of Kaseya as soon as he found Monique.

Mama Apoline was relieved to find that all was well on *Avenue Kindu*. When the shooting started, *kambo* Colette and the children locked themselves in the house; they had only come out at night to get some water at a public fountain. Mama Apoline's clothes were safe, too. *Kambo* Colette had Gilbert and N'Kongolo dig up a hole in her vegetable garden and bury the two suitcases of clothes there; then they planted some cassava offshoots on top.

One week after our return to Kongolo, the fighting started again. In the middle of the night, we heard gun shots coming from the airport and business district. As the night wore on, the gun shots got steadier and louder. Papa and Mama Apoline gathered our things while we slept. Before dawn, Papa woke us up.

"We have to leave now. Things are getting worse."

It didn't take long for us to get ready. After all, we didn't have much to pack any more. And off we went again along the same country paths. This time, however, Papa took us on the four-hour trip to Kimama, a pygmy village, where the chief was a good friend of his. Because they were different, people made fun of the pygmies and some readily believed negative things said about them, but not Papa. Papa visited the pygmies often, bringing them salt, cigarettes, and clothing from town, which they treasured. Papa would return from these visits with plenty of meat, one of the treasures of the forest.

As we approached the pygmy village, it started to rain, but Papa said we had to keep on going. He cut some thick tree branches that he gave to each of us to use as umbrellas. That kept most of the rain off of us. Papa always seemed to know what to do to protect us. Finally, we came to a clearing through which we saw the village with its round houses. The pygmies lived in round huts that looked like huge mushrooms made of straw. They always kept a fire going in the center of their houses, and I could not figure out how they managed to keep their houses from burning down. The chief's house was near the center of the village, but we stopped at almost every compound to say hello. The chief was honored that Papa had come with his family to seek refuge in his village. He and his family evacuated their house and turned it over to us for the duration of our stay. That night it seemed that the entire village brought us food: bowl after bowl of cooked fresh cassava, sweet potatoes, cassava leaves, and smoked meat, the first meat we had seen in a week. As hungry as we were, we couldn't come close to finishing all that they had brought for us.

The pygmies treated us like visiting royalty for the three days we stayed in their village. Josée and I, and even Benjamin, had great fun playing with their children. Then Papa received word from a friend who had gone near Kongolo that things had settled down. Despite the pygmy chief's repeated invitations to stay longer, Papa insisted that we go back.

When we arrived, we found that Kongolo was indeed calm for the moment. We stayed at that same empty, two-room house, behind our compound in Kangoy, waiting for life to return to normal.

A few days after our return, Mama Apoline was sitting in the yard under the shade of some mango trees with Benjamin asleep on her lap. N'Kongolo and Marie had come from *Avenue Kindu* to stay with us. They were playing with Josée and me on the other end of the compound, close to the remains of our burnt house.

Suddenly, we heard people shouting and booing on *Avenue des Fonds d'Avance.*

"Look at that woman!"

"She must be crazy. She's almost naked."

"Who is she?"

Josée, N'Kongolo, and I ran to the corner to see what was happening. A grown-up woman walking on the avenue was carrying her clothes on her head. She had a little piece of cloth hiding her private part in front; it was held up by a thin string around her waist. There was nothing covering her behind or her breasts as she headed toward the center of the city. When she got closer to our yard, Josée and I looked at each other and froze. We didn't know what to say or do. We were sure the crazy woman marching almost naked down the street was *ma* Monique Alingite! After a long pause, Josée finally spoke.

"Geolo, go tell Mama. I'll stay here."

I got to Mama Apoline in no time and told her what we had seen.

Mama Apoline ran with me to the avenue. The woman had passed our yard, but a group of children was still following and booing her. Mama Apoline sped up to get a closer look. It was indeed Monique Alingite. Mama Apoline shook her head, took us by the hand, and led us home.

CHAPTER 6

Chaos

In February 1961 the world learned that our imprisoned Prime Minister Patrice Lumumba had been murdered. The one man with the intelligence, energy, and charisma to truly lead the Congolese nation had been flown to E'ville and delivered into the hands of his enemies, the Katangese rebels. Only later did we learn that the man who put him on that plane, the man who sentenced Lumumba to death, was none other than his own protégé, the Army Chief of Staff, Joseph Désiré Mobutu.

It was less than two weeks after our second return to Kongolo. Mama Apoline was inside the kitchen cooking *bukari*, a doughy starch made of cassava flour that is the staple of North Katanga, *matembele* [sweet potato leaves], and *ndankala* [small dried fish]. I was hungry, as usual.

"Georgette is always hungry," Papa said. "She eats like a grown-up, but we can't figure out where all that food goes. She's thin as a broom-stick." Josée didn't eat nearly as much as I did, but she was chubby.

"She's always hungry because she never stops moving," Mama Apoline said. "And she's always playing rough games with boys. The food doesn't have enough time to stay in her body."

Suddenly, we heard a loud boom coming from *Avenue des Fonds d'Avance*. Papa went to see what it was all about, and Josée, N'Kongolo, and Gilbert followed him. I stayed put, because, after all, lunch would be ready soon. Then we heard gun shots and saw lots of people running past our compound in the direction of the countryside.

"No, not again," I grumbled, "not just when we're getting ready to eat. This time I won't leave the food behind. I'll take it and eat it later when we stop. We'll have to stop some time, won't we? We can't be running away forever."

Gilbert, N'Kongolo, and Josée came running inside, with Papa right behind them. "Let's grab whatever we can," Papa shouted. "We're getting out of here. There's no time, we have to take off—now!"

We had all been instructed beforehand what each of us would take if trouble broke out. The only things we would carry with us were blankets, water containers, and two or three pots. I grabbed my responsibility, a water container. Papa, Josée, and N'Kongolo were ready and waiting. Mama Apoline wrapped Benjamin on her back, took her bundle, grabbed my hand, and told Gilbert to carry Marie.

What about the food? That was my main concern. I dropped the water container, let go of Mama Apoline's hand, and raced to the kitchen. That food was not going to stay behind. I put everything in one pot, put the pot on my head, and held on to it with one hand. Then I ran behind Mama Apoline, who had taken the water container, and we all left. I was wearing one of Mama Apoline's *pagnes*; earlier that day Mama Apoline had cleaned my only remaining dress, and it was still drying in the sun.

Gilbert and Marie were behind me, and as I glanced around, it seemed that hundreds of people were running with us. Mama Apoline called to Gilbert, "Hold on to Georgette and Marie so that they don't get lost in the crowd." People were shouting, and they were running as fast as they could. They cut in front of us again and again. Somehow, in the chaos, Papa, Josée, and N'Kongolo got separated from the rest of us. Papa and Mama Apoline had discussed what to do in case they were separated from each other while fleeing from fighting: it was too dangerous to waste time looking for each other, the important thing was to get the children out of harm's way. So we ran forward with the surging crowd.

Soon, we spotted Josée's bundle on the ground. Gilbert told Mama Apoline not to worry about Josée and N'Kongolo.

"They're with Papa, they'll be okay," he said. We had no time to look for them. The shooting was right behind us, we could hear the bullets getting closer.

When we got to the Kangoy River, it was several feet high, higher than usual as it was the peak of the rainy season. I wondered how I was going to make it across with the pot of food on my head. Bullets were still flying in every direction. We saw some dead bodies by the banks of the river. Some people were wounded and blood covered, but still moving and moaning. Many people were running along with us. Clothes and pots and other possessions were scattered everywhere. I had trouble holding on to my pot of food as we crossed the river. Then my *pagne* opened up. It started slowly flowing away from me, taken by the current. I couldn't go around in only my underpants; so I let go of my pot of food and grabbed the *pagne*. Just then, the pot fell off my head, and the food spilled into the river. I froze and stared, with anguish, at my meal floating away downstream. Gilbert, more practical, grabbed my hand and pulled me across the river.

Josée and N'Kongolo followed Papa. He strode a little ahead of them to make sure the path was safe, but constantly turned to see that they were behind him. Then, suddenly, a throng of people cut in between. "Papa, where are you?" Josée cried out. Then somehow, above the din, they heard his voice crying out their names. Josée and N'Kongolo looked around. Finally they spotted Papa within the crowd ahead of them, right by the banks of the Kangoy River.

N'Kongolo lifted his mat high up waving it to attract Papa's attention. It seemed like Papa saw them, but then they heard another *ratatata,* closer to them, to the left. Perched high in a mango tree, there was a man, a soldier, with an automatic gun shooting down at the people on the run.

Papa started back towards N'Kongolo and Josée, and they moved forward towards him. But then some people between Papa and the children fell to the ground. Papa gestured to N'Kongolo and Josée to stop. He took a few steps in the opposite direction, toward the river. Dust flew up in the air around him from the bullets. The soldier in the tree seemed to be aiming at Papa! Papa spun around to look for the children. Then he plunged into the river. N'Kongolo and Josée held their breath for a few seconds, waiting to see Papa stand up again and look back in their direction. But he didn't stand up. He disappeared. Had Papa been hit by a bullet? They stood still, frozen by fear.

After a short while the soldier in the tree stopped shooting, and the people stopped falling. Josée and N'Kongolo raced forward. They got to the river bank where they had seen Papa fall and stared into the water. Papa was not there. Josée and N'Kongolo stared at each other without saying a word. Too scared to stand still any more, they crossed the river where the water was shallow. When they got to the other side, bullets started flying again. They were terrified without Papa, but they remembered Papa's stories about how soldiers try to avoid getting shot during a battle. So they did what Papa said soldiers do, they crawled on the ground.

They zig-zagged through the cassava fields by the river. When they were far enough away from the flying bullets, they stood up and ran back to the path. They followed the other refugees, walking at a fast pace. They kept going for what seemed like hours until they decided it was safe enough to take a rest. N'Kongolo opened up his mat, and they both lied down. They slept for an hour or so, and, when they awoke, there was no one in sight.

N'Kongolo folded his mat, and they continued trudging all

alone through the countryside. They didn't know where they were headed, they just hoped to find a safe village before nightfall. All was quiet, except for the chirping of crickets and the croaking of frogs. Josée and N'Kongolo didn't talk; they just kept on going. They walked for hours.

Finally, when the sun was about to set, they found a hut in the middle of cassava and corn fields and went inside. It was comfortable and looked like it had been used recently. "Maybe we should sleep here for the night," N'Kongolo said. "We've gone such a long time without meeting anyone."

Suddenly, they heard footsteps outside. They stood up and cried out, "Who's there? Who's going there?" N'Kongolo grabbed his mat, and they raced out of the hut shouting, "Papa, Papa, we're dead!"

A strange looking man came out of the field. He had a funny looking mouth with his teeth sticking out. Terrified, Josée and N'Kongolo ran from the hut, while continuing to shout for help. The man didn't run after them. He was, instead, making gestures, urging them to keep quiet.

"*Shhhhhhh*, please stop making noise, children. I am also running away. I mean you no harm. Please, stop."

Josée and N'Kongolo stopped and turned back to look at the man. They quickly realized that he was unarmed and appeared to be no threat to them.

"Are you all by yourselves? Where are your parents?" the man with the funny mouth asked.

"We lost sight of our father, and we don't know where our mother is," Josée responded.

"We don't even know where we are," N'Kongolo said. "But Papa said we have to get away from the city."

"I am headed to Lubunda," the man said. "I can take you to a village where I will spend the night. Your parents might be there, or there might be people who know your parents. It's not safe to be all by yourselves. Let's go while it's still clear."

Josée and N'Kongolo lined up behind the man and followed him. They felt better under his protection. While walking, the man offered them water and raw cassava. Josée and N'Kongolo hadn't had any food all day; they finished what the man gave them in no time. It was already dark when they got to a village just before the one where the man was headed to spend the night. They saw many people sitting in circles around large campfires or standing by straw-roofed houses, all engaged in serious conversation about what was going on, about who were the good guys and who were the bad guys. N'Kongolo and Josée went around shouting, "Mamaaaa, Mamaaa, Papaaaa, Gilbeeert, it's us, Josée and N'Kongolo!" But nobody responded. The man with the funny mouth found one man who knew *Monsieur* Benoit, but nobody had seen him or his wife. It was time to move on to the next village, where the man had friends.

They got there in less than an hour, and the man took them to the simple house of a couple who were originally from Mama Apoline's home area, Maniema Province. The woman, Zabibu, said she knew Mama Apoline very well. In fact, she and Mama Apoline were distant cousins. In Congolese culture, that means they would call each other "sister." She and her husband said they would be delighted to look after her "sister's" children. They would return the children safely to her when they saw her or her husband. The man with the funny mouth said goodbye and left.

Zabibu and her husband didn't have children of their own. They gave Josée and N'Kongolo food and fixed two places in the living room where the children could sleep. Zabibu's husband told Josée and N'Kongolo that if their parents didn't show up, he would go look for them after the war. But Zabibu told them a different story.

"If your parents don't show up," she said, "my husband and I will keep you as our children." After a few days, Zabibu asked them to call her "Mama," not "*ma* Zabibu."

After walking for many hours in the blazing sun and then the dark shadows, Mama Apoline, Gilbert, Marie, Benjamin, and I got to a village late in the evening. The village was already packed with people fleeing from Kongolo. We were all very tired and happy to hear Mama Apoline say that we would spend the night there. "In the morning," Mama Apoline said, "we will go to a nearby village where I know some people from Maniema who might be able to help us." Gilbert found a spot far away from the road, near a vegetable garden, where we could camp for the night. He collected dead, dry branches to make a fire. Mama Apoline got water and food in the village; she cooked us *bukari* and smoked fish, which we ate with great appetite.

While we children slept, Mama Apoline went around to get the latest news of Kongolo from people who had arrived after us. No, they hadn't seen her children, some said. Others said that they were sure they had seen two wounded men in the backyard of our home back in Kongolo. One had been seriously wounded, and the other was dying. Some told Mama Apoline that they had seen her husband fall under the bullets of a soldier shooting from a tree near the river. Her two children, they said, had been following their father before he was shot. The children had probably headed back to the city.

The next morning Mama Apoline told us that we were not going to any other village. "We will stay where we are for a day or two to let you little ones rest. Then, we are going back to Kongolo."

"If it's true that Papa Benoit has been killed or wounded," we heard her tell Gilbert, "I have to find out before we go any further. If he is dead, I will bury him. My husband won't be left to rot like a dog. And we need to see if Josée and N'Kongolo are indeed back in Kongolo."

Gilbert tried to persuade Mama Apoline not to return to Kongolo. "Josée and N'Kongolo must be with Papa," he told her. But she wouldn't listen. She was determined to return home before we took the long journey to Samba in Maniema Province, where we could stay with her relatives until the end of the war. It was a distance of more than 150 miles.

That day, I played with some children who were also camping there like us. But I missed Josée a lot. *Was she all right? Did she and*

N'Kongolo stay together? Were they with Papa? They must be with
Papa, like Gilbert said. And what could possibly go wrong if they were
with Papa? Mama Apoline's talk about dead bodies in our yard made
no sense to me; after all, none of these pretend soldiers could do anything to hurt *Monsieur* Benoit.

The following morning, we returned to Kongolo and headed
directly to *kambo* Colette's house. *Kambo* had refused to go into hiding.

"What's an old woman to do with their politics? Take the children instead," she had said to Mama Apoline when they saw each
other last. She was delighted but very surprised to see us return.
Unfortunately, she had no news of Josée, N'Kongolo, or Papa. After
explaining why we had returned, Mama Apoline said that she had to
leave immediately for our compound to see if Papa was there.

"If I am not here by sunset," she told *kambo* and Gilbert,
"keep the children in the house. Wait until dawn. If I am still not here,
take the children and go back the way we came. Go back to the village
we stayed at. Ask there how to get to the next village. People there can
help you get to Samba."

"Why are you talking like that, Apolina," *kambo* replied.
"You're just scaring the children. You'll be back, and we'll wait for you
right here."

Mama Apoline walked quickly over the largely deserted streets
and in got to our compound in no time. Her heart pounded loudly as
she neared the back of our burnt house where people had told her
there were two wounded men. Would one of the two wounded men
behind the house be her husband? If one of the bodies was his, what
was she going to do? How was she going to tell the children? And Josée
and N'Kongolo, were they still alive?

She went around the house. At the corner she smelled a
funny, foul odor: there were indeed two dead bodies behind the
house. Tears started flowing down her cheeks.

"Is Benoit really dead? Why wasn't I there when he was
dying," she murmured.

As she neared the bodies, she saw that one was facing up. The other one was facing sideways, his face almost buried in the dirt. The one facing up couldn't be Benoit, he was too short. Sure enough, when she looked at his face, it wasn't her husband. She headed toward the other corpse, her heart pounding.

"Please, Almighty, I need a miracle. Please, make this body not be my husband's. He is a good man. I need him."

She gathered all her courage, bent over and looked at the corpse's face. It was not Benoit. She fell on her knees and sobbed. Then she held her nose with her fingers, as the odor from the two dead bodies started to make her nauseous. Running to the far end of the compound, she threw up. When she felt a little better, she stood up, wiped her eyes, and started her way back to *Avenue Kindu*. On the way, invigorated and full of hope, she stopped at some cassava fields to pick fresh cassava and sweet potato leaves for dinner

Early the next morning, before the sun had risen, she woke us up, and off we went to the countryside along the same route we had come from two days earlier. When we got to the first village, it wasn't as crowded as it had been before. We were lucky this time. We got a room to spend the night in and were given food by the kind people of the village. "My legs are hurting badly," I wept. Mama Apoline said I had no choice but to keep on walking. I trudged on tearfully. I missed Papa and Josée so much—even if Papa punished me the most and even if Josée bossed me around so much.

The following morning, on our way to the next village, I could barely put one foot in front of the other. Big blisters scraped inside my thighs.

"Mama, my feet are hurting worse," I said.

"All right," Mama Apoline responded. "We can take a rest now, and then we'll walk a little more slowly."

"But I can't walk any more. My blisters are ready to burst!"

"She's just putting on a show because she wants to be carried like I'm carrying Marie," Gilbert interjected.

Mama Apoline asked me to show her my legs. The anguished look on her face made me start to cry. Were my legs so bad?

"Gilbert, put down Marie. Take Benjamin instead. I'll carry Georgette. Marie can walk, we're not that far away anymore."

She took off Marie's dress that I was wearing. It was soiled with pus coming from my wounds. She tied one of her *pagnes* around my neck and wrapped it around my body. Then, she put me on her back, and we continued.

When we got to the next village in the afternoon, Mama Apoline asked for the house of her "sister" Zabibu. We were led to the fourth house from the entrance to the village, where Mama Apoline stood in front of the open door and called out, *"Hodi huku?"* [Anybody home?]

A voice inside responded *"Karibu"* [Welcome]. A woman came out, looked at Mama Apoline and said, "Apoline, is it really you? Where have you been?"

Before Mama Apoline could respond, we heard "Mamaaa, Geoloo, Mamaaa!" I turned around to see Josée and N'Kongolo running toward us. Despite my blisters and pain, I started running toward them.

Josée jumped on me and said, "Why are you walking funny? I missed you. I thought I'd never see you all again. *Ma* Zabibu says that N'Kongolo and I are her children now." Josée hugged Mama Apoline and picked up Benjamin. *Ma* Zabibu gave Mama Apoline an ointment made from herbs to put on my wounds. It stung really bad, but Mama Apoline said it would help me heal faster. "We'll stay here until your wounds get better," Mama Apoline said. I was delighted to stay in one place for a few days. Above all, Josée was with me, and we could play together, eat together, and sleep together. I felt safe when Josée was next to me.

Mama Apoline's "sister" Zabibu didn't seem too pleased that she was there to take back her two children.

"I think you need to give me some kind of reward," we heard *ma* Zabibu say to Mama Apoline. "I have taken good care of your children. I deserve something in return from you." She went on and on talking of a reward while Mama Apoline grimaced. Finally, Mama Apoline replied, "Of course, my sister. Once the war is over, we will give you some money for your trouble. For now, all I have to offer are these *pagnes*." Mama Apoline gave *ma* Zabibu two of her nicest *pagnes*, but she didn't look very happy about making this gift.

After hearing Josée and N'Kongolo's story of how they were separated from Papa, Mama Apoline decided that we had to go back once more to Kongolo.

"*Baba* Josée might still be around town looking for us. Or he might be in the hospital or somewhere in Kongolo. We have to go back again to Kongolo, children, and stay with your *kambo* for a couple of days. I know this is too much walking, but your father might be looking for us. Besides, people coming from Kongolo say that things seem to have quieted down."

We rested in *ma* Zabibu's village for a week to let my sores heal. Then back to Kongolo we went. Mama Apoline said that if we had to leave town again, she would convince *kambo* to come along, for she couldn't have peace of mind leaving her mother behind.

"Next time, I promise, if we leave Kongolo, we will not return."

Meanwhile, as I learned later, my father had faced death in the Kangoy River. Benoit had one foot in the river when he suddenly realized that he had a better chance of escaping from the mad soldier up in the mango tree by going down into the water. The soldier had been shooting at random targets, and it looked then as if Benoit had become his bull's-eye. Before jumping in the water, Benoit turned around one last time to gesture to his children. He thought he saw Josée still carrying her bundle and N'Kongolo holding his mat. Next to them he saw a woman with a baby on her back.

"It must be Apoline. She's caught up with the children. Thank God," Benoit said to himself.

As he gestured to tell his family to stay back out of the soldier's target area, a bullet grazed his left shoulder. Instinctively, Benoit took a deep breath, jumped in the water, and headed to the other bank and downstream where the water was deeper. He had no chance of getting to the cassava fields, a few feet away from the river. He would stay at the riverbank for as long as the bullets rained down from the tree.

As Benoit swam underwater, he heard the noise of bullets hitting the river. The water was muddy and dark. He couldn't see anything underwater, but propelled himself forward by an innate sense of direction. His head hit what felt like floating threads—probably plant roots. He was then far downstream from where people were crossing the river. His lungs felt ready to explode; he couldn't hold his breath any longer; he had to come up. Slowly, he lifted his head until his face surfaced, then he took a long, deep breath. He couldn't stand for fear that he might be spotted. He stooped, then lifted his head a few inches higher and turned to the tree. A shower of bullets rained down from it. "How much ammunition did that lunatic take up there with him?" he mumbled. *Why would he shoot at fleeing, defenseless civilians? And how could he aim his gun at women and children? Then Benoit's thoughts went back to his children. Did they get across the river? Or did they turn around and run back toward Kongolo?*

Benoit could still hear the noise of people crossing the river upstream. The screaming, crying, shouting of the people and the banging of the gun shots went on and on and on. He stayed by the riverbank for what seemed like an eternity. Finally, the gunfire stopped. The river was calm once again save for the croaking of frogs. The sun was starting to set. It seemed safe but Benoit decided to stay where he was until dark. It had been hours since he plunged into the river. His shoulder ached some, but he had only a superficial wound from the bullet. His legs, though, were getting numb from staying stooped all that time. It seemed like the sun took forever to disappear.

Finally, darkness set in, and he started to get cold. Benoit stood up shivering and looked around, but couldn't see far. He had decided that Apoline and the children had probably headed back home to avoid the soldier in the tree. But with things so chaotic and dangerous, he knew they couldn't stay in Kongolo. He had to get them out of town, into the relative tranquility of the countryside. He walked stealthily toward the town. It was quiet, very quiet in the city. He got to the house where we had been staying and found the door open—but nobody was inside. He felt relieved; surely, Apoline had left with the children. But then he became terrified by the thought that they might not have made it past the sniper. *No*, he thought to himself, *this was not the time to be pessimistic. They had made it; God was with them!*

Benoit picked up a tin water jug on the ground. He would need water to sustain him, because he had a long trip ahead. He and his wife had agreed that if the situation deteriorated, they would go to the town of Samba, where Apoline had relatives. Apoline and the children must be on their way there. They couldn't be very far; there was no time to waste. After he filled the water jug, he instinctively closed the door behind him and followed the same road that his family had taken hours before. Bodies littered the streets. In the darkness, he tripped on some of them. He picked up his pace to get away from the nightmare, crossed the Kangoy River on the outskirts of town, and kept on going all night long.

As the first rays of sunshine emerged, he decided it was safer to go off the road into the woods. He would rest during the day and travel at night, at least until he got closer to Samba. So far, by ducking off the road at the sound of footsteps, he had managed to avoid all contact with people, but he knew his luck could not possibly last during the daylight hours. He had to avoid being seen. His character, his reputation, his good deeds no longer mattered. All that seemed to matter to the lunatics with the guns was tribe and home region. And he happened to have been born in another province. After all these years of living in Katanga, he still spoke a very poor, heavily accented kiSwahili; his native language was Lingala, spoken in the northern and western parts of the Congo. He would be in danger as soon as he opened his mouth. It would be better in Maniema Province, where Samba was located; it was home to many people from Eastern Congo.

Far from the path, Benoit found a tree with branches strong enough to hold his weight. Up there he could keep an eye on the surroundings. He looked down to make sure he was well hidden. "You never know who else might pass this way," he said to himself. He tied his jug of water around a branch, stretched his legs as far as he could, then turned his attention to the now far-away path. Overwhelmed with fatigue, he fell into a tumultuous sleep. He dreamed that he had been caught and was standing in front of a firing squad. He woke up just as the squad was ready to shoot.

It was hot, and sweat poured down his face and back. The sun was high in the sky. He didn't want to sleep any more. It was not safe, he might fall off the tree or miss someone coming into the area. Anyway, he did not want to dream the nightmare again. How could he have fallen so fast asleep up on a tree anyway, he wondered. Later in the afternoon, as the heat eased off, a pleasant breeze swayed the leaves back and forth like green fans. He would be on his way soon.

CHAPTER 7

THE MUZZLE
OF THE RIFLE

After our return to Kongolo, we stayed with *kambo* on *Avenue Kindu*. Mama Apoline searched in vain for news of Papa at the hospital, the prison, and all over town.

"I think *baba* Josée is on his way to Samba," she told us as if trying to convince herself. "When he hears that things are settling down here, he will come back."

We spent some days helping Mama Apoline gather food from the fields on the outskirts of town. Gilbert usually stayed on *Avenue Kindu* where he was less likely to be arrested; he was old enough to be a prime target for nervous, inexperienced Katangese soldiers.

One day, about a week later, a group of Katangese soldiers stopped us on the way to the fields. "You are under arrest," they told us. As they rounded us up, I winced, looking at Mama Apoline, N'Kongolo, Josée, Marie, and even baby Benjamin wrapped on Mama Apoline's back. They didn't explain why we were being arrested, they just said it was for our own protection.

They protected us by marching us to the military camp and locking us up in the camp prison. We were stuffed in a tiny cell with a wet floor, a single narrow bench to sit on, and the overpowering stench of stale urine. We hardly slept that night. The next morning, all prisoners with small children were transferred to a convent at the Mission Parish that the soldiers were calling the "children's camp." Our family lagged behind; so a soldier named Kakuji Honoré was ordered to march with us at our pace.

Mama Apoline started a conversation with Honoré and learned that he had two boys and a girl and was originally from Kasai Province in central Congo.

"Your girl here," he said, pointing to Josée, "looks just like one of our girls from Kasai. She's very pretty. I tell you what," he said to Mama Apoline with a smile and a wink at Josée. "I'll give you a nice dowry for her. She'll be my oldest son's fiancée." Mama Apoline tried to take advantage of the winks and smiles and asked him to let us go.

"I wish I could," he responded, "but I've got orders to take you to the children's camp. So that's where I'm taking you."

Suddenly, it started to rain. Honoré pointed us toward a nearby school, "We'll take shelter there." I looked around. Most of the school's windows were smashed during the fighting; books and other school materials littered the grounds. We entered one of the classrooms to wait for the rain to stop. Honoré entertained us with more stories about his family and talked again and again about Josée marrying his son. I began to fear that he might be serious about this even though Josée was only a child.

"When my battalion is ready to pull out of town, I will take Josée with me," he said. "My wife and I will raise her for our son. That's how people from my region take care of our children's future."

It looked like it would rain forever. The children started to get sleepy, so we stretched out on benches and dozed off. When Mama Apoline put her head on a desk to rest, Honoré stood up, exited the classroom and marched back and forth in the hallway. After a few minutes, he returned to check on his "prisoners." Finding us asleep, he left again and, soon, we heard no more footsteps.

As the rain eased into a drizzle, Mama Apoline awoke suddenly. She shook us frantically one by one and whispered, "Wake up quickly, children. We might be able to get away now." I wanted to stay and sleep a little longer, because we hadn't slept much in that horrible cell the night before. But I'd learned that in this game of war I had to do whatever Mama Apoline told me to do without any questions. We went out quickly in single file: N'Kongolo in front, then Josée, Marie, me, and Mama Apoline with Benjamin wrapped on her back.

A block away from the school, it seemed like our escape had succeeded. There was no sign of Honoré or any other soldier on the road. Then suddenly behind us we heard, *"Click click clack!"* We turned around and saw Honoré holding up his rifle and aiming it straight at us. He was angry, very angry. His right index finger touched the trigger of the rifle. Mama Apoline ran right at Honoré. He hesitated, and Mama Apoline grabbed the muzzle of the rifle and pushed it up in the air. They struggled momentarily, then Honoré took control of the rifle and pushed Mama Apoline to the ground. Mama Apoline began pleading desperately for our lives.

"I cannot believe that you want to kill us," she said. "You also have a family, don't you? What would you and your family do if you felt threatened? I'm very sorry I decided to run away. I was afraid, that's all. Please don't hurt my children. In the name of your family, spare us, spare us."

She sat on the ground absolutely still and repeated again and again in a remarkably calm voice that she had made a big mistake, but it was a mistake that anyone would make in these circumstances.

Finally, Honoré lowered his rifle. He told us to go ahead of him. He was not friendly any more. The conversation, the winks, the laughs were over. But our lives were spared. It had stopped raining, but there were puddles of water everywhere. My shoes, or what was left of them, were soaking wet and filthy with mud. My stomach started to grumble. I knew if I asked, I would be told there was nothing to eat, but I thought that maybe we would find some food at the children's camp. Just the idea gave me such strength that I let go of Mama Apoline's grip and started running ahead of everyone.

"Geolo, come back here," Mama Apoline called out. "Don't you go far from us. We have to stay together." I stopped in my tracks and ran right back to Mama Apoline's side. None of us wanted to upset Honoré anymore. When we arrived at the convent, it was already full beyond capacity; so we were brought to the orphanage about five minutes away. We were put in a small room that already had two families in it. Two or three rooms down the hallway, there was a woman gone crazy who shouted all night long. We were told that she had been shouting like that for a week and that every day it got worse.

The good news was that there were many children at the orphanage. The soldiers let us out during the day, and we played all day long in the courtyard under the mango trees. We got a daily ration of food, mainly *bukari* with cassava leaves and sometimes dried fish or smoked meat. There wasn't really enough food to go around, and each day the daily ration got smaller and smaller. After about a week, the soldiers sent parents out to look for food to bring back to feed their children. The children had to stay behind, because the soldiers knew that people would run away if they had their children with them.

A few more days passed. Parents got permission to take their children out to help look for food. Mama Apoline told us that we were all going to look for food downtown and that we'd come back to the orphanage in the late afternoon. But I could tell by the look in her eyes that she was not telling the truth: we were not coming back to this place at all. Willingly, that is. Once we got past the railroad, Mama Apoline told us to walk very fast.

"Hurry up, children! We're going to *kambo's* house. If *kambo* and Gilbert are still there, we'll all leave town together." Our luck held, and we arrived at *kambo's* house without incident. Mama Apoline explained our situation to *kambo*.

"This is a chance for us to finally get away from Kongolo. Things are not going to settle down for a very long time, Mama." *Kambo* finally

agreed that it was time for her to leave Kongolo. Mama Apoline didn't
sleep well that night. She still didn't know if her husband was dead or
alive. Or if the soldiers would find us and lock us up again. Or how she
would manage the long walk to Samba with an old woman and six children. As the sun rose, she looked drained.

Seeing her daughter's fatigue, *kambo* Colette said, "Apolina,
you need to rest. How will you travel if you're not rested? You can't go
on like that. Put everything in God's hands. Try to get some sleep."

Mama Apoline didn't protest at all. She went back to bed and
soon fell into a deep sleep. Later she woke up sobbing and told *kambo*
about a dream she was having. "I saw one of the two dead bodies I
found behind our house, and it turned out to be Benoit after all."

"It's good," *kambo* said. "That means he is still alive and in
good health. Had you dreamt of him being alive, that wouldn't have
been a good sign. Now, try to sleep. I will keep the children busy.
There is no way we can travel today."

Later that afternoon, *kambo* Colette asked me to go with her
to get some water at the public fountain. I didn't linger or forget my
tasks like the rest of my brothers and sisters would often do. And she
reminded me to take my "bike" with me. My "bike" was actually a bicycle wheel that I pushed with a stick and ran behind. That made me get
a lot more quickly to wherever I had to go. *Kambo* loved me very
much, I could tell just by the pet names she always gave me. One of
her favorite pet names for me was *kampulumayamba, nyoka havale
mukaba*, which literally means "the restless, full of energy one who
slides from place to place like a snake with no belt."

As we walked to the fountain, I saw that the neighborhood was
starting to come back to life. Many families had returned to town. The
secession of Katanga from Congo seemed to have been accomplished.
Katanga was its own country. We saw white soldiers, mostly Belgians,
patrolling along with the Katangese soldiers. When we got to the fountain, there were a few people ahead of us.

"*Kambo*, can I go get some dry palm nuts, over there?" I asked.

"Don't go very far. Don't go near the railroad. Our turn will be up soon, do you hear me?"

I went to a nearby palm tree, cracked open a couple of nuts with two rocks, devoured them, and proceeded to search for more. Then I stopped, because I heard an unusual noise that was getting louder and louder. I turned to where *kambo* was waiting on the line and saw that her turn was next. But everyone at the fountain was looking up at the sky, first to the right, then to the left. A loud noise was coming from both sides. Two planes were up in the sky, and something was coming out of their tails. From where we were, it looked like confetti.

"Geolo, come back quick. We have to go, now!" *Kambo* Colette's voice snapped me out of my sky-gazing reverie.

"Are those planes the good guys or the bad guys?" I asked.

"I don't know, and we're not staying around here to find out."

Kambo helped me put my bucket of water on my head and then put hers on her own head. We walked a little, then we heard people at the fountain shouting. We turned and saw them running toward the descending confetti.

"It's the new Katangese money," they shouted.

People were running all over the street picking up paper money. *Kambo* and I put the buckets down against the wall of a house and ran back to try our luck at getting some free money. Free money! That's what the planes were dropping. I saw a couple of bills lying in the grass, not far from the railroad. Off I ran in that direction. I was excited, already imagining how I would show off my bills to Josée. Two or three steps away from the grass and ready to grab some cash, I was suddenly knocked to the side by a strong hand that then scooped up my bills. I fell to the ground and looked up to see a big woman stuffing my bills into her bra. She didn't even notice me, she was too busy searching for other bills to grab. I started to cry. *Kambo* had had more luck; she managed to get a couple of bills.

"I almost got two bills," I told her, "but that woman over there pushed me aside and took them."

"It's all right, dear. Let's go home now and tell everyone."

The new money was unlike any money we had ever seen before: it had a picture of a black man on it! "It's Tshombe, the President of Katanga," Mama Apoline said.

The following day, things were still quiet. Mama Apoline and *kambo* left Gilbert in charge while they went to get water at the public fountain. On their way back, they could hear our voices a block away from *kambo's* house—even though they had given us many warnings about making too much noise. But they had too many other things on their minds to worry about scolding us.

"Mama, I don't know what I will do if Benoit has been killed. What am I going to do with Josée and Georgette?"

"You know what you will do. You will take care of those children as your own, as you've been doing up to now. When the war is over, if we still don't have any news of their father, then you will look for their mother." They continued to chat and started to laugh about the way Mama Apoline had tried to talk Honoré, the Katangese soldier, into letting us get away.

"Can you believe it, I even started to call him '*Ba Mukwe*' [father in law], even though in my mind I was saying 'Over my dead body, you idiot!'" As they arrived close to the compound with the water buckets on their heads, they noticed that they couldn't hear our voices any more.

"Mama, listen! Can you hear anything? The children have suddenly gone quiet. I have a very bad feeling. Let's hurry home."

Then they heard a boy's voice screaming, "Mamaaa, they're going to kill me, Mamaaa, Mamaaa!"

"That's Gilbert's voice," Mama Apoline said.

Throwing down her bucket, she started running to the house. She arrived at *kambo's* compound in a matter of seconds and found two soldiers with the children. One was aiming his rifle at Gilbert. Mama Apoline ran to that soldier and grabbed his rifle. She started struggling with the soldier for the rifle, just as she had done with Honoré. When the soldier wrestled it away from her, Mama Apoline wrapped the palm of her hand around the rifle's muzzle and said defiantly, "You'll have to kill me first before you kill him! Don't you see he's only a child! Please, sir, don't do it. You'll be killing an innocent child."

By this time, kambo arrived at the house, all wet from spilling the water on herself. She couldn't believe her eyes. Two soldiers were standing in her own yard, threatening to shoot one of her grandchildren! She noticed that Gilbert was wearing the *camouflage* shirt he had found on the street. She had warned the silly boy not to wear it, because the soldiers might think he was a *kartel*, a member of one of the vigilante groups that had been terrorizing the population.

"If he is a child like you say," responded the soldier aiming his rifle at Gilbert, "why is he wearing this soldier's uniform? He must be a *kartel*. He's old enough to be one."

Kambo joined Mama Apoline in pleading. Josée, N'Kongolo, Marie, Benjamin, and I stood still, silently watching this latest crisis unfold. After a few long seconds of silence, the other soldier told his colleague to put his gun down.

"I've seen *kartels* before. He's not one of them. *Kartels* usually wear amulets and all sorts of tattoos. If the boy were a *kartel*, he would have tried to get away when he saw us coming. Take off that shirt, boy, burn it once and for all." He turned to Mama Apoline and added, "You're very lucky this time. Many of my comrades wouldn't have given him a chance. But I also have children his age. Now don't let these children run around outside of the compound. This town isn't safe for children. If you have any safe place you can go to outside Kongolo, you ought to take all your children there right away. You should leave while you can."

Mama Apoline bent down low, practically touching the ground with her knees, and clapped her hands softly together saying over and over again, "Thank you, sir, thank you, sir."

When the soldiers left, Gilbert stumbled to the ground with a blank gaze in his eyes. He didn't talk for a long time. *Kambo* took his hand and led him to the kitchen, where she poured some cold water on his head. Then she sent him into the house to rest. Mama Apoline grabbed a stool and sat down. We were all quiet for some time. Finally, Mama Apoline broke the silence.

"Tired or not tired," she said with iron-clad conviction, "tomorrow at dawn, we're leaving this town."

CHAPTER 8

ONLY BY NIGHT

For several weeks, Benoit walked in the darkness of night along the railroad tracks heading toward Maniema Province. As dawn approached, he'd dart into nearby woods to find a place to hide during the daylight hours. His strategy was effective: he had yet to run into soldiers or any other kind of trouble. But this day he would take his chances with the sunlight. He knew that just a few more hours of walking should get him to the village of Casimir where one of Apoline's relatives, whom he knew well, lived. Maybe Apoline had already passed through there on her way to Samba. Or maybe she was still there waiting for him to arrive. This might be the day when he would see his family again. He could not wait until nightfall.

He splashed a few drops of water from his jug on his face and took a couple of good gulps down his throat. He chuckled as he thought that, even if he didn't find his family at Casimir's house, at least he would finally get a hot meal. He'd been scavenging for food for weeks and had eaten nothing but cassava, sweet potatoes, sugar cane, and other raw crops from fields.

He walked fast along the snake-like path of the railroad tracks, knowing he could rest when he got to Casimir's house. After passing some cassava and corn fields, he approached the village. Suddenly, he felt very uncomfortable, as if somebody were watching him. He accelerated his pace. Then, from the other side of the railroad, a male voice cried out, "Stop right there!"

Benoit turned around and saw three men dressed in beat-up soldiers' uniforms with animal skins across their chest. They were wearing hats with feathers on top and were armed with bows and arrows.

"Oh Lord, *kartels!*" Benoit said to himself. The oldest of the three started shouting at him.

"Where are you coming from? Where do you think you're going? You look like a soldier in disguise. You think you can fool us? After him!"

It was clear to Benoit that these fools would follow standard *kartel* practice: beat a suspect to death and maybe then inquire about his guilt or innocence. No time to explain that he had nothing to do with what was going on or that he had nothing against any side in this crazy war. He turned around and ran like he'd never run before. He was, quite literally, in a race for his life. The three *kartels* started shooting arrows at him. Benoit ran in zig zag fashion toward the village. He was not far anymore. But would he get there before getting struck down by one of those arrows?

Ping! An arrow deeply scratched his left leg. With blood flowing down his leg, he kept on running, not once glancing down for fear that it would slow him down. The tin water jug on his back felt like it weighed a thousand kilograms. He reached to his chest and opened the strap that held the jug on his back. The jug flew behind him and crashed to the ground.

The *kartels* screamed out in horror, "A grenade, he's thrown a grenade!"

The *kartels* thought the tin jug was a grenade! They stopped shooting arrows and ran for cover in the cassava field by the railroad.

Seconds passed, and they heard no explosion. They gingerly approached the object and kicked it in frustration when they realized what it was. "The enemy is getting away," they shouted, and they resumed their chase.

The unintended diversion gave Benoit breathing room. He arrived at the village before the *kartels* got back into shooting range. Some of the villagers stared apprehensively at the man with blood flowing down his leg, who was running as if he had devils at his feet.

"Where's Casimir's house? I'm his son-in-law," Benoit shouted while gasping for breath. When he saw them staring at his bleeding leg, he added, "There are three *kartels* chasing me for no reason at all."

The villagers didn't say a word, they just pointed in the direction of Casimir's house. It was only two compounds away. Benoit sprinted there and found Casimir sitting on the front lawn under the shade of a palm tree.

"*Monsieur* Benoit? Is that you?" Casimir asked. "What's going on? Why are you running like that? For heaven's sake, you're hurt!"

By this time, Benoit was completely out of breath. He tried to explain but couldn't, so instead he pointed behind him where the three *kartels* were racing toward Casimir's compound. Casimir instantly understood the whole picture. He hugged Benoit and stood in front of him as the three *kartels* entered his compound. He pointed to Benoit as he snarled at them.

"Do you know this man? Why are you chasing him? Why in God's name are you trying to kill him? That's not the way you protect this village. We want to keep away people who bring trouble here. But now, you are creating trouble. I'll speak to your chief about this, you can count on that."

The three men didn't say anything. They looked extremely cross and embarrassed, like children being scolded by their teacher. They hesitated, then shifted their feet back and forth before complying with Casimir's command that they return Benoit's water jug. Benoit glared at the three thugs and saw that two of them were in their early teens, while the one who asked questions couldn't be more than twenty. Just children!

As soon as Benoit caught his breath, he asked Casimir about Apoline and the children. He was crushed to find out that Casimir didn't know anything about Apoline's whereabouts. "She might have gone past this village without stopping," Casimir said. "Many groups of people have been passing through these days. It might have been easier for her to just move on."

"Then I've got to move on," Benoit said. "I've got to get to Samba to see if they're there."

"Tomorrow, Benoit, you can leave tomorrow. I can't let you go like this. Apoline and the children are in God's hands. You are tired and hurt. Please rest here tonight. I'll send two of our most trusted men to take you all the way to Lubunda. You can stay with my brother Ramazani in Lubunda. From there you won't have any problems like you had today."

After having his first bath, cooked meal, and night spent in a bed in weeks, Benoit took off the next morning to Lubunda with Casimir's friends as escorts. They arrived with no incidents and went straight to the house of Ramazani, who was a cousin of Mama Apoline. Again, Benoit found no news of his wife and children. He did get some good news, however: Ramazani told him that the train was operating between Kibamba, the next major town on his route, and Samba. The next morning, Benoit set out for Kibamba. Soon after, he arrived finally in Maniema Province, where he felt it was safe to travel during the day. He inquired about his family at every village along the way, but no one had any news of them. His feet hurt badly, but he had no time to think about it or to let pain slow him down. He had to get to Samba as soon as possible.

It took him another week to get to Kibamba, where he spent the night at the train station and learned that the train to Samba was scheduled to depart the next day. He woke up early the next morning and anxiously paced back and forth on the station platform. A couple of other travelers joined him outside, and they talked about the train, the war, and all the suffering people had gone through. There was dew on the grass, and birds were chirping in the orange and mango trees. Benoit felt full of life again.

"This is going to be a good day," he said to himself. "A glorious day." He grabbed some mangoes and an orange for breakfast.

The train departed on schedule later that morning and arrived in Samba three hours later. The trip would have taken several days on foot. Benoit could barely believe that he had made it to Samba alive. From the Samba train station, Benoit headed straight to the nearby home of Apoline's uncle, Raphaël Sumaili. Benoit was considered Sumaili's *mukwe*, or son-in-law. Sumaili was Muslim and had three wives and many children. He worked for the railroad company.

Benoit heard noise coming from behind the house. Children were playing. Could that be Georgette's voice or Josée's? He couldn't tell. All he knew was that he was there, and he was ready to finally be with his family. He entered the compound, went to the front door, and knocked. The windows were open, and he could see *ba* Sumaili inside chatting with two friends.

When Sumaili heard knocking, he stood up without hesitation and went to the door. He was accustomed to people dropping by unexpectedly. But it was quite a surprise to see *Monsieur* Benoit of Kongolo at his door.

"*Monsieur* Benoit, are you all right? We've been getting only bad news from Kongolo. You've made it safely here, *Allah Amdulilayi*" [may the name of Allah be praised]." His eyes seemed to be looking for something behind Benoit. "Where are Apoline and the children?"

The words dropped like a bomb on Benoit's head. From the look on Benoit's face, Sumaili understood that either he had no news of his family or there was bad news. He reached for Benoit's arm, steadied it, and took him to one of the empty chairs where his two friends had been seated. He introduced Benoit to his friends, then asked them to leave him alone with his son-in-law. As Benoit explained what had happened, he could not hold back his tears. They were the first tears he had shed in his adult life.

"I've lost all of them. My whole family. Are they all dead?"

"No, my son, they're not gone," Sumaili responded. "May *Allah* be my witness, I cannot believe that Apoline and the children are gone. We're talking about a woman with small children. They're not a threat to any government. On the contrary, I've been worried about you."

Benoit sat silently, so Sumaili filled the void. "Apoline must still be on her way here. She has small children with her. The little ones can't walk that fast. It might take them a few more weeks to make it. They are alive." He said it with such conviction that Benoit started to hope again.

"I will use my railroad connections to send word around about them," said Sumaili. "I will do all that can be done to find out about Apoline and the children."

"I must go back along the railroad tracks and find them," Benoit said.

"I can't let you do any such thing, especially after what I've heard about the mercenaries slaughtering anyone suspected of being against the secession. No, you arrived in Samba by the grace of God and under the protection of your ancestors. We mustn't tempt fate and risk such an important life. The only safe and wise thing to do is to sit tight and wait."

"They will come," Sumaili said with a smile, touching Benoit's hand. "You will see. They will come."

CHAPTER 9

SCAVENGERS

Late at night, when it was dark and no one passing by could see, Mama Apoline and Gilbert dug out her two big, metallic suitcases and Papa's two guns that were buried in *kambo*'s vegetable garden on *Avenue Kindu*. Mama Apoline woke us up before dawn, and off we went again. The two women carried the two suitcases, while Gilbert carried Papa's guns and a couple of blankets. Josée and N'Kongolo carried blankets and a bundle of food, and N'Kongolo, of course, hung on to his mat. Marie and I carried water containers. Our target for the day was the second village from Kongolo, where *ma* Zabibu and her husband lived. This time, it seemed that we were going away for a very long time. Samba, our final destination, was about 150 miles away from Kongolo.

We got to *ma* Zabibu's house late at night and stayed there for three days before heading out for Samba. Mama Apoline thanked her "sister" Zabibu once again for taking care of her children.

"We might also leave for Kindu, where we have family, if the situation starts to deteriorate here," Zabibu said. "But we'll wait and see. We know the area very well. We can get away pretty fast if we have to."

My sores were much better now, and I could walk without any problem. Excited to get back into the hide-and-seek game, I didn't complain about being tired for that whole day. The children marched way ahead of Mama Apoline, Gilbert, and *kambo* Colette, who were slowed down by the big bundles they carried. After a while, the plastic water container I was carrying got heavy, and I started lagging behind the other children.

"Can I pour out some of the water to make it lighter?" I asked Mama Apoline.

"No, we'll just have to walk slower. We'll soon take a rest and drink some of your water. Then the container will be lighter."

By the afternoon, we were more than halfway to our next targeted stop, a railroad station where we could spend the night. We stopped to rest under a mango tree in a cassava field, not far from the road. Mama Apoline took out roasted cassava and peanuts from the bundle that N'Kongolo and Josée took turns carrying. After resting and eating, we got back on the road and went for hours, stopping now and then to rest under the shade of a tree and nibble on our modest supply of food. Onward we marched, even as the sun descended and darkness began to surround us. We could barely see where we were putting our feet.

"Can't we sleep here by the road? I'm tired," Marie said.

"We're not far from the station at all," *kambo* replied. "We can go slower, but we need to go spend the night there."

Finally, we came out of the woods into a clearing, from which we could see the train station. As we passed a group of people sitting around a campfire, some of them stood up to welcome us and help Mama Apoline and *kambo* with their bundles. They'd seen this kind of scene before. Many people with children had been fleeing lately.

Three houses down was the train station. There were already a good number of people inside. Gilbert ran ahead to find us a space to sleep. We had another meal of roasted cassava and peanuts, and then we spread out on our mats. Like everyone else, I fell asleep as soon as my head hit the ground.

From that station, we would follow the railroad all the way to Samba. It was the only way Mama Apoline and *kambo* knew to get there. The next day, we walked for hours at a time with only toilet stops for breaks. When the sun was high up in the sky, the little rocks by the rails sizzled below my bare feet. I didn't have shoes any more, my last pair of shoes had simply fallen apart from all the walking. "The hot rocks hurt my feet," I complained.

Mama Apoline told me "Keep your feet off the rocks." This advice didn't help much, as little rocks were everywhere. Later, *kambo* eased my discomfort by tying some leaves around my feet with a string.

"Hey, look, Geolo is wearing bushes on her feet," N'Kongolo teased me, and everyone laughed, even me. I was a funny sight to behold. But it worked, my feet didn't hurt any more, and I didn't care how silly I looked. How far was Samba from here, anyway? Even with my feet protected, I was sick and tired of all the walking.

"Why can't we take a train? It will be a lot faster!" I grumbled to Mama Apoline.

"There are no trains any more," she replied with more than a little frustration at my failure to understand the situation. "There's a war going on. People are doing bad things to each other. That's why your Papa isn't with us, and that's why we're not at home." If Papa were with us, I thought, he'd find a train to get us to Samba. He would figure something out. He wouldn't let me suffer like this.

After a few hours, my natural shoes started falling apart. *Kambo* had to make me many pairs over the course of our march. As we followed the railroad's path, we met many people going in the same direction as we were, though they all soon left us far behind. We were not walking as fast as everyone else, that was for sure.

Late in the afternoon, we heard noises on the rails as if a train were coming or going in the far distance, but we saw nothing on the tracks. Then, far behind us, we saw a speck moving in our direction. Even from a distance we could see that it was too small to be a train. As it got closer, we saw that it was not even a single train car; it was nothing but a metal bar with two wheels and two men sitting on it.

The two men were moving the wheeled metal bar by pushing sticks against the tracks as if they were riding in a canoe. They each carried a backpack and wore a funny looking hat. When they reached us, they gave a silly wave and barely comprehensible shouts, then continued on their way "paddling" down the track. Now why couldn't we ride those bars? My feet were hurting again, and I gazed at the two men with envy as they disappeared far ahead of us. Mama Apoline said they looked like troublemakers, like *kartels*.

"Did you see their eyes? They were as red as chili peppers! They smoke *diamba* [marijuana]! I'm glad they didn't stop to rob us."

During our long trip to Samba, we spent almost every moment of every long day walking, following the general path of the railroad tracks. Some nights we slept in train stations. Sometimes one of the children was sick or we were all hopelessly exhausted, and Mama Apoline and *kambo* decided that we should rest at a station for a day or two before hitting the road again. Occasionally we spent nights in villages and, rarely, we slept in someone's house. But, for the most part, we slept outdoors in the countryside between villages and train stations. Our "beds" consisted of dead leaves and straw that we all collected; we even turned it into a game to see who could make a fluffier bed. We covered ourselves with Mama Apoline's *pagnes*. When there was moonlight, *kambo* told us stories before we slept. We were all so tired from walking that, even though it was very uncomfortable, even though we often heard strange noises, even though sometimes we were cold and wet, we always fell fast asleep in no time.

Sometimes it rained when we were in the middle of nowhere, without any shelter to protect us. Usually we just continued walking under the downpour and after it ceased, we would let our clothes dry right on our bodies. If it rained at night, we just lay there, getting some protection from tree branches but mostly getting soaked.

We lived by scavenging for food from fields and trees that we passed. On the first leg of the trip, not far from Kongolo, many of the villages were deserted. Mama Apoline and *kambo* went inside empty houses and looked for whatever edible things they could find for us. Gilbert and the rest of us helped a lot when it came to climbing trees to get mangoes or papayas.

Most of the time we ate whatever we came across in the fields and woods. On good days we found cassava, sweet potatoes, peanuts, or termites. Sometimes we ate vegetables that I never knew could be food, such as hibiscus leaves, which were very sticky and had a taste similar to that of okra. We searched through dead and rotten palm trees to find different types of caterpillars and other insects that Mama Apoline and *kambo* fried without oil. We ate many different kinds of roots and tubercles. No one was picky about their food any more. Anything that stanched the constant hunger was appreciated. Some days we ate only once during the whole day, and some days we found nothing to eat. In the beginning, I asked for food when I got hungry. But as the days went by, I learned not to ask for something that wasn't there. Instead, I concentrated my energies on looking for any edible thing visible from our path.

We had no plates or silverware. We all ate with our fingers from the same two pots that Mama Apoline found in a house in one of the villages outside Kongolo. Every time we passed by a crop field, Mama Apoline and *kambo* took all the food we could carry, because we never knew how long it would be before we found something to eat again.

Mama Apoline and *kambo* usually took only a few bites and left the rest for us children. There were times, especially when it was dark, when I had only two or three mouthfuls before the pots were empty. Later, we found out that fourteen-year-old Gilbert had been taking more than his share. When we weren't looking, he'd scoop out a sizable portion of the food and hide it behind his back in one hand. Then he'd proceed to eat, very fast, with his other hand what was left in the pots. As soon as we finished, Gilbert would announce that he had to go urinate, but he'd really leave to eat up the portion he had hidden.

We drank any water that we came across, from wells, streams, and rivers. We bathed in streams that we passed. Of course, there was no soap to wash our bodies or clothes. But Mama Apoline and *kambo* beat some plants, which resembled cactus, with a wooden stick until some bubbles came out. The bubbles mixed with wet clothes, and this process effectively removed dirt and stains. The drawback was that the mixture was so strong that frequent use of it tore fabric to shreds.

As we trudged on, not only I, but the others developed blisters and calluses. The nasty blisters on my thighs returned, and some pimples that looked like boils developed on my back, chest, and stomach. One day, a woman who had been marching near us told Mama Apoline to make sure that the pimples I had on my body didn't have any worms inside. She came up to me and showed Mama Apoline how to check for the worms. With her forefingers and thumbs, the woman squeezed one of my pimples at its base. A white worm, about the size of a grain of rice, popped out. I shrieked with fear, but Mama Apoline held me tight and insisted on popping all my pimples to get the worms out. The lady showed her how to treat the popped pimple sites with ashes of banana peels to help them heal. From that time on, Mama Apoline checked me regularly and did what the woman showed her. The ashes stung terribly and made me cry. *Kambo* hugged me and calmed me down by promising that I'd soon feel better. Later, I got up the courage to pop the pimples by myself as soon as they emerged.

Sometimes, in a train station, I saw myself in the reflection from a window, and I got scared. The girl who stared back at me had skin pockmarked with scars that would take years to disappear. Her face was gaunt from poor nutrition. She was about the skinniest little girl I had ever seen.

After several weeks of walking, we arrived at the town of Lubunda in the thick of the night and went straight to the home of Ramazani, Mama Apoline's cousin. Mama Apoline knocked on the door, and a male voice inside asked who it was.

"Is it you *kaka* [brother] Ramazani? It's me, Apoline Bahati. I'm here with Mama and my children." Before she finished explaining, the door opened, and a man with a kerosene lamp came out. He raised the lamp higher to get a close look at his visitors.

"Welcome, welcome *da* [sister] Apoline. Come in. Why are you traveling like this at night with children? Come on in. How are you doing, Mama?"

"Everything is chaos in Kongolo," *kambo* said. "Even old people like me are no longer left alone."

"Where is Monsieur Benoit? Has he found you?"

Mama Apoline's heart skipped a beat. "Do you have news of my husband? We've been separated for over six weeks now. The children told me they saw a man firing at him."

"I saw Benoit about a month ago. Why, he even spent the night here at my house. I think he's on his way to Samba. That's where he said that you and he had agreed to go if things got worse."

Papa was alive! Papa was alive!

"I told you, Apolina. I told you he's alive," *kambo* Colette said with a great big grin. We all laughed and laughed; the children were so excited that we started jumping up and down. Even Marie and I understood that something wonderful had happened, that we had escaped the worst blow of all.

The following day we went back on the road as soon as the sun rose. There were many other people with children trudging along the railroad tracks. But, on this day, nobody passed us by. For, on this day, Mama Apoline and all of us were filled with boundless energy. We did not walk, we marched. We no longer felt the blisters on our feet, the sores on our thighs, or the stinging heat of the sun beating down on our heads.

He was alive! He was alive!

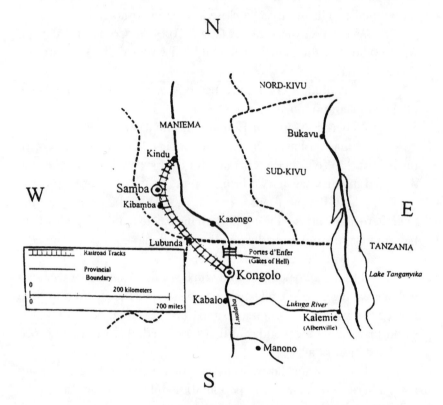

The road from Kongolo to Samba

CHAPTER 10

BETRAYAL

At the station after Lubunda, a surprise awaited us. Mama Apoline's "sister," Zabibu, and her husband were there.

"The village is no longer safe," they told Mama Apoline. "Strangers are fighting in the streets with people and gunfire can be heard now and again. No one is safe anymore. We figured we'd better leave quickly."

"But how did you get here, past us, so fast without our seeing you?" *kambo* asked. "We took a short cut," Zabibu replied. They would accompany us along the railroad until Kibamba, where they'd catch a train to Kindu. *Kambo* was pleased to have them join us, but Mama Apoline didn't seem very happy about it. She had not been comfortable with them since Zabibu had talked on and on about getting a "reward" for taking care of Josée and N'Kongolo.

"I don't think they really care about us, especially Zabibu," she told *kambo*. "They're just after what we have."

"That's nonsense," *kambo* said. "Zabibu is family; she's your sister. How can you talk about her like that? Don't be suspicious of everyone, Apolina. Don't you see how happy they are to travel with us?

They'll give us a hand with the children. It will help us get to Samba sooner."

N'Kongolo and Josée agreed with Mama Apoline. They were not at all pleased with our new travel partners.

A few days later, very late at night, we were asleep inside a train station with many other refugees. Suddenly, we heard shouting from outside.

"*Sergeant Major, leta bunduki na masasi!*" [Sergeant major, bring the guns and bullets]. Trampling footsteps came near. It sounded like a group of soldiers was coming to get us. Everyone snapped awake and ran out of the train station to the nearby cassava and banana fields. Mama Apoline and *kambo* managed to get us ready in no time, and we all fled into the moonless night. We didn't go very far, we hid in the thick fronds of a group of banana trees behind the outhouse. The shouting soldiers soon arrived at the station house. And now we heard the sound of guns going off and bullets hitting the walls.

"Keep quiet and absolutely still," Mama Apoline whispered to us.

But how could we keep quiet and still when thousands of mosquitoes were sucking our blood? I felt like I had a blanket of mosquitoes all over my body!

"Quiet! Don't slap yourselves!" *kambo* whispered. "We might be discovered. Just wipe them off. The mosquitoes will go away after a while."

Everyone somehow kept still, terrified by the thought of getting arrested and sent to some prison, or even worse. Meanwhile, the mosquitoes were partying, and we were their feast. Contrary to what *kambo* had promised, they didn't go away at all. They buzzed off for a few seconds, and then they swooped back for another attack. I could hear Josée quietly crying, as I was. How long were we going to stay in these trees? I wanted to go back home. Papa might be there. If he were here, he would have gotten us out of here. Where was he now? He would have gone after those soldiers. He would have taken his two guns and scared them away!

I hated this. This was no game. Games had beginnings and ends—my favorite part. There was laughter and good times and make believe when games were played. No, this was no game. It was hideously real. I hated it. I wanted to eat my favorite dinners. I wanted to sleep in my own bed at night. I wanted to hear Papa's bedtime stories, the stories that his grandma Ibumando told him when he was a little boy. How I missed those stories, even though I usually fell asleep halfway into them.

To help my fears go away, I tried to think of one. I started to remember the story about a boy named Amundala. Amundala's parents lived in a village that was wiped out by a giant, mean beast who swallowed everyone and everything in his path. The mean beast, Nunda, used to live far away in the forest where no one ventured. Then Nunda finished all the animals that lived in his area of the forest. He moved closer and closer to the part of the forest where people from Amundala's village went hunting. Soon, the beast ate everyone who went hunting. Nunda got so big with all the people he swallowed that he couldn't move very fast any more.

When Amundala's mother was pregnant with him, she had a terrible craving for *simbiliki* steak. *Simbiliki* is a huge rodent similar to a guinea pig, but twice the size. It lives in the forest and could only be found where Nunda lived. No matter what Amundala's father would give his wife, she wouldn't be satisfied until he brought her *simbiliki* steak. Both of them knew that, because of Nunda, he risked his life every time he went hunting for *simbiliki*. Then one day, he didn't come back. He was one of the last persons in the village to be eaten by Nunda. Amundala was born shortly thereafter. He grew up to be a strong man who vowed to find Nunda, kill him, and liberate his father and the people of his village.

One day, he packed his bow, arrows, and a big knife in a skin pouch made from *simbiliki* skin. He then headed out for the forest where Nunda lived. The *simbiliki's* skin had magical powers for anyone who owned it. When Amundala arrived where Nunda lived, he started singing very loudly: "Nunda, are you the one who ate all the people from my village? You have eaten my father, so come and swallow me, too."

Sure enough, Nunda came and swallowed Amundala. Once inside the belly of the great beast, Amundala found his father and everyone who had disappeared from the village. Amundala then opened his *simbiliki* skin pouch, took out his bow, and shot an arrow through Nunda's heart. The monster was killed instantly. With his long knife, Amundala cut open Nunda's belly and, thus, liberated everyone who had been captured by the beast. The people made Amundala's parents King and Queen of the village, and Amundala became the Prince.

All of a sudden, I was awakened from my sweet dream of Papa's tale by shouting. The cries were very close, dangerously close to us. As a matter of fact, they were coming from right where we were hiding. Suddenly I realized it was Mama Apoline; she was the one who was screaming her lungs out! Why was she shouting? Wouldn't the soldiers come and get us?

"People, those are pygmies, they are not soldiers," Mama Apoline shouted. "Don't be afraid. Please come out, and let's go after them! There are no soldiers here. Listen for yourselves. These pygmies are here to rob us of the little we have left. Please, all of you men, come out; we need each other!"

Gilbert was terrified and thought his mother had lost her mind.

"Mama, quiet, be quiet. You're going to get all of us shot! Those are soldiers."

"Quiet, Apolina," *kambo* said sternly.

"Listen carefully, Gilbert. Even you, Mama. Listen to their accents and the noises. Those aren't gun shots. They're throwing rocks on the station roof. Listen!"

As if by miracle, the shouting of the "soldiers" suddenly stopped. We heard a group of people running away. Mama Apoline pulled us out of our hiding place. Thank heaven! The mosquitoes were about to reduce us to skin and bones. Mama Apoline kept on shouting, calling out to all the men and women to join her and go after the pygmies before they got away. Although they had not responded to Mama Apoline's before, one by one, people started coming out. Some started running after the "soldiers." Everything happened so fast, but thanks to Mama Apoline, not all of the pygmies managed to escape with their loot. Some of the men who had been sleeping in the train station grabbed three fleeing pygmies.

Clothes and other possessions lay on the ground outside the station; the pygmies must have dropped them in their haste to escape. Back in the station, we found that most everything had vanished. Mama Apoline's two suitcases with her clothes were gone.

"These pygmies, they will hear from me," she said furiously. "They will learn how crazy I can get!"

She asked *kambo* to look after us and took Gilbert with her to join the men who were holding the three pygmies. They threatened to torture the pygmies if they didn't get their things back. The pygmies quickly relented; they took the men on a path leading to the pygmy village. Along the way they discovered more things discarded here and there in the rush to escape. Almost everyone from the train station found their belongings. But Mama Apoline and Gilbert couldn't find her two suitcases or the bundles in which we had wrapped our most essential possessions, Papa's two guns. Mama Apoline threatened the pygmies in every way possible, but they insisted that none of their group had taken her possessions. Somebody else had taken them.

"Who?" Mama Apoline asked, with a continuing menace of violence in her voice. "Someone from your village? Let's go to your village."

"No," one of the pygmies said.

"It is one of your men and one of your women," said another pygmy. "They came earlier, during the day, to our village. They told us that there are people at the station who have stolen their things. And that we should go and pretend to be soldiers so that they can take their things back. They said they will share some things with us and also give us a reward."

The three pygmies described the couple to Mama Apoline. She frowned and said, "That description sounds very much like two people I know and now distrust." When Mama Apoline and Gilbert returned to the station, she explained to *kambo* what the pygmies had told her.

"Mama, do you know where Zabibu and her husband have been all this time?"

"They left a long time ago, they said they were looking for food, but they haven't come back yet. They weren't with us at the station when the pygmies came."

"That's what I thought," Mama Apoline said appraisingly.

"Do you think that they had something to do with this? Oh, that's not possible. She couldn't do such a thing, she's your sister," *kambo* objected.

"She is what she is."

"Who do you trust? The pygmies? Listen, Apoline. We've lost those things, but remember we still have our lives. Let's concentrate on getting to Samba alive. You might alienate yourself from your relatives for something they didn't do. Haven't they been helping you with the children? Please, get some rest. We have another long day tomorrow."

We woke up early the next day and started marching again on the road to Samba. From the cock's first crow, Mama Apoline and *kambo* talked about nothing but *ma* Zabibu and her husband. By midmorning, Mama Apoline's suspicions grew even greater.

"Every day they'd spent lots of time with us. But since the pygmy incident last night, they've been keeping their distance. Don't you think they're acting strangely?"

Kambo no longer rushed to her relatives' defense. N'Kongolo said, "We don't need Zabibu and her husband with us," and Josée immediately seconded his statement. They were afraid that, somehow, *ma* Zabibu and her husband would steal them.

"Don't worry, my children," Mama Apoline reassured them. "They won't get you. They got my clothes, but I'm going to get them all back, you wait and see."

By the afternoon, Mama Apoline could no longer control herself. "I'm going to catch up with them and see what they're carrying," she said to *kambo*. "It seems to me that they're carrying much bigger bundles than they were before the pygmy incident. I'll be back soon."

As soon as the couple saw Mama Apoline headed toward them, *ma* Zabibu stopped walking. She turned her back to Mama Apoline, opened one of her *pagnes* and shook it; meanwhile her husband carried some things to the woods next to the railroad tracks. When Mama Apoline reached where Zabibu stood, she immediately asked her "sister" what she thought of the attack the night before.

"That was terrible," Zabibu replied. "To fool people during a time like this! Those pygmies are the lowest of the low." She seemed very much ill at ease.

When Mama Apoline returned, she told *kambo,* "Mama, they have our missing stuff. I have no doubt about it."

"How do you know for sure?"

"I just feel it, Mama. They got rid of the suitcases and put everything in her *pagnes*. When I was there, I saw some long things hidden in the woods not far from where they were seated. Those long things, I bet, are *baba* Josée's guns. But I won't let them know that I know.

"I'll let them carry our things for us. When we get near Kibamba, that's when I'll confront them. I'll be as nice to them as I was before last night. That way they won't catch on and disappear on us in the night. I just have to keep a close eye on them. We're not very far from Kibamba anymore. A day or two, and we'll be there."

It was almost dark when we got to a little train station where Mama Apoline said we would spend the night. We went directly into the station and settled down. But *ma* Zabibu and her husband didn't come to the station house like they would have done before the pygmy incident. Instead, they said, they were going to the home of some people they knew near the station.

"How come Zabibu didn't mention to me before that they know people here?" asked Mama Apoline. "Mama, I won't wait to get near Kibamba anymore. I'm going to confront them right now. If I wait for tomorrow, it might be too late. They might hide our things some place where we will never find them. Gilbert, come with me. Children, you stay here with Mama."

Mama Apoline raced out of the station with Gilbert; they followed Zabibu and her husband and saw them enter a compound. Zabibu and her husband were greeting their friends, but then they noticed that Mama Apoline had followed them. They turned to their friends and said something, and the friends started lifting their bundles.

"Gilbert, let's run now!" Mama Apoline called out. "If the things go inside the house, they'll disappear. Let's run fast!"

Meanwhile, *kambo* and all of us children had followed Mama Apoline and Gilbert outside of the station. When we saw them running toward the house, we all ran after them. Mama Apoline soon stood between the house and Zabibu and her friends. Panting with fatigue, she barked out commands.

"Zabibu, open up these bundles right now! I used to think of you like a sister, but now I despise you. Open up fast before I show you how crazy I can get."

Zabibu and her husband stood motionless, stunned. Mama Apoline grabbed from Zabibu's friend a long bundle wrapped in clothes. It was one of Papa's guns! She turned around to see Zabibu's husband holding another bundle that obviously contained Papa's other gun.

"Gilbert, go take the other gun," Mama Apoline shouted.

She opened up another bundle—her clothes! Zabibu tried to touch Mama Apoline's hand, but Mama Apoline pushed her away hard, knocking her to the ground. Zabibu tried to plead for mercy.

"I'm sorry, Apoline, I'm sorry. I was going to give you back all your things. Sure I was. I've just been helping you by carrying them for you, that's all. I only wanted to help you, my sister."

Mama Apoline snarled at her "sister." By this time we were all in the compound watching the scene play out. As Mama Apoline tore open the bundles, we started collecting the things that Zabibu and her husband had taken from us.

Kambo was stunned. "Apolina has been right all along. Zabibu, you are family. How could you do this to us?"

Zabibu, on bent knees, tried to salvage something from the disaster. "Apoline, my sister, at least leave me some *pagnes*. I carried your things for you, *da* Apoline. Two or three *pagnes* won't make any difference for you."

This drove Mama Apoline over the edge: she lost control and slapped Zabibu across the face. "You took care of my children, I thank you for that, even though you didn't have any right to scare them with stories about keeping them for good. I have given you a thank you present and promised to give you more after the war. How dare you come and do this? You don't deserve anything from me, as God is my witness!"

When Mama Apoline took a step to leave, Zabibu tried again to touch her hand. Suddenly, Marie jumped on Zabibu, bit her behind, and didn't let go. She was hanging on with her teeth! Zabibu screamed as she tried to shake Marie off her butt. This was one time when Josée, N'Kongolo, and I were not going to pull Marie and her killer teeth off her victim's flesh.

"Please, *da* Apoline, tell the child to let go," Zabibu screamed. "I'm sorry I took your things. Please, get the child off of me!" Gilbert finally pulled Marie off.

"I'm sorry," Zabibu's husband said. "This was all Zabibu's idea. Since you left our house, she couldn't stop talking about all your clothes. When she told me about getting the pygmies involved, I told her it wasn't right. I tried to talk her out of it but she wouldn't listen. She said your husband has so much money that you wouldn't miss the things we took. I'm sorry."

Mama Apoline looked at him with disgust. We picked up our things, and returned to the station. I looked back and saw that Zabibu was still clutching her aching rear end.

CHAPTER 11

REUNITED

Our trip continued for many more days before we got to Kibamba. It had been more than a month since we'd left Kongolo. Limping, weary and having had little to eat for what seemed to me forever, we exhaustedly approached Kibamba's train station. There we saw a beautiful sight: thick, rich variegated green branches of mango and orange trees filled with lush ripe fruit lining both sides of the railroad. All at once, I felt better. I knew that we wouldn't go hungry here. We saw people at the station ahead of us, some sitting in groups, others walking under the trees. We heard children playing *kange. Kange!* It had been so long since Josée and I had played it. Mama Apoline told us to stay together until we found a spot in the train station. Then we could go play.

"Look over there, Mama, that man looks just like Papa," said Gilbert, pointing to a man sitting on a concrete bench outside the station. The man stood up and looked in our direction.

"*Baba* Josée?" Mama Apoline called out with a tone of uncertainty. The man started to walk in our direction.

"Apoline, is it really you?" he called out. He started to run toward us.

"Papa! My Papa is here!" cried Josée as she dropped what she had been carrying. She ran ahead of us and was the first to jump on Papa. Papa held her high up in the air.

"Papa, I knew all along that you would come to get us," I said as I awkwardly ran to him. I couldn't run very fast. I had sores again on my thighs, and they hurt badly. Papa lifted me up and held me for a while. Then Mama Apoline told him of my sores, he looked at them with concern, felt my skinny arms, and hugged me again. He looked overwhelmed, as if he didn't quite grasp that we were really there. We had been separated for more than eight weeks since that terrible day when we fled Kongolo. "Papa, you've found us," I cried. "Now we are safe." I knew Papa would never let anything bad happen to us ever again.

Mama Apoline had been waiting her turn. Papa went toward her, helped her put down her bundle, and they embraced. They talked briefly, softly, then Papa picked up Benjamin. He went to *kambo* Colette, and they shook hands. Even in this moment of great elation, he could not be any more affectionate with her: the customs of the area forbade a man from hugging his mother-in-law or touching her in any way other than a handshake. It was one of the greatest taboos. Papa then shook hands with Gilbert and N'Kongolo and gave Marie a hug. We all went inside to sit down at Papa's spot in the train station.

"So have you eaten yet?" Papa asked, just as he always did in Kongolo. "Is anyone hungry? I bet I know one person who's hungry. Eh, Georgette?" Papa looked at me with a smile, then gave us a bunch of mangoes and oranges that we devoured.

Papa told us all that had happened to him since we separated, "Friends of *ba* Sumaili who worked on the railroad told me they had seen a woman, fitting the description of Apoline, with a baby and other children walking along the railroad tracks toward Kibamba. I couldn't be sure it was you, but it gave me hope. I couldn't sit in Samba waiting; I had to come to Kibamba to greet you and help you get to Samba quickly." He'd been waiting at the Kibamba train station for over a week, gazing at each group of newcomers. Finally, he saw what he was waiting for.

Papa said, "The next train will come in three days." He told Mama Apoline how glad *ba* Sumaili would be to see us all.

"He insists that we stay with him until the war is over. But I think as soon as we get settled, I'll figure out something I can do. I can't just sit and wait for the war to be over. As kind as he and his wives are now, I don't want us to become a burden for him. He already has a huge family to support."

Finally, the day came for the train's arrival—but the train didn't arrive. We began to think that it would never come.

"Will we have to continue on foot again?" asked Josée. "I'm so tired of walking all the time."

"Me, too," I echoed.

"If we have to wait here for weeks until the train comes, then let's wait," Josée added.

"There's no need to worry," Papa said. "The train has kept its schedule pretty well up to now. It will come, maybe late, but it will come."

Three more days passed without sight of a train. Then, in the afternoon, as we were about to lose all hope, we heard that magnificent sound, *tchooooo tchooooo*, in the far away distance.

"Yippeeeee! The train!" Josée, Marie, and I jumped up and down, excited. There was a commotion as people at the station started to get ready. After we boarded the train, Josée, Marie, and I stood at the window, peering outside. Then we heard the whistle. Slowly, we started moving. What a joy, what extraordinary pleasure to move so fast without wearying our calloused and blistered feet, to know that our horrible journey was about to end, to have Papa there to smile at us. We passed through village after village. Then, just as the sun went down, we arrived in Samba.

When we arrived at *ba* Sumaili's house, we got more than just a happy welcome. They gave us a great, big *shangwe* [party]. His second and third wives busily made us dinner, while his first wife took us to the house we would stay in. Each of *ba* Sumaili's wives and their respective children had their own houses. All three women used the same kitchen, though wives number two and three did most of the cooking. Then we all took delicious showers, the first time in more than eight weeks that we had been able to wash with hot water and soap. Only N'Kongolo refused to shower. He said he was too tired. Some things never seemed to change.

The next day, Sumaili invited his friends and some relatives who lived in town to come and thank *Allah* for saving his "daughter's" family. We hadn't seen so much food since our nights in the pygmy village. We all ate to our heart's content, and no one did so with more gusto than I. *Ba* Sumaili sent for some palm wine, even though as a Muslim, he didn't usually drink alcohol. Everyone was so happy that Papa even let us taste some of the sweet, sweet palm wine.

For us children, the party lasted for days. Josée, Marie, and I had all of *ba* Sumaili's children to play with. How many were there, nine, ten, twelve or more? We played with them all the time. It felt almost like being at home.

Somehow, Papa had managed to keep some Congolese money with him since our departure from Kongolo. This would support us for a few weeks, but then he said determinedly, "I'll have to find other ways to make a living for my family." At least that was how he viewed the situation. From *ba* Sumaili's point of view, Papa was worrying needlessly. *Ba* Sumaili epitomized all that was good and gracious about the African extended family.

"This is my territory, *Monsieur* Benoit," *ba* Sumaili said. "If I can provide for more than twenty people, I can certainly provide for nine more. Don't you worry yourself like that. You and Apoline and the children will stay under my care until the war is over and you can return to Kongolo."

But Papa insisted that he needed to work, if for no other reason than to keep busy and sane. He decided that hunting offered him
the best prospects.

"*Ba* Sumaili has helped us more than enough," Papa told
Mama Apoline. "Nobody knows when the war will end. It could be
today, tomorrow, or years from now. I can't just sit and wait. I don't
want my family to be somebody else's responsibility. Besides, if we
make some money selling meat, it will help us after the war. Otherwise,
we will have to start from ground zero."

Mama Apoline supported Papa's hunting plans, in part
because it would free her from the long shadow of Sumaili's first wife,
Sakina, who was starting to boss her around as she did her *wake-wenzake* [co-wives]. So, one day soon after our arrival in Samba, Papa and
two of *ba* Sumaili's friends, Amédéo and Simon, left at sundown for
the forest. When they came back at nightfall three days later, they were
carrying loads of smoked meat.

"Apoline, go get *ba* Sumaili," Papa said, grinning from ear to
ear. "I want him to be here when we open the bags. Josée, please bring
some water for my two good friends here."

Sumaili said he felt honored that Papa decided to have him
present for this great occasion. Papa then silently sealed two bags of
meat and presented one each to Amédéo and Simon, who were obviously very grateful. They had never had so much game during one trip
before; they were used to hunting with traps, not guns.

"Any time you want us to go back, *Monsieur* Benoit, just let
us know," Simon said as they left with their reward.

And that was the beginning of Papa's very profitable hunting
business. Every two to three weeks, Papa, Amédéo, and Simon went
into the forest, while Mama Apoline sold at the house what Papa had
brought from his previous trip. We began to contribute a great deal
of food to *ba* Sumaili's household. This tremendously improved the
relationship between Mama Apoline and *ma* Sakina, *ba* Sumaili's
first wife. She even started helping Mama Apoline sell the meat. But

she always found some way to let Mama Apoline know who was the boss of the Sumaili compound.

Two months after our arrival in Samba, we moved to a two-bed-room house about a thirty-minute walk from *ba* Sumaili's compound. It was much closer to the forest, where Papa went hunting and where he planned to start farming. There was a smaller house in the backyard where *kambo* Colette, Marie, and the boys slept. In between the two houses stood a tremendous palm tree; further back, there was an out-house enclosed by a fence made of palm branches. Just beyond the out-house was a small vegetable field, where *kambo* planted cassava, sweet potato leaves, sugar cane, and green vegetables that we call *lenga lenga* and *ngai ngai*.

Josée and I shared a bamboo bed that Papa made for us. Since our compound was not very far from the forest, we heard all kinds of animal noises at night. Josée trembled and squeezed my hand whenever we heard a spooky noise. "I wish Maman was here," she'd often say. She didn't like to sleep on the outside part of the bed, she always wanted to sleep against the wall with me between her and the window. I protested because sometimes I got scared at night, too.

"Let's take turns," Josée suggested. "You sleep one day in front, me against the wall. The next day, it's my turn to sleep in front."

But almost always, when I woke up at night, I found her hud-dled against the wall. I'd push her back to the outside, but in the morning, there she'd be wedged against the wall again. I never under-stood how she managed to do that. One night I decided to sleep with my hand hanging on the side of the wall so that if she started pushing me I would wake up. This strategy worked, because that night when I woke up, I was still on the inside. But Josée wasn't on the outside, she had disappeared. I reached out in the dark and touched Benjamin's sleeping space. He was by himself, no sign of Josée. I went to knock on Papa's door.

"I need to go pee," I called out. Papa came out with his flash-light. As he took me to the outhouse, I told him, "Josée isn't in our bed,

Papa. I'm all alone. I can't sleep by myself. It's her turn to sleep in front tonight."

"She's in our bedroom," he said with a yawn.

"Then I'm also coming into your bedroom."

"Oh no! I'll bring Josée back when we go inside."

When we returned, Papa carried Josée to our room and dropped her into our bed on the side away from the wall. In the morning, as usual, I found myself on the outside. "Josée, it's my turn. Why do you always do that?" She told me that she had heard an owl, humming at the window. And she had seen strange shapes! And she had heard footsteps by the window!

CHAPTER 12

THE LIGHTNING'S VENOM

An old couple who had no children lived across the street from our house in Samba. Most of our neighbors called them *balozi* [witches] and told their children to stay away from the couple's house. They said that the couple might eat their children. I never understood why people thought they were witches. Mama Apoline told us not to talk to them or go near their house, but Papa disagreed.

"It's always like that when people are a little different, they get called names and people create all kinds of stories about them," Papa said. "Don't pay any attention to that nonsense. It's just ignorance, that's all it is."

In fact, Papa was one of the few people in the neighborhood who ever went to visit the old couple. Josée and I went with Papa sometimes to visit, and they always treated us kindly. A couple of times, I climbed their trees to get them some ripe papayas. They even gave me some papayas to eat. Mama Apoline said that they had already "eaten my heart"; they had bewitched me.

Early one sunsplashed afternoon, Mama Apoline, *kambo*, all

of us children, and some of our neighbors were sitting on the side of the main house under the shade of palm trees. Suddenly, the sky started darkening, then quickly cleared. But it became windy. Abruptly, a flash of light rent the sky, then immediately a tremendous roar sounded. It rained often here, and the rains were usually preceded by dramatic displays of thunder and lightning. Papa had often told us not to take any chances with the lightning in Samba, that storms were much more dangerous there than they were in Kongolo.

Before we could race indoors, a bright, purplish light hit the top of the trees and traveled down to where we were sitting. The next thing we knew we had all been knocked off our chairs and thrown to the ground. We had no idea how, but some force had blown us off our seats in a matter of seconds.

"We're leaving," our neighbors said as they hurriedly gathered their children. "Quick, children, we have to get home before it starts to rain." As they ran to the entrance of our compound, another bolt of lightning struck again at the exact same place. We all started running to *kambo*'s house.

"Fast, children," Mama Apoline called out. "This one is really bad!"

This was one time Mama Apoline didn't have to tell me twice to get out of trouble's way. Once inside the house, the children sat on the ground by *kambo*'s bed, *kambo* perched on a stool, and Mama Apoline sat on the bed. It was drizzling now, with all sorts of rumbling noises coming from the sky. *Kambo* and Mama Apoline talked nervously about what had just happened. Then, we heard "*Crraaack paaackt!*" Another bolt of lightning, like a cannon ball, struck our compound. Mama Apoline began to rock back and forth on the bed, as she stared straight ahead and spoke.

"I have been told that people here have magical powers, so they can send lightning to get back at people who have wronged them. When you owe somebody something, and you don't want to pay back, they send the lightning to get you. First, you get warnings, then *kaput.*"

She punctuated her final words by running her fingers across her throat in the universal sign of throat slitting.

"We don't owe anything to anybody," *kambo* said. "*Ba* Benoit doesn't have problems with anyone. On the contrary, people owe him money and a lot of other things. Why is this lightning threatening us and our children?"

She was about to make another comment when a big bright orange light bathed the room. It was immediately followed by a tremendous boom. Instantly, my mouth became warm as if filled with hot vapor. A whitish, fuzzy smoke filled the room. All of us children started to cry. *Kambo*'s bamboo bed cracked, and its legs buckled under.

Mama Apoline screamed out in pain, as she held her left leg, "Mama, I'm dying, I'm dying. It's broken, Mama, it's broken."

Pieces of the bamboo bed scattered across the room. The lightning bolt must have hit Mama Apoline. *Kambo* came to her side, held her wounded leg, and began bending it gently, up and down, up and down. While doing that, she looked toward the roof and cried out, "We don't owe anybody anything. We haven't killed anybody. You, lightning, you can't do anything to this family. What we have, *ba* Benoit has earned from his own sweat."

She put Mama Apoline's leg down and told her to continue rubbing it at the joint. *Kambo* then took a long, wooden spatula, went to the door, and started wagging it from left to right in the doorway while talking to an invisible adversary. It was only then that I realized that the straw roof was on fire. Gilbert threw a bucket of water on it, and the smoke started to dissipate. Moments later, the rain stopped, and the mischievous sun snuck out from behind the clouds again.

Gilbert and *kambo* helped Mama Apoline stand up. "You need to try to walk right away, that will help you get some feeling back in your leg again. You'll be all right; you'll be all right," *kambo* told her frightened daughter again and again as she helped her walk to the main house.

Gilbert tried to put the pieces of *kambo*'s bed back together, while the rest of us followed *kambo* and Mama Apoline to the main house. As we left *kambo*'s house, we saw that the tall palm tree standing in our backyard was smoking. Its green branches had turned brown.

Mama Apoline recovered with no ill effects, but two days later, the tree started to exude some whitish bubbles.

"Is it palm wine?" I asked *kambo*.

"No, it's the lightning's venom. It didn't have any reason to harm us but instead ended in the tree."

I stood there incredulous. So much venom! I felt grateful toward the tree for somehow taking the blow that could have destroyed us.

Two days later, after Papa had come back from his hunting trip, I saw him out the window beginning to cut down the tall palm tree that had absorbed all the lightning's venom.

I hurried outside, "No, Papa," I said. "Don't do that! That tree saved our lives. It sucked in all the venom that was meant for us!"

"Georgette, let me tell you something," Papa replied. "There was no venom meant for us. Nobody sent lightning to hit us. People can't control lightning, only God can. The lightning came into our yard, because the tree was here. Lightning hits tall things. Do you understand?"

"Yes, Papa," I said, much relieved to learn that no one had cast a spell upon us.

One rainy evening, in 1962, Papa was on a hunting trip, and Mama Apoline asked *kambo* to come to the living room to tell us a story. *Kambo* brought a small charcoal grill from the kitchen to warm the cold room. We sat or lied on mats in a semi-circle around the grill facing *kambo*. I lay behind Mama Apoline, in front of Gilbert. *Kambo* began telling us a legend story from her tribe, the Lubas of Katanga.

Halfway through the tale, Mama Apoline decided to put Benjamin to sleep in her bedroom. Gilbert then told me, "Geolo, you can cover yourself with my blanket." He helped put it over me up to my neck. I was delighted by how nice he was treating me. Gilbert was fifteen years old, and he usually paid no attention to his younger step-sister.

Then he whispered to me, "You can come closer to me, the blanket isn't very large." That was a very sweet thing to do, I thought. He usually didn't share much, but this night he was sharing his blanket with me. But why was he whispering this way? Maybe he thought *kambo* would shush him for making noise while she told a story.

Then Gilbert started to press himself against me, against my behind. I started to feel uncomfortable. I knew something wasn't right, but I didn't say anything. If I said something, Mama Apoline and *kambo* would know, and I might get in trouble. This could be *mambo mbaya* [bad things]. But then he started pulling my underwear down with one hand. He pulled me against him, and I instinctively flipped around. As I turned over, the blanket fell off. *Kambo,* who was behind me, saw my underwear halfway down my thighs. She instantly lifted the blanket up off Gilbert. I was stricken by terror!

"Get up, Gilbert, now," *kambo* said with great anger. "Take your blanket and go wait for me in your room. Now!" Gilbert quickly stood up, wrapped his blanket around his body, and left without saying a word.

"Why are you sending the child away like that, Mama? You haven't finished telling the story. What's going on?" asked Mama Apoline, who had just returned to the room.

"I will tell you later," *kambo* snapped at her. "You have to open your eyes, Apolina, when you have boys and girls, especially if they are grown-up boys." Mama Apoline looked at her without under-standing what could possibly have put *kambo* in such a rage.

"I'll finish the story tomorrow. Georgette, come with me to the bathroom," *kambo* said as she grabbed my hand and led me out-side. Mama Apoline looked closely at me and saw that I was pulling up my underwear. She now seemed to understand what had hap-pened.

Kambo didn't say anything to me at first. I also was quiet. Finally she spoke, and the only thing she said to me that night was that she would talk with me in the morning. First thing the next morning *kambo* took me with her to her vegetable field.

"You know why I want to speak with you. What happened between you and Gilbert last night?" she asked me. After I explained to her how it all started, she shook her head and looked straight at me.

"Do you know that it is very bad for a brother and a sister to see each other naked? And it's even worse for them to touch each other while naked. In fact, it's bad for any boy to see you naked. Before this time, when did Gilbert ask you to pull down your underwear?"

I looked at her with great surprise. "He never asked me to pull down my underwear before. Just yesterday he started."

"How come you didn't say anything when he started pulling your underpants down?"

"I don't know. I guess I was afraid. I thought he would just stop when I turned around."

"Do you know what your father will do if he hears about this? If this happens again, go tell your Mama and come tell me. You hear me? Now, it's not your fault. You are the younger one. Gilbert will not do anything to you. He will be punished. Go now."

I was greatly relieved to hear *kambo* say that it wasn't my fault. When I went back to the house, I met Gilbert by the outhouse; it was his turn for a private talk with *kambo*.

"If you try again to pull down my pants like yesterday, I'll tell on you," I said to him defiantly. *Kambo* had told me not to be afraid to tell.

Gilbert looked at me without saying a word and continued on to the vegetable field. I went to play with Josée and some of our friends in the front yard. Somehow, Josée already knew about the incident with Gilbert. Apparently, Mama Apoline had told her about it when

Josée asked why *kambo* Colette wanted to talk with me alone. Mama Apoline had also told her that Papa mustn't hear a thing about this.

"If Papa knows, he will kill you," Josée whispered to me. "You're in big trouble." She went back to playing with her friends, while I sat down by *kambo*'s house and started to cry. *Kambo* discovered me sitting there and asked if it was Gilbert who had made me cry. When I told her what Josée had just said to me, *kambo* shook her head.

"Go play with your friends. Your father will not kill you. It's not your fault, it's Gilbert's fault. If it comes to killing, he is the one who will be killed, not you. Go play." She wiped away my tears and gently pushed me toward the front yard. I joined the others, and soon enough, thanks to *kambo*, I was back to having fun.

At the dinner table that day, Gilbert didn't look at me at all. I didn't know what *kambo* had told him, but it must have been something big to bring Gilbert to that state. Later that day, I heard *kambo* talking with Mama Apoline.

"You must be more careful with boys that age around little girls with whom they really didn't grow up together. What will happen to Gilbert if Geolo's father finds out? He will be kicked out of the house and maybe even sent to prison."

"Why didn't Georgette say anything when he started pulling down her underpants?" asked Mama Apoline. "It seems to me that she was cooperating, and..." Before Mama Apoline even finished her thought, *kambo* cut her off.

"Apolina, you listen to me, listen to me good. In this world when you get a man like Benoit, you don't go behind his back and not look after his children. You know full well those two children have a mother who has left because of you. *Ba* Benoit takes care of all your children as if they were his. Who among the men you married before did that? Tell me! You're speaking with a devil's mouth."

But Mama Apoline still wanted to blame me. When she was alone with me the next morning, she told me, "You're too wild. Don't play dirty games any more with boys; do you hear me? If your father hears about this, we will both be in trouble, you and me."

From that day on, *kambo* always asked me and Josée if any of the boys were trying to do *mambo mbaya* with us. Gilbert stopped telling us the stories he used to tell us, about what a man and a woman do all night long. He spent even more of his time with his friends in the neighborhood.

And, after that day, Josée got to sleep against the wall, almost every night. Every time that I tried to insist upon my right to the cherished inside position—at least every other night—she'd say, "Wait until I tell Papa about what you did with Gilbert!" I was so petrified of what might happen that I let her decide almost everything. If I did anything that displeased her, especially taking attention away from her when we were with her friends, she simply said, "I'll tell Papa." I knew what she was talking about. So I gave in and let her rule uncontested.

We had been in Samba for more than a year, when Papa told us that it was time for us to go to school. "I want to go to our old school," I protested.

"When the war is over, you can go back to your old school in Kongolo," Papa said. "Education is very important. We can't let a silly thing like a war get in the way of studying." So, I went into first grade, and nine-year-old Josée started third grade.

Papa continued with his hunting business and also bought some land in the forest where he and Mama Apoline worked at least three days a week. They planted cassava, corn, sweet potatoes, wild yams, and tropical vegetables and spices. *Kambo* usually stayed home to make us dinner and do other chores.

On the weekends, everybody helped in the fields. We spent all day there and didn't come back home until the evening. Mama Apoline, Papa, and *kambo* plowed the field with hoes. The children picked weeds and put them in big piles to use for making charcoal.

Papa dug a shallow hole and started a small fire with dry logs. Then, when the fire was well lit, we helped Papa and Mama Apoline put big, freshly cut tree logs on top of the fire until it formed a tower, like a pyramid, about four feet tall. A little opening was left to provide access to the fire. Then we put the fresh weeds on top of the pyramid and soil on top of the weeds. At this point it looked like a giant termite mound with smoke coming out of it. Two or three days later, the freshly cut logs turned into charcoal to be used as fuel in the kitchen. Charcoal was easy to sell, because it didn't produce billowing smoke as logs do, and it was much more efficient than dry wood.

As our fields grew larger, there was more and more work to do. Papa spent most of his time there, chasing away monkeys and other animals from eating up the crops. He still went hunting, but less frequently, maybe just one or two trips per month. Sometimes he hunted around our field for some *liulumba* [big, dark grayish brown monkeys]. He got a couple of them every week, some of which we ate and some of which Mama Apoline sold. I liked smoked *liulumba* meat, but I couldn't quite get used to the sight of their heads, with their teeth flashing a human-like grin. They looked too much like people. Papa knew that seeing the heads upset me; so he usually gave them away. It wasn't hard for him to find takers, as many people considered them to be delicacies.

In 1963, Papa learned that the war was over. The Tshombe government had agreed to end Katanga's secession. The central government had won, thanks to the help of the United Nations soldiers. There was a cease-fire throughout the country. We were all excited, especially at the thought of returning home to Kongolo—but this time, by train! Even though we had a very good life in Samba, Kongolo always remained our home. No matter how well Papa did with his hunting and farming, no matter how many friends Josée and I made at school, we remembered that we had come to Samba as refugees and we still felt like refugees. This sense of apartness was accentuated by our kiSwahili accent, which was quite different from the accent heard in Samba.

"I will go first by myself to see how safe Kongolo is," Papa told Josée and me. "After that, I'll decide if we can go back now or if we have to wait a little longer. And when I'm in Kongolo, I'll try to send a letter out to your Maman." We had not been able to exchange letters with Maman for the three years of the civil war, and we weren't even sure where she was.

Papa stayed in Kongolo for two weeks. He returned with some bad news, but lots of good news, too. "We've lost everything. My truck is nowhere to be found. Many of the houses and buildings downtown have been destroyed. But people are coming back. Life is starting to go back to normal. I spent my time there getting people to fix the TRANGEN house in the business district."

Papa decided to sell our house in Samba and most of our things that could not be easily carried with us on the train. There really wasn't all that much to sell, since Papa hadn't spent a lot of money on buying big things like furniture. Instead, he saved most of what he earned. Papa sold our house and our fields in the forest—well below market price—to his hunting friend Simon. Simon had just taken a second wife, and his present compound wasn't big enough for two wives. Papa then went back to Kongolo one more time before taking all of us home.

But all was not tranquil in his absence. During Papa's trips to Kongolo, Mama Apoline started to go out at nights. She usually stayed out very late, some nights even past midnight. She always told us that she was going to *ba* Sumaili's house, or to see this friend or that friend. Now and then, I heard arguments between her and *kambo*.

"If you want to stay out late," *kambo* said, "you should first find out if your children are well fed and healthy. This isn't my marriage, it's yours. What if your husband comes back late and doesn't find you here?"

Then one day, Mama Apoline left in the early afternoon to see someone who supposedly owed her money. After supper, we all went to *kambo*'s house to hear stories of her youth. Suddenly, we heard some women screaming outside.

Rows of burned out homes in one of the dozen African villages in the province of Kasai (bordering the province of Katanga), August, 1961.

A Katangese family hurries down an Elisabethville street in search of safety after hearing reports of a massacre of women and children, December, 1961.

A boy with bandages over his eyes is led by another barefoot youngster as they walk past the food line in the Baluba refugee camp in Katanga province, December, 1961.

Soldiers of the National Congolese Army bringing in suspected rebel prisoners after the battle to free the town of Bukavu from the rebels, August, 1964.

Dead bodies lying on the roadside near Bukavu airport, after the town was freed by the National Congolese troops, August, 1964.

Rebel troops responsible for the revolt in Stanleyville, September, 1964.

In Kindu, white mercinaries employed by the Congolese government prepare to head towards Stanleyville, the last rebel stronghold, November, 1964.

Rebels captured by villagers in the northeast Congo are beaten to death, December, 1964.

New Congolese President Lt. Gen. Joseph Mobutu delivering a speech before the Congolese parliament in Leopoldville, November, 1965.

A group of
Congolese rebels,
the *simba mulele*,
believed they had
powers that made
them invisible and
invincible.

Renamed Mobutu
Sese Seko, Zaire's
president poses with
George Foreman
and Muhammed Ali,
after the "Fight of
the Century" in
Kinshasa, September,
1974.

President for a
total of 31 years,
Mobutu Sese Seko
was ousted from
office in 1997,
and succumbed
to cancer the
following year.

"She's getting away, she's getting away! Where did she go?"

We heard running footsteps behind *kambo*'s house. We all stopped talking and listened closely. Who was running into our compound through the backyard at this hour? *Kambo* stood up and said, "Go on children, tell yourselves some stories. I'll be right back." She went behind her house, and we soon heard voices whispering. It was *kambo* talking to someone who sounded like Mama Apoline. What was she doing behind the house? And why was she running? Those women, were they screaming about her?

After a while, *kambo* came back, picked up the front house keys from Josée, and told us she'd be right back. When she returned a minute later, she looked upset, but she managed to finish the story she had been telling us. I could hear someone taking a shower. That must have been Mama Apoline. When *kambo* took us to our house, Mama Apoline was already inside, sleeping.

In the morning when we were outside playing with the neighbors' children, we heard that two women, both wives of the same man, had been in our neighborhood the previous night looking for a woman who had been fooling around with their husband. They said the wives had caught her with their husband while he was walking her back to her house from the bar where they had been meeting. They had started hitting her, but she got away from them and disappeared near our house.

When Mama Apoline woke up late that morning, her lower lip was swollen, and she had scratches on her neck.

"What is that you have on your neck?" Josée suspiciously asked her. "And why is your face fat?"

"I scratched a mosquito bite too hard. And I'm feeling sick, that's why I look this way," Mama Apoline explained while looking away from us. After that day, she didn't go out as often as she had before.

A few days later, Papa came back from Kongolo. We were all happy to see him, but in the next few days, I could hear angry voices coming from his and Mama Apoline's room. Things were not going very well between them. I didn't understand much, but I knew it had something to do with her scratches. Papa's friends started telling him things about Mama Apoline. But Mama Apoline was sure that it was Josée who told Papa about how she had stayed out late when he wasn't in town. She knew that Josée hadn't really forgiven her for causing the separation between Maman and Papa. Josée continued to compare Mama Apoline to her Maman and constantly reminded me that Mama Apoline was not our real mother.

I began to realize that Mama Apoline was indeed treating Josée and me differently from her other children, especially when Papa was away. As mean as Josée could be to me at times, she never left any doubt that she considered me "hers" to protect. I could no longer say the same about Mama Apoline. She always seemed more interested in her natural children, and she clearly favored them when it came to assigning household chores. One day, when Josée saw that I had many chores to do and Marie next to none, she marched right up to Mama Apoline to complain on my behalf.

"Geolo can't do all those chores. Why don't you give Marie the same amount of work that you give to Geolo?"

"You are such an impolite child," Mama Apoline replied. "I treat Geolo the same as I treat Marie, they are both my children."

"No, you don't. And Geolo is not your child. Geolo is my baby sister. Our Maman will come back one day soon. I'll tell Papa when he comes back what you're doing to us."

The two of them battled frequently like this when Papa wasn't home. Mama Apoline usually rewarded us for Josée's impudence by sending us to bed without dinner. Fortunately for us, *kambo* Colette would always feed us without telling her daughter. When Papa returned from his trips, Josée or I would tell him everything that had happened. Often we would hear Papa and Mama Apoline arguing about how she treated us.

"You're the one who treats those children differently from the other children," Mama Apoline would say to Papa. "You treat them like princesses, as if the Virgin Mary herself gave birth to them. I need to be able to discipline them when they ought to be disciplined."

"You are never to touch either one of those two children, Apoline," Papa would say calmly but firmly. "Report to me if they do anything wrong. I will punish them."

When the time finally came for us to leave Samba, Papa thanked *ba* Sumaili again and again for all he had done for us. To demonstrate his gratitude, he gave *ba* Sumaili two new pairs of pants, two shirts, and a pair of decorative antelope horns. Papa also bought each of *ba* Sumaili's three wives two expensive *pagnes*. All three of them were very pleased.

"What's so important in Kongolo that you can't find here in Samba?" *ba* Sumaili asked Papa. "You're doing very well here, why don't you make Samba your home?"

"I can't really explain it," Papa replied, "but Kongolo is our home and we must be there."

Josée and I knew it was our home. We were born there.

CHAPTER 13

SPIRITS

Early in 1964, shortly after I turned eight, more than two years after our arrival in Samba, the day of our train trip to Kongolo finally arrived. We waited at the station for the train with great impatience. All sorts of questions swirled through my mind about what we would find at the end of our voyage: *How bad did Kongolo get during the war? Were there still dead people lying in the streets? What had happened to all our friends?*

A couple of freight trains came and passed, each time raising our hopes only to crush them.

"When is it coming?" we asked Papa again and again. As time passed, we started to wonder if our train would ever arrive. Then, we heard an almost inaudible buzz coming from far away. A few minutes later came the clear, long *tchooo tchooo tchooo tchooo!* Was it really our train, the one that would take us home? A clerk came out of the train station office with a loudspeaker.

"Train to Kongolo! That's the train to Kongolo. People traveling in that direction, please get ready in line. Families with children and *wakambo* [senior citizens] go first."

Finally. As we boarded the train, we took one last look back at the mango and palm trees around *ba* Sumaili's compound, which could be seen from the train station. Once on board, Josée looked at me and started to sing, *"Leo, leo njo leo, leo Kongolo na siye leo"* [Today is the day that we will see Kongolo]. Marie and I joined in, and we sang louder and louder and louder, while clapping our hands and swaying back and forth—until Mama Apoline told us to stop making so much noise. When all the people had boarded, we heard a whistle blow three times, and then the train started pulling slowly away, honking as it crept along the tracks.

"We're moving, Geolo!" Josée shouted, standing at the window with a great big grin on her face. I stepped up onto the bench and looked at the trees marching past the window as we pulled out of Samba. I waved back at some children who were waving at the passing train. I used to do that a lot when we lived at *ba* Sumaili's. I would fantasize then that it was me sitting in the train. And now, I really was headed back to Kongolo!

I had mixed feelings about Samba. It had been both a safe haven for my family and a place where I had lost my innocence. We led a normal, good life in Samba, making many new friends and benefitting greatly from their kindness. But Samba was also where the war between my stepmother and my maternally protective big sister escalated out of control, where my father's marriage began to disintegrate, and where I came to live in daily terror of Papa finding out that I had done *mambo mbaya*. How excited I was to return to Kongolo, where my memories of life before the war were only those of fun and joy.

We saw again all the villages by the railroad tracks which we had passed through on our way to Samba. I remembered how it had taken us days to go from one village to the next while traveling on foot. During that long journey, I had come to believe that we would be marching in our bare feet forever, traveling endlessly, never having the chance again to go to school. But, now, in just one day, we would be in Kongolo. We would be home again.

Late in the afternoon the train pulled past *kambo* Colette's *Avenue Kindu* neighborhood. Everyone rose, anxious to see what the town looked like. We had arrived, we were in Kongolo! *Kambo* stood up to look for her shiny tin roof that was usually visible from the train— but it was nowhere in sight. She sat down discouraged. Nobody said anything, but soon she smiled as if saying, it's all right, what will be will be. When we got to the train stop near the Mission Parish, we saw some nuns standing outside the convent looking at the passing train. I wondered if they had ever left during the war. Some people at the station, mostly children, waved at us. Josée, Marie, and I waved back. We could barely sit still any more, we were so excited.

When we passed the railroad company's housing complex, we saw that many buildings had indeed been reduced to rubble. Otherwise, the town looked pretty much as it did before the war. At last, we arrived at Kongolo's main train station by the Lualaba River. Everybody had to get off at Kongolo because the bridge over the Lualaba that held the train tracks and roads heading south had been destroyed during the war. Now all the people headed for E'ville had to take a boat to Kabalo, the next important town south of Kongolo, and then re-board a train there. To get to all the villages on the other side of the river, people had to take a taxi canoe.

From the station, it took us about thirty minutes to get to our old house downtown, TRANGEN's Kongolo headquarters. Papa had had it all cleaned up, so it almost looked as it did before the war. Other families had also come back, including Papa's good friend, *ba* Joseph, and his family. His eldest child, Godeliève, who was between Josée's age and mine, soon became our best friend. The best news was that school had started again in Kongolo.

But there was plenty of bad news as well. We learned that some people we knew had been killed during the war. *Ma* Monique Alingite died during the war years, though no one knew when or how. Many other people had disappeared, and no one seemed to know what had happened to them.

Papa was devastated when he learned that the terrible rumors we had heard were true. Father Michel Vanduffel, Papa's friend, the priest who came by so often to share a drink with Papa, who never condemned Papa for not going to church but accepted him as a good and God-fearing man, was dead. He was brutally murdered along with almost all of the white priests based in Kongolo on New Year's Day 1962. Twenty priests, mostly Belgians, and two European laymen, were surrounded at the parish by a group of central government soldiers and then taken to the Lualaba River, not far from the military camp. Two of the priests were brothers, and most were young men. Some were good men, friends of the people, while others still had the colonialist, racist mentality. But none were any threat to either side in the war—certainly not our good friend, Father Michel. Many of the soldiers during the war, however, were completely out of control; they did as they pleased with no concern for right and wrong and no fear of being held responsible by higher authorities.

And so, the madman who ordered the arrest of the priests charged them all as spies. It was his job, he said, to show them who was now in charge of Congo. The Belgians had treated his people badly for many years. The priests shouldn't think, for one moment, that they were beyond the reach of the new powers just because they called themselves "messengers of God." He ordered his men to line the priests up. As they prayed to their Lord and sang hymns of praise, the officer gave the fatal command, and his men let loose a shower of bullets. One by one, twenty priests fell into the water, and their bloody corpses floated downstream. One priest, Father Jules D'Armond, was left alive to bear witness to the madman's accomplishment. To this day, he lives in the Kongolo area, where he continues the work of his fallen colleagues.

When we got to *kambo* Colette's house for the first time, we understood why we hadn't seen it from the train: her glittering tin roof was gone.

"Filthy thieves," *kambo* muttered over and over. "While people are suffering and dying, they have time to go and kill them twice by stealing what's theirs."

"Don't you worry now," Papa told her. "We'll get you a new and better roof. In the meantime, you'll stay with us." And Papa did fix her roof, it was one of the first things he did. When *kambo* moved back to *Avenue Kindu,* Gilbert and N'Kongolo went with her.

There was one very noticeable new group of people in Kongolo, the blue helmets. They were the United Nations soldiers whose support for the central government had helped turn the tide against the secessionists. Papa said the blue helmets were still here because the government soldiers needed help in restoring order and defusing all the mines that were left by the Katangese army and their white mercenaries. Many spots in town were off limits because of possible mines. Despite these precautionary measures, there were a number of tragic incidents in which children had stepped on mines while playing in their backyards. Most of the blue helmets were Moroccans, who we found to be friendly and even funny. Many tried to speak kiSwahili and mingle with local people. Conversations with them often turned out to be something like a Charlie Chaplin movie.

One Sunday after mass, as we headed to *kambo's* house, we came across a couple of blue helmets standing on each side of Kongolo's main soccer field. They tried to say *jambo* [hello] to us, but when we started heading toward a short cut behind the field, they hurried to step in front of us.

"*Barabara kule, barabara kule. Hapana huku. Mbaya kabisa. Kaboum huku!*" [Road over there, not here. Here, very bad, kaboom!] they said in hilariously broken kiSwahili that led us to burst out laughing. Fortunately, they were good humored and laughed with us; they even let us try to teach them how to say it properly. We had to use only main roads to avoid stepping on mines, they said, while vividly acting out a big explosion in pantomime.

Kambo quickly re-established the vegetable garden behind her kitchen. After two or three rains, her garden would be in business again, she told us. She also fixed up her ancestors' "houses" on the side of her main house. These were two earthen structures the size of large doll houses. Inside each of these houses was a clay statue of the living spirits of her ancestors in the Luba tribe. In one house was a statue of the spirit called Mbuyi, while the other structure housed the statue of the spirit called N'Kongolo.

Kambo made them offerings from time to time during the year. She would cook two chickens for the occasion; then she'd put a large portion of *bugari* in each of two bowls and divide the chicken parts among two additional bowls, making sure that each chicken bowl had a gizzard. *Kambo* said that a gizzard represented a complete chicken.

"Are we going to see them eat, *kambo*?" I asked her.

"Absolutely not. You don't go disturb them while they eat. It's forbidden to hang around there for at least an hour."

That was okay with me because it was time for us to eat chicken and *bugari*, too. Still, I was curious to see whether the statues could really eat food. Would they turn into people, eat, and then turn back into clay statues? Or would the statues somehow eat the food? How I wished I could see them do that.

"The spirits protect and look out for all the baLuba descendants," *kambo* explained in great earnestness. "From generation to generation, Mbuyi and N'Kongolo live within some of their living descendants. Right now, N'Kongolo's spirit lives within Apolina. That's why she named her boy N'Kongolo. When she was pregnant with him, the spirit showed himself to her in a dream. That was when we knew the spirit of N'Kongolo lived within your mother Apolina."

I couldn't quite follow what she meant, but I tried hard to understand. "So, Mama has a statue in her stomach?" I asked. *Kambo* soon ran out of patience with my questions and busied herself in the kitchen preparing dinner.

"Well, we're not baLuba," Josée announced to me. "Papa says

we're *batokachini* [natives of northeastern Congo], from Stanleyville. And our real mother is muTabwa from Baudouinville."

"That's all true," said *kambo*, who had overheard Josée's comments. "But since Apolina is now your father's wife and taking care of you, she is also your mother. That's why I am your *kambo*."

"Still, Geolo and me are not really baLubas," Josée insisted with her typical stubbornness.

As for me, muLuba or not, I was so curious to know what went on in those ancestors' houses that I couldn't think of anything else. Since I really wasn't muLuba, I didn't think N'Kongolo and Mbuyi would mind me dropping by in the middle of their feast. It would be just a quick visit, mind you. I didn't want to disturb them, after all. That day I finished eating before everyone else, which was awfully unusual for me.

"Are you sick?" *kambo* asked, eyeing me suspiciously.

"No, I just have to go to the potty," I replied while crossing my fingers behind my back. On my return from the outhouse, I snuck past the back door where I might be seen by *kambo* and went straight to the ancestors' houses. The two ancestors' houses were covered with one long tin roof, on top of which *kambo* had put a big brick. I went on my knees and peeked through the little doors. I looked first in N'Kongolo's room: the food was still there, untouched! Then I looked in Mbuyi's room: same story. So, when were they going to eat? Maybe they weren't hungry. Or maybe they didn't like the food. That was hard to believe, I had just had the same food, and it was delicious. After all, *kambo* was a great cook. I was afraid *kambo* would be very disappointed. Without wasting any more time, I went into the house.

"*Kambo*, when are N'Kongolo and Mbuyi going to eat? Their food is untouched, exactly the way you left it. Except for a couple of little black ants on it."

Kambo reminded me that I wasn't supposed to go near the ancestors' houses. I soon realized, to my relief, that she was neither surprised nor upset that they hadn't touched the food she had so meticulously prepared for them. Later, *kambo* took back N'Kongolo and

Mbuyi's food, and scraped some small, black ants off the plates. Then she gave us the food to eat!

"Why didn't they eat the food?" I asked *kambo*.

"They did," she replied. "Did you see those little black ants? It's a sign that they've enjoyed the food."

I was as confused about the food as I was about Mama Apoline carrying a statue inside her belly. I couldn't keep my eyes off Mama Apoline. It took me a couple of days to stop thinking about it. Then one day, we went to pay *kambo* a visit after Mama Apoline had been sick for a week.

"Our ancestor, N'Kongolo, will help us know what has caused Apoline's illness," *kambo* said aloud to no one in particular. "If Apoline has forsaken her ancestors, then the spirit of N'Kongolo will tell her what to do."

We were playing in the yard when we heard *kambo* start to sing some songs in kiLuba and clap her hands. Then the singing and clapping stopped. We heard *kambo*'s voice talking—and then a man's voice responded! Josée, Marie, and I looked at each other and then dashed into *kambo*'s kitchen. We entered in silence and looked around. There was no one else there but Mama Apoline and *kambo*, no third person, no man in sight. Mama Apoline, seated on a stool, didn't even turn to look at us as we all entered the room. Her eyes seemed to go through *kambo*.

"Quiet, children," *kambo* said, while continuing to look straight at Mama Apoline. "N'Kongolo is here. He is speaking through Apolina."

I thought Mama Apoline would look like the statue when the spirit within her came out. But she hadn't changed at all, only her voice. It had become a deep, man-like voice. She also had a very different glare in her eyes. She was telling *kambo* that his person, Mama Apoline, had done things that she shouldn't have done. She—or he— was now telling *kambo* what Mama Apoline should do to be absolved.

This went on for a few minutes until *kambo* decided that

Mama Apoline's strength couldn't take any more. Then *kambo* started singing again and clapping her hands rhythmically. Mama Apoline's upper torso began shaking, and she rolled it forward and back in a circular fashion. *Kambo* kept on singing until Mama Apoline closed her eyes and the shaking stopped.

Kambo then called out, "Apolina Bahati, is it you?"

Mama Apoline slowly opened her eyes. She looked around as if she had just come out of a deep sleep and slowly realized that there were other people in the room. She looked at us and then at *kambo*. She asked *kambo* what had happened. *Kambo* explained to her what the spirit had said and what she had to do. All this seemed like it was news to Mama Apoline.

A few days later Josée asked her, "Where are you when N'Kongolo speaks?"

"I don't know," Mama Apoline replied. "It's like I'm sleeping the whole time."

Sometimes the spirit came out of her uninvited. *Kambo* said this happened when he was very angry with Mama Apoline. One evening Papa was not at home, and Mama Apoline was telling us some stories. Suddenly, she stopped talking and, just as suddenly, she started to shake. She went into the circling motions with her upper torso that she went through when *kambo* sang the songs inviting the spirit to come. We couldn't take our eyes off of her. Her spirit's deep voice started talking on and on in a language we could not understand.

Shortly after, Papa arrived. Papa had obviously had a few drinks and was in a very jolly mood. He said hello to all of us and asked how we were doing and his usual question: "Have you eaten yet?" We barely paid him any attention, we were so transfixed by seeing the spirit talk through Mama Apoline.

"Papa," Josée said, while continuing to stare at Mama Apoline. "Mama Apoline's spirit is here."

Papa hooted. "That's nonsense that your mother and your

kambo put on." Then he turned to Mama Apoline and said, "Apoline, may I have something to eat, please? I'm starving."

Mama Apoline, or rather the spirit of N'Kongolo, turned to Papa and spoke with a very angry and thundering voice, this time in kiSwahili.

"My person hasn't been doing what she is supposed to."

That voice made Papa step back and look closely at his wife for a few seconds. Then he hooted again and said, "Now, cut that out, Apoline. I said I'm starving."

But the same voice spoke out again through Mama Apoline. Papa now saw that Mama Apoline was truly under some kind of spell. Before Papa even sat down to witness what was going on, the voice started speaking directly to Papa. It told him about many things that Mama Apoline had done. Apoline hadn't performed deeds to absolve herself as she had been instructed by her ancestors' spirits. Apoline had eaten food that he had forbidden her to eat, such as fish with no scales. Apoline had fooled around with some man in Samba. Apoline hadn't taken very good care of her husband's children. And now, Apoline was starting another affair, and still she hadn't bothered to do the specific deeds he had told her to do to absolve herself.

Somehow I sensed that Mama Apoline was in big trouble and not only with the spirit. After a short while, she came out of her trance. She looked at all of us for a minute or two before gradually realizing that the spirit had taken her. It was clear that she didn't know what the spirit had said. Papa aimed a look of disgust at her. He was sober now and no longer jolly.

"When did you get here?" she asked Papa.

"I've been here long enough to hear what N'Kongolo had to say," he answered softly. "I'll speak with you later."

Then Papa said good night to us and went outside. I was disappointed that Papa didn't come back in time to tell us a bedtime story that night. N'Kongolo's spirit had ruined his good mood. After that evening, things started to get bad again between Papa and Mama Apoline.

One night, after we went to bed, I overheard Mama Apoline and Papa arguing.

"It's yours. It happened in Samba when you came back between your trips here," I heard Mama Apoline say. Then they lowered their voices, and I couldn't hear any more.

A few months later, late in 1964, we didn't find Mama Apoline at home after school one day. I didn't give it a second thought because she sometimes went out in the afternoon. But that evening Papa told us that there was an addition to the family.

"I took your mother earlier today to the hospital. She's just had a baby girl." We all jumped up and down with excitement. We had a little sister!

When was Mama Apoline pregnant? I asked myself. *She was a little chubbier these days, but her stomach hadn't grown big at all. Did she just get pregnant these past few days? Didn't it take months and months before the baby came out?* I was too excited to have a younger sister to worry much about my questions. Papa and Mama Apoline gave the baby the name of Papa's late sister, Dalane. And since the baby was born during a difficult time, she got the French name of *Misère* [misery]. So there came into this world our little sister Misère Dalane Suruba. She was very cute. Papa smiled, sort of, when many people said that she looked just like Josée.

CHAPTER 14

A Fresh Start

Upon our return to Kongolo, Papa decided to go into the transport and trade business. But first he needed to get a truck. He announced that he would try to salvage our old Mercedes truck, the one that Biriki drove past us on the first day of the war. The truck had been found, almost totally wrecked, by the road near the destroyed bridge.

Evidently Biriki had been ordered to leave the truck with Katangese soldiers watching over the bridge. He had a hard time explaining how he had come to be in possession of such a vehicle. Fortunately for him, he was muHemba, a local tribe, hence not a threat; if he had been from another area, like Papa, he would have been shot. The Katangese soldiers let him cross the bridge on foot and took the truck for their own use. Unfortunately, during their use, it got trashed.

Papa had the truck towed to our house and hired three mechanics to fix it. The day it arrived, I couldn't believe my eyes.

"Is this the same truck that we were going to take to the airport that day? The truck that *ba* Biriki was driving?" I asked Papa.

"Well, it doesn't look good, does it? But with new engine parts, it will one day ride like brand new. This truck is going to pay for our *bukari* and *sombe*." I believed Papa when he said that, but I might have been the only one who did.

He spent some of his savings on auto parts ordered from Albertville. When the mechanics said it was ready to drive, we all gathered around to watch "Paul." That was the name that one of Josée's friends at school gave the truck, and it stuck. Many people came to watch; most of them thought Papa was crazy to spend so much time and money on a truck that was in such bad shape. Since the keys to the truck had been lost, the men needed to push to get it started. Papa, the three mechanics, and a few other men pushed the truck into the street and up a little hill to the right of our house. One man placed two big rocks underneath the back tires to keep the truck from rolling down the hill. After all, the brakes were not working properly yet either.

After they got up the hill, the driver stepped up into the truck. He gave the signal that he was ready, and the rocks were taken away from the tires. The truck moved slowly down the hill, but the engine did not come to life. Back up the hill the men pushed the truck to try again, but still there was no roar from the engine. Some of the people watching started to laugh. That made me angry, but Papa just smiled and said they would keep on trying. Finally, after many tries, the truck descended slowly, then picked up speed as the engine emitted a harsh, gurgling sound. It roared to a stop, and the whole crowd watching howled with delight. Everyone applauded wildly. A giant grin of satisfaction brightened Papa's face. I could just guess what he was thinking: *I knew it would work, I told them it would work!*

The sound of the truck improved somewhat after a while, but not completely. You could still hear it puffing and chugging along from a long distance. Josée's friends teased her about all the noise that Paul made. But Papa didn't pay any attention to all the naysayers, for he was in business again! He, the driver, and two mechanics started making trips into the area around Kasongo, northeast of Kongolo.

On the trip out from Kongolo, the truck carried passengers for a fee. They didn't get a seat for their fee, just a place to stand in the open air back of the truck. It was not very comfortable, but it was the best anyone could find. On the way back, the truck carried sacks of cassava and rice, smoked meat, plantains, sweet potatoes, and many other food items to be sold in Kongolo. If there was enough space, they would even carry a few passengers.

It took Papa only a couple of months after our return from Samba to have a thriving business. The truck would break down from time to time, but the mechanics really knew their job. Word soon got around that there was cassava for sale at *Monsieur* Benoit's house. People came to buy it early in the morning before we even left for school. The merchandise didn't last long.

Papa and his three aides went on the road every two to three weeks; they were usually gone for three or four days at a time, though sometimes they were gone for a whole week. The front of the house was now full of sacks of cassava and rice, as was another smaller room on the right side of the building. Papa's business was booming—all thanks to a truck named Paul.

"I've got news from your Maman," Papa said to Josée and me one day, with a letter in his hand and a great, big smile on his face. He had written to Maman soon after our return to Kongolo. This letter brought our first news from her in three years.

"Where is she now? Is she coming back here?" Josée asked. Josée had never stopped asking about Maman since we left Kongolo during the war.

"No," Papa said to Josée's great disappointment. "Maman is not coming here. But she's doing fine, and she's very happy that you two are safe. She was very worried about you during the war."

"So where is she living? When is she coming here?" Josée asked impatiently.

"Well, she's living in Manono, that's a small town about 200 kilometers south of here. And she has very wonderful news. She has a new husband. Not only that, but she and her new husband had a baby girl born in 1961. You girls have a new baby sister. Her name is Jeanne Marie-Edmondine."

Josée was thrilled to hear that our mother was doing fine and that we had another little sister. But she wasn't very happy to hear that Maman had married another man instead of coming back to Papa.

"Your Maman misses you two very much," Papa explained, "but she's happy with her new husband, and that's a good thing. She and I are still good friends, and we will continue writing to each other."

One day, after Papa's business trips had become routine, he called Josée and me to him.

"I have some big news to tell you," he said. "You are going to have another mother who will come to live with us. She's very nice. Your mother Apoline welcomes the idea. You'll like her very much, you'll see. I have told her all about you children, especially about you two girls."

"Another mother? What other mother?" Josée asked, obviously upset by the idea. "I want our Maman to come back, that's who I want, Maman Thérèse!"

Papa explained that he was going to have two wives like so many of the other men that we knew.

"Is she bringing her children, too?" I asked.

"No, she doesn't have any. That's why she's so looking forward to meeting you girls."

Afterward, Mama Apoline shared with us her feelings about this major development in our lives. "Your father is getting a second wife. It's all right with me. I'll welcome her with open arms. But what I know is that she won't last very long, or my name isn't Bahati Apoline."

Late one evening, Papa returned from a trip with *ma* Catherine Zaibu. She was a lot younger than Mama Apoline, soft-spoken, and very pretty. Papa lit up around her. She was very polite to Mama Apoline and called her *bi mukubwa* [first lady]. Mama Apoline seemed to enjoy having someone to order around and take over most of her routine chores.

While working around the house, *ma* Zaibu told us many stories in kiNgwana, an offshoot of kiSwahili with many Arabic nuances. Many of her stories were about Arabs and Muslims. She herself was a Muslim. Just like Papa said, she gave Josée and me special attention—and we liked it.

"You are for me just like my own children, the children, *Inch Allah* [Praise the Lord], I never had," she'd say. People who knew Maman said that *ma* Zaibu reminded them of *bibi* Thérèse. That only made Josée and me like her even more.

The first few months went surprisingly well. *Ma* Zaibu said she didn't mind getting married to a man who already had another wife. In her first marriage she had been the fourth wife. Her *bi mukubwa* then was fine, but she had had serious problems with wives number two and three. They hadn't wanted their husband to marry another woman, so they caused a lot of trouble for her. Their husband, she said, wound up listening to them because she was unable to have a child. In the end, he took her back to her parents. She then started to sell plantains, smoked meat, and other things to earn a living. That was when she met Papa.

"Your father was very different from the usual haggling businessmen I was used to. He was always so kind and considerate. A true gentleman. He never tried to cheat me or take advantage of me to make money. He always offered a fair price. I started to pile up merchandise only for him. I even found other good wholesalers for him. When he asked me about becoming his second wife, I accepted without reservation, even though I had refused many other marriage propositions after my divorce."

Ma Zaibu was a very good cook. She made the most delicious chicken in the world. Even Mama Apoline said it was good. She showed Josée and me how to iron pants and shirts and how to fold them so that they looked neat even weeks later.

"I sure do like her a lot," I told Josée.

"Yeah, me too," Josée said. "But it would have been even better if Maman had come back instead."

Sometimes, I got the impression that Mama Apoline was upset when *ma* Zaibu gave Josée and me so much attention. One day, I heard her talking to *ma* Zaibu about it.

"I have raised these two girls, they are my children. All that talk about loving them is just a story to take their father's attention and love away from me. You're wasting your time."

"It's nothing like that, *bi mukubwa*," *ma* Zaibu replied politely. "I just like these girls, that's all there is to it."

Slowly but steadily, relations between Mama Apoline and *ma* Zaibu started to sour.

Ma Zaibu, who had never had a drink of alcohol in her first few months with us, started to drink a lot, even though she said it was forbidden in her religion. And when she drank, she talked a lot—too much. I didn't like it when she drank a lot. She was always nice to Josée, me, and Papa. But when *ma* Zaibu was drunk, she lost all her politeness around Mama Apoline. She would tell Mama Apoline exactly what she was thinking, and it usually wasn't nice things about Mama Apoline.

"*Bwana* [Mister] Benoit will kick you out soon. I will stay here with all the children. I'll become his first wife." *Ma* Zaibu would spit out the words like a machine, with a strange, cruel look in her eyes. I was afraid that one day she and Mama Apoline would start hitting each other. Every time I saw *ma* Zaibu drinking I went to my room to hide. I didn't like it when big people got angry at each other. It kept me from sleeping at night. It didn't take much to disturb my sleep. Since the war, I had become a very light sleeper. Any sudden noise at night—an owl hooting, a baby crying, a drunken man singing on the streets out-side our house—would startle me awake and into a momentary panic. Upon seeing the four walls of my room I'd ease back to my slumber. But since *ma* Zaibu started drinking, I had also been wetting my bed often, which was pretty embarrassing for a nine year old.

Mama Apoline now had a strong weapon against her rival. She sometimes pretended to be nice to Zaibu and invited her to share a drink. And sometimes she did mean things that made *ma* Zaibu want to drink. Things quickly went from bad to worse between them, and this made Papa miserable. Soon he decided that he'd had enough headaches with his two wives. The easiest thing to do was to return *ma* Zaibu to her family. On the day that she left, she told Josée and me that she would always love us, even when she was gone. We never saw her again.

After *ma* Zaibu's departure, Papa and Mama Apoline became friendly again. Mama Apoline started treating Josée and me nicely. Was she trying to be like *ma* Zaibu had been to us? Josée and I wondered.

One day I told her that I missed *ma* Zaibu. "*Ma* Zaibu was very nice to us, a lot nicer than you are," I foolishly said.

"Is that so?" Mama Apoline responded furiously. "That's wonderful. Well, then I think you're not going to eat what I've cooked today. Why don't you wait for Zaibu to come and cook for you?"

When Papa found out about this, he shared his food with me. The next day, Josée heard a heated argument between Mama Apoline and Papa about me not eating her food. That day I could tell that Mama Apoline was angry with me, but she never forbade me again from eating her meals. As time went by, I talked less and less of *ma* Zaibu. She became just a fragment of memory, floating in the recesses of my mind, somewhere beside the image of Maman Thérèse whom Josée talked about incessantly.

Slowly life in Kongolo started to return to normal. The stores were open again, and many of the expatriate merchants were also getting back to their businesses in town. If not for some destroyed buildings still left in rubble, one wouldn't even have known that there had been a war. Soon Papa was invited to Albertville to meet with his old TRANGEN boss, Constantinides Papadopoulos, to discuss business. Constantinides and his wife had left Congo for Cyprus at the outbreak of the war, and they had lost almost everything. For now, Constantinides was concentrating his efforts only in Albertville. As for Kongolo, he asked Papa to oversee all his real estate, rent the buildings out to businessmen, and use the money to properly fix all of the TRANGEN properties. If things got better in the future, maybe the export-import operations would start again in Kongolo.

Papa started fixing, with his own money, all of the TRANGEN buildings and then rented them out. Constantinides had promised Papa that he would be getting his salary as soon as the business was back on track in Albertville, and Papa trusted him. Papa didn't mind risking his own money, he knew he would get it back. After all, Constantinides was a man of honor, just like our Papa.

Just a few months after our return from Samba, Josée became seriously ill. She'd wake up at nights complaining about intense pain in her ribs. Lying on her belly hurt, and she could only get to sleep when she was propped up against something or someone. She would ask me to sit up against the wall on our bed, then she'd sit up against me. We struggled all night to find a position that would ease her pain. When I was too tired to sit up for her, she'd moan all night long and neither of us got any sleep. I finally got some restful nights when Papa let Josée sleep against him. Mama Apoline was not with us; she and the other children were staying with *kambo* on *Avenue Kindu*. Papa said Mama Apoline was on vacation.

Almost all the medical equipment at the Kongolo General Hospital had been destroyed during the war. Even simple blood tests couldn't be done. The doctors gave Josée medication to calm her pain, but she didn't really get any better. Papa said that Josée would have to go to Albertville to be examined and treated there. He would send her there by plane, and she would stay with *Monsieur* Constantinides and his wife; they had told Papa that he didn't need to go with Josée himself, that they would take care of her. So two days later, Papa and I took Josée to the airport. She was excited to go on a plane for the first time in her life and forgot about her pain for a few brief moments.

Papa told Josée that our sister, Louise Kalundi, Maman's oldest daughter from her first marriage, lived in Albertville with her husband

and children. When Josée felt better, he said, she should go and visit Louise before coming back home. Papa also sent Maman a letter telling her about Josée going to Albertville for treatment.

In Albertville, the doctors found that Josée had an advanced case of schistosomiasis, a parasitic disease, transmitted by contact with infected water, that can cause fatal damage to vital organs such as the liver and spleen. She was also heavily infected with amoebas and other parasites. Had she stayed longer in Kongolo, her health would have deteriorated fast, and she probably would have died. Her treatment started right away. She got shots every day and lots of pills to take. *Madame* Constantinides saw to it that she did exactly what the doctor ordered. Within a week, the pain in Josée's ribs disappeared. She started to sleep again through the night and to eat well. Soon she got back to her old chubby self. After two weeks in Albertville, she finished her treatment and got a clean bill of health from the doctors.

One day, *Madame* Constantinides told Josée that she would have a surprise visitor. First, Josée thought it was our big sister Louise, but that wouldn't be much of a surprise because Louise had been coming regularly to visit her. Then Josée thought that it was Papa coming to take her back home. That afternoon, as she and *Madame* Constantinides were sitting on the balcony, she saw *da* Louise coming with her baby wrapped on her back. She was not alone, another woman was with her. The woman looked a little familiar but Josée couldn't see her very well from the balcony. As they got closer, Josée's heart started to race. Could it be possible? She shouted her lungs out, "Maman, Maman," and ran to the door. She jumped on Maman, and they both started crying.

"Are you all right now, Maman?" *Da* Louise asked. "Maman arrived in Albertville today. She thought that Josée was still very sick and wanted to see her right away. When Maman received Papa Benoit's letter, she thought Josée was dying!"

Maman thanked *Madame* Constantinides for taking care of Josée and asked if Josée could go with her to Louise's house. Not only did *Madame* Constantinides say yes, but she said Josée could spend the last few days of her stay in Albertville with her. Josée was in heaven. It had been six years since she had seen Maman.

Josée met our little sister Jeanne for the first time, and also *da* Louise's husband, Louis Kabila, and their children and two of Louis' children from his first marriage. Louis Kabila was a muLuba from Manono and a well-educated man. He was very nice to Josée, and she had lots of fun with his son, Déo.

Back in Kongolo, I missed Josée terribly. She had always been with me, showing me all the amazing things she could do, while I would show her my daring, tomboy tricks. I thought about how I would turn an old car engine cover into a canoe. Even though she called me crazy, she would nonetheless sit in the front of my "canoe," with two long wooden sticks and help me propel it up and down the shallow Kangoy River.

"When she comes back," I said to myself, "I'll be very nice to her. I won't smash a rotten papaya on her head like the other day when I was angry with her after I got punished because of her."

About three weeks later, I was playing in the backyard, and I saw a truck stop in front of our house. I saw Papa go to the front of the truck, then to the back. My heart jumped. I dropped the rocks I'd been playing with and started walking towards the truck. And there she was getting out of the passenger seat.

"Josée, Josée," I shouted as I ran to the truck.

She was wearing a beautiful flowery brown dress. She turned in my direction and ran toward me.

"I've missed you so much," I said.

"I did too, you know, our *kampulumayamba* [the restless one]," she said, always ready to tease me. "But I have so much to tell you. Guess what? Maman, our Maman, has been with me at *da* Louise's house. They've sent you lots of presents!"

That night we didn't go to sleep until very late, as I soaked up every detail about her stay in Albertville. Most of all, I asked her to describe to me what it felt like to fly.

CHAPTER 15

BULLETS INTO WATER

A few months after Josée's return from Albertville, we started hearing rumors about another war breaking out in different regions of the country. The rebels were sympathetic to the memory of our martyred first Prime Minister, Patrice Lumumba. They blamed some of the central government leaders for actively participating in the plot to kill Lumumba, and they blamed the entire government for selling out Lumumba's ideals of integrity, national unity, and autonomy from Europe and the United States. Many of the rebels called themselves *simba mulele*, Mulele being the name of their leader, Pierre Mulele, a former cabinet minister, and *simba*, the kiSwahili word for lion. People said the *simba mulele* had magical powers that protected them against bullets. Before they became *simba mulele*, they went through a series of initiation rites through which they were given powers that made them invisible and invincible.

The *simbas* first started going after the secessionists who had fought against Lumumba's vision of a unified nation. Then they attacked those who worked with the central government. Later they began attacking anyone who worked in an office or had been educated.

The rebels liked to chant: "*Mulele mai, mai; mulele mai, mai,*"
[Mulele water]. This meant that their powers turned bullets into drops
of water. Bullets couldn't harm them, they actually believed it! What
was worse, many of the central government soldiers seemed to believe
it, too. When confronted by government soldiers, the *simbas* charged
fearlessly, armed only with bows and arrows. Their madness worked
miracles: the government soldiers would typically flee at the sight of
advancing *simbas.*

During 1964, the *simbas* took control of one area after another
in Congo. Their warriors, mostly boys in their early teens, instituted
reigns of terror in the towns they captured. There were many reports
of brutal rapes, even of young girls, and horrible massacres of defenseless people. They forced many young boys to join their ranks under
the very real threat of torture. Many people were taken from their
homes and never seen again.

Papa told us that if it looked like the *simbas* were coming to
Kongolo, we wouldn't take any chances. He feared that, during this war,
we might not be lucky enough to escape as we did during the first war.

"No," Papa said repeatedly, "if the *simbas* come near
Kongolo, we will leave immediately and go into hiding."

In August 1964, Stanleyville, the largest city in the northeastern
part of Congo, Papa's home region, fell to the *simbas.* The *simbas* held
many white expatriates hostage there, and quite a few were killed. The
simbas even killed Congolese nuns who refused to sleep with them. We
heard that the *simbas* were now raping girls as young as three years old
and brutally torturing and killing any family members who protested.

In early fall we heard that the *simbas* had arrived at some towns
near Kongolo. Papa decided that it was time to go. We didn't want to
leave our home and our friends. We didn't want to walk for days on end
and sleep in the forest and scavenge for food and run to hide whenever
we heard someone passing. But we were afraid of the *simbas.* So, once
again, we took only what was essential and headed out of Kongolo. But
this time we all left together: Papa, Mama Apoline, *kambo* Colette,
Gilbert, N'Kongolo, Josée, Marie, Benjamin, baby Misère, and me. And

this time our destination was a lot closer than Samba. We drove for a little while in Papa's truck, until the roads became impassable. Papa tried to hide the truck in the bush; we helped him by smoothing out the tracks that the truck tires had left in the dirt roads. Then we headed off on foot to the village of Papa's good friend, *ba* Chui, who lived by an estuary of the Lualaba River, near the *Portes d'Enfer* [Gates of Hell]. It took us a day to get there. *Ba* Chui set us up in one of his houses, and we became villagers for the time being.

Papa said we had enough cash to get us through this crisis, but he soon learned that cash didn't mean much in this village. Twice a week people met at the market place to "buy" things, but in this time of renewed crisis, no one was very interested in paper money. Most of the people with food to sell would only sell it in exchange for other things, mainly other types of food. Fish were plentiful in this village by the river, but meat was rare. Papa still had his two guns and his hunting skills, so we temporarily went back into the hunting business. He didn't get as much meat as he had in Samba, but it was enough for ourselves and for exchanging to get whatever food and other essentials we needed.

A week or two after arriving in *ba* Chui's village, we learned that the rebels had taken Kongolo. Some of the *simbas,* we heard, were headed toward outlying villages. Almost every day, people from the village brought news about what was happening in Kongolo. I was so very happy that we hadn't stayed around the city as we did during the first war. I had no desire to ever again hear the *ratatata* or *kabooms* of war. Since we were more prepared this time and we all stuck together, life in the village was almost like going on a long vacation. No school, just playing all the time. Josée, N'Kongolo, Marie, and I learned how to trap fish in a pond from our new friends in the village. We didn't dare go into the Lualaba River, however. The water was very turbulent in that area, and people from the village told us frightening stories about children getting trapped underneath the huge rocks in the water and drowning. Their bodies would emerge only days or weeks later. I was a big girl of nine years old, and Papa and Mama Apoline didn't have to tell me twice any more. I played in the water only in the places we had been told were safe.

Then one day, Papa told us that people in a nearby village had spotted a small group of *simbas* in their area. The *simbas* were setting people's houses on fire and beating villagers to death for no apparent reason. The village leaders decided that everyone in our village had to move to a small island near the middle of the river. If, after a day or two, the situation stayed calm, we would return to the village. Otherwise, we would all move together to the other side of the river. The people of the village began shuttling back and forth with their canoes to take their families and some belongings to the island.

Most of the men, including Papa, stayed behind until everyone else had crossed to the island by the late afternoon. The last men to leave the village said everyone had to start moving directly to the other side of the river. The rebels were getting closer to the village, so the island was no longer a safe haven. Soon after, we saw smoke rising to the sky from the village, a clear indication that the *simbas* had arrived.

It was late in the evening when Mama Apoline and all of us children crossed from the island to the other side of the river. Papa and a couple of other men were among the last scheduled to cross the river. Three men had been on the edge of the island observing the village. They saw that the *simbas,* furious about not finding anyone in the village, were headed toward the riverbank carrying a canoe. Apparently, in the rush to leave, one of the villagers had left a small canoe on top of his house. It appeared that the *simbas* were heading straight toward the island.

The three lookouts raced to where Papa and the others were waiting for them.

"We have to cross the river fast," they shouted while gasping for breath. "They must already be on the island."

Instead of leaving immediately, Papa and the others got into a big argument over whether they should flee or stay to fight the *simbas*. After a long discussion, they finally decided in favor of discretion and took the path to where the canoes were docked. Sitting in a canoe, Papa had his guns on his shoulders, both loaded and ready for action. A short distance from the island riverbank, they saw four or five men emerge from the trees—the *simbas!* The *simbas* started shouting, then they shot arrows at the canoes. One of them aimed a rifle at the canoes and started shooting. But they were too late, the canoes were just out of reach, close to their destination on the other riverbank. As Papa and his friends cheered and talked about how narrowly they had escaped, Papa's canoe headed straight into a ferocious stretch of rapids. The canoe started spinning out of control and tilted upwards, immediately tossing all its passengers into the water.

On the riverbank, we heard people shouting that one of the last canoes had capsized and that a couple of the other canoes had gone to search for survivors. We all waited anxiously.

"I felt something bad was going to happen," Mama Apoline said as the rest of us stood still and silent in disbelief.

The first rescue canoe came back, but Papa wasn't among the rescued. Mama Apoline started to sob, and we followed her lead by sobbing and whimpering. When the next canoe came in, two wet people were sitting up, obviously shaken, but a third wet person was lying down. The first two stepped out, and one said that it was Suruba Benoit lying in the boat. We then started to wail as mourners do. Papa was dead, he must be dead!

But the man who had been guiding the canoe pulled it to land, looked at us reassuringly, and said, "He's just weak, that's all. He'll be fine." Mama Apoline waded into the water toward the canoe.

"*Baba* Josée!" she called out.

Papa mumbled something in response. Mama Apoline and the man helped Papa out of the canoe and led him to the shore. Later, Papa told us that the weight of his two guns had pulled him all the way to the bottom of the river, thirty or forty feet deep. As good a swimmer as he was, he couldn't pull himself and the rifles up. He had to put the guns down and soar up to the surface to take a deep breath. Then he plunged down to the bottom again to try to find the guns. He couldn't locate them and, when he surged to the surface again for air, the current started spinning him around like a top. At that point he gave up on the guns and managed to fight the current and swim toward the riverbank, where a canoe picked him up. Those guns meant a lot to him, they helped us get back on our feet again, but they weren't worth his life.

The *simbas* never followed us to the other side of the river. Apparently, the group of rebels that took our village were few in number and realized they would have difficulty with the large group of villagers on the other side. Papa and the villagers quickly made temporary shelters with bamboo sticks, palm tree branches, vines, and mud in which we lived for almost three months. Then we heard that the fighting had stopped, the *simbas* had been defeated. We could go home once again to Kongolo. Our house in town had been seriously vandalized, so Papa said that we would live in the house next door. It had fewer rooms, but wasn't as badly damaged.

Our flight from the second round of fighting was much less painful than the first time. We didn't see any fighting, no dead bodies. We stayed mainly in one place and didn't march endlessly on foot through the forest. We had regular meals and got to play to our heart's content. We were away from home for but a few months, not a couple of years. But, most of all, we were together, with Papa to take care of all of us.

Other people were not so lucky. After our return to Kongolo, we got a letter from Maman. She and Jeanne were fine, but she had bad news from Albertville. Louis Kabila, *da* Louise's husband, my brother-in-law, was gone.

Louis had no involvement in politics, and he was repulsed by the murder of Lumumba. He knew some of the *simba* leaders in Albertville, and he could not believe that they would ever see him as any kind of threat. Louise was concerned for his safety, but he thought she was being irrational. So he kept on working at his office job even after the rebels took Albertville. Some of his colleagues at work had gone into hiding, but he was confident nothing would happen to him.

Then one day, Louis was taken from his office by three rebels who said they were bringing him to their headquarters for questioning.

Louis had no reason to be alarmed, it all seemed to be routine and, if there were any problems, he would smooth it out with the *simbas* that he knew. He told his staff that he would be back soon.

But as Louis entered the rebel car, he probably got a little nervous when two of the three rebels sat with him in the back seat and put him in the middle as if he were a prisoner. How frightened he must have been when the car raced past the rebels' headquarters and went straight on towards the airport. By the time they got to the Lukuga River, the rebels started beating him. As they dragged him out of the car, Louis somehow found the strength to escape momentarily and dive into the river. He almost made it all the way to the opposite bank, but the rebels commandeered a canoe, followed him, and pierced his flesh with a barrage of arrows. They killed Louis Kabila, office manager, husband, father, my brother-in-law, the man who'd been so kind to Josée when she was being treated in Albertville. And they left his body in the river, to be picked apart by the fish and crocodiles.

CHAPTER 16

HAPPY GIRLS

By Fall 1965, Josée and I were back at school in Kongolo. Even though I was nine years old, going on ten, the previous years had been so chaotic that they put me in second grade. Twelve-year-old Josée was put in fourth grade. Things returned to normal a lot quicker this time. It seemed like people were getting used to running away and then starting over again. Papa found his truck unharmed and went back to his transport and food selling business, while also managing TRANGEN's properties in town.

Every now and then, Papa reminded us of how we should escape to the countryside if trouble started again when he was out on a trip.

"You always have to be ready to escape on a moment's notice. I don't know when or if the country will ever calm down. The fighting has stopped for a while, but many, many people are still unhappy with the government in Léopoldville. The political parties keep on arguing all the time, and nobody seems to be able to get everyone to work together for the good of the country."

Josée and I fully expected that we would have to run away

again. Maybe, if we were lucky we'd get to stay in Kongolo for two or three years before the next war. Running into the forest to hide from soldiers and cannons and mines, wasn't that what all children did?

Late in November we heard that the army chief of staff, Joseph Desiré Mobutu, had taken control of the government. We didn't know much about him, but he said he would bring peace and stability to the country. That sounded good to us.

I was very happy in our new house, I actually liked it better than the one we had lived in before the war. It had a nice balcony in front, where I could sit and watch everything going on in the street. Best of all, I could slide down the pipe that ran from the balcony to the ground floor. Of course, I never did this when Papa or Mama Apoline was around.

"That's dangerous. What if you fall?" Josée asked me.

"I'm holding on tight, I won't fall. Do you want to try it, too?"

"No, I'm not that stupid!"

Sometimes I didn't understand how Josée could be so scared of doing things. I was never scared of trying anything. I guess she couldn't understand me either. Mama Apoline said I didn't act like a girl. *Kambo* said I was a tomboy if ever there was one. I just wanted to have fun.

When he came back from his trips, Papa often brought us a sack or two of fresh peanuts. One day I asked if I could take some to sell.

"I'll make some pocket money for myself. Please, can I, Papa?"

"Pocket money? What do you want to do with pocket money?"

"Well, I'll buy some roasted peanuts and *beignets* at school during recess. And I'll also buy myself a couple of crayons. I always need crayons."

Papa laughed. "So, you want to go into the retail business? Well, that's all right with me."

He gave me a giant helping of peanuts to sell. I boiled my stock of peanuts and put them in a bowl, which I carefully covered with a clean cloth and placed on the table in our bedroom. After school, the following day, I took my peanuts and an empty sack to the front of the house, by the street. I diligently swept the sidewalk clean and put the empty brown sack on the ground. Then I put my merchandise in piles on top of the sack. Each pile cost one franc.

"Welcome, welcome clients," I shouted out with a big, friendly smile on my face. "Plenty of boiled peanuts here. Only one franc a pile!" I put on a big show, imitating the adults who sold things at the market.

My first client asked if she could have a taste before buying. "Certainly," I said, oozing confidence in the quality of my product. I gave her a couple of peanuts, and she rewarded my marketing savoir faire by asking for two piles. We didn't have plastic or paper bags to put things in, so I did what everyone at the market did. I took a piece of used notebook paper, shaped it into a cone, and put the two piles of peanuts inside. In return, she gave me two francs, pure profit for the fledgling entrepreneur. I was actually making money. I couldn't wait to tell Josée.

"Eh, Joséeee, Joséeee, come and see," I shouted to the balcony. "I'm selling my peanuts!"

When Josée came to the railing of the balcony, I showed her my two coins while jumping up and down and skipping back and forth. I turned to the street again and cried out the news about my incredibly delicious peanuts. When it was time to close shop that day, I had made five francs.

Josée sometimes helped sell Mama Apoline's *beignets* in front of the house. "But I can't shout for clients the way you do," she said. "You shout like a crazy person."

"Maybe you think I'm crazy, but people come to buy from me, anyway. If I'm so crazy, then don't ask me for roasted peanuts and *beignets* when I get some at school."

That evidently inspired Josée to teach her baby sister a lesson. She went to ask Papa for her own stock of peanuts and began selling them after school right next to my stand. I shouted to attract clients for myself, but since she was right next to me it brought her customers, too. Most customers insisted on getting a sample taste from each of us, and they quickly discovered that Josée was a much better peanut roaster than I. She started to get the lion's share of the sales, which upset me to no end.

"Well, now it's your turn to attract the clients. I won't shout anymore!" I vowed.

We argued for a while, and after a few minutes of boring silence, I went back to shouting for customers. If I shouted loud and long enough, I thought, maybe we'd get so many customers that they'd finish Josée's peanuts and have to buy mine. Sometimes it actually worked out that way, but not often.

In the evenings, Josée and I often made up plays and dance shows to perform for the family. Sometimes, I tried to dress up like a *mbuli*, a Hemba traditional dancer who wears a goat skin on top of a raffia skirt, a straw hat, and some amulets around the neck, arms and waist. Of course, I didn't have such a sophisticated costume; instead I wore a *pagne* and put palm branches around my waist and head. I danced and danced until my audience begged me to stop, so they could have some peace and quiet. Josée often joined me. *Kambo* Colette sometimes joined in, and eventually, so did Mama Apoline. I felt like I could dance forever!

The most fun was when Papa danced with us to *Tango ya ba Wendo*, Congolese popular music from the 1940s and 1950s. Papa was a unique dancer, so unique that he might have been the single worst dancer in all of Congo. But it obviously brought him great pleasure to stand up and dance with his girls. Mama Apoline said he danced like a soldier on a battlefield. He'd start by moving his whole body from one side of the room to the other and then back, sort of like someone doing a partner-less tango. When he began to tire, he'd hold his hands behind his back and just shuffle his feet, left, right, left, right. After that, he didn't move his feet any more, but just swayed from left to right and right to left. His next move was back to his favorite chair.

"That's all for me," he'd say as if he had just run a hundred miles. "Go on without me. I'm an old man, I get easily tired!"

One thing Papa never got tired of was telling us stories about his younger days. And I never got tired of listening to Papa's wonderful tales. Every time he finished one story I'd ask him to start another. I asked him about Wendo and all the other old musicians. I asked him about the games he played as a child, about the market in his village, about his Maman and Papa. I asked him about the house he lived in and the school at which he studied. I asked him to tell us about the days that we were born and how that made him feel. After each question he'd smile, heave a sigh of pleasure, and lean forward to answer as if he were telling us a great, big secret. Then he'd lean back and finish his story and, somehow, each tale always ended with something funny that made us all laugh. All of us except Mama Apoline.

Mama Apoline never got used to the way Papa let us ask questions. I guess it wasn't really her fault: she wasn't brought up to talk to her Papa that way. Neither were most girls in Congo. Girls were supposed to start distancing themselves from their fathers as they got older. That way, when they had to talk about "women" things, they'd know that they had to do it only with their mothers.

Sometimes, when Papa was on his trips, Mama Apoline told us we should stop asking Papa so many questions. One day I couldn't pretend that I agreed with her, so she came at me with what she thought was an unbeatable argument.

"You're starting to grow up now. What are you going to do when you start seeing the moon? Are you going to ask your father about it?" She laughed at the very idea.

"What do you mean?" I responded naively. "I've been seeing the moon for a very long time."

"No, silly child, I don't mean the moon in the sky. That's just an expression for when a girl starts to have her period every month."

"What's a period?"

Mama Apoline smiled. This was as it should be, the mother talking to the girl about the women things.

"When girls are about twelve or thirteen, but sometimes even at eleven, they start bleeding once a month from their private part," she explained. "Your sister will start having it real soon."

"You mean that blood will come out of my private part when I pee?" I asked.

"Yes, it can come out when you pee," she said. "But it will also come out when you don't pee. After a few days it stops and goes away for about a month."

I found the whole thing pretty repulsive, so I rushed to tell Josée about it. To my surprise, Mama Apoline had already spoken with her about it. This period business started to worry me. I didn't want to pee blood every month. I had peed blood once before, a side effect of an infection. Peeing blood hurt, and I had to take a lot of medicine for a long time to make it stop. Now Mama Apoline was telling me I would be doing it every month! For a few hours I thought of nothing but all that bleeding I was destined to get. By the end of the day, however, I stopped worrying about it and concentrated on playing.

A few days later, Papa was telling us a bedtime story, and my fear of peeing blood suddenly, inexplicably returned. I couldn't help myself, before I even knew what I was doing, the words came out.

"Papa, is it true that when a girl is about twelve or thirteen blood will start coming out of her private part, sort of like she's peeing blood?"

As soon as I said "private part" in front of Papa, Josée put her hands in front of her mouth and gave me the signal to shut up. Mama Apoline looked at me and shook her head, then looked back at the clothes she was ironing. She didn't appear to be worried. She seemed confident that, even Benoit with all his crazy ideas, would never let a girl get away with talking about such a thing in the presence of her Papa. Even Benoit would have to tell his daughter that there were some things that a girl just mustn't ask her father about. Finally, she'd heard a question from one of the "princesses" that Benoit would refuse to answer.

Papa looked at me for a few seconds. Then he smiled, leaned forward, and started to talk.

"Yes, that's true," Papa said. "But I'm told it usually doesn't hurt much, and you sort of get used to it." He leaned back in his chair and continued. "Besides, you wear something called a hygienic napkin near your private part, so your clothes stay clean and you hardly feel a thing."

I was disappointed that it was true but at the same time delighted to hear that it wouldn't hurt so much and that my clothes would stay clean and dry. It looked like Josée was happy about that, too. Mama Apoline stopped ironing. She was too shocked to even shake her head.

A year passed, then two, and no war came to Kongolo. It seemed that the new president, Mobutu, had kept his promise and brought peace to the country. In 1967, when I was in fourth grade, there was a rebellion of soldiers and white mercenaries in Stanleyville and Bukavu, but it didn't spread far or last long. Nobody in Kongolo appeared to be afraid, and, soon enough, the government won, and the rebels fled to another country. That same year, we were told that there would be no more political parties, there would only be one party for all Congolese to join—Mobutu's party. We started to get used to the idea that we would be staying in Kongolo, and we wouldn't have to run away any more.

Godelìève was our best friend. During vacations, she'd often sleep over at our house, and we'd sleep over at hers. Her father had two wives, and sometimes the second wife took us to their fields where we'd pick our own rice. After we'd harvested quite enough, we each carried basins full of rice back to Godé's house. Her mothers would lay the rice down on the ground to dry under the sun, and we'd go off to play near a little stream under the late afternoon sun. We'd frolic in the sand and roll around like crazy people. We'd run, shout, sing, and get dirty all over. Sometimes we'd take off all our clothes and play naked in the stream. Then we'd go roll in the sand again and get the sand all over our naked bodies before heading back to the stream for more swimming and games. When we heard voices coming, we'd grab our *pagnes* fast. Who would believe that these happy girls had ever been war refugees?

After school, Josée usually headed straight home without any stops or detours. I, on the other hand, often stopped along the road to play or stare at things and usually fell far behind her. I didn't blame her for not waiting for me, I knew that I must have driven her crazy sometimes.

One day, when I was twelve, Josée was way ahead of me on her return home from school. I couldn't even see her any more, not that I was looking since there were so many things along the road that had captured my attention. When I passed the railroad company's housing complex, a couple of older boys, around Josée's age, started to tease me. I had grown tall for a girl my age, but I was still extremely skinny. My head, however, was normal-sized, which made it look disproportionately large on top of my pathetically thin frame. The boys shouted at me: "*Double tête, double tête*" [double head]. I started to cry and raced forward to catch up with Josée, who was furious when she heard what the boys had said. She sometimes teased me about my head being big, but, she said, she was my sister. Anybody else who dared tease me like that would have to answer to her!

"Don't you cry," Josée said with a wisdom well beyond her years, while wiping away my tears. "If you do, then they win the game because they get what they want, and they'll continue to tease you. Just ignore them, because they aren't worth it. There's nothing in their little chicken heads." She took my hand and held it tight for the rest of the walk home.

The rest of the week I stuck with Josée for the walk home, and I didn't hear anything from those boys when we passed the housing complex; they didn't dare tease me when I was with Josée. But one day the following week I fell into my old tricks and let Josée get ahead of me. As I passed that housing complex, a boy named Claude approached me from behind, startled me, and began taunting me mercilessly. But this time Josée hadn't gone too far ahead.

"Dada, dadaaa," [sister] I called out loudly.

Josée heard, turned around, and came running back to me. At that point I started to cry. She looked around and asked, "What's the matter? Is anyone teasing you?"

"He's teasing me," I said, pointing to Claude, whom Josée and I knew.

Before I even finished telling her the details, she stuffed her things in my hands and grabbed the boy by the collar.

"Don't you dare tease her anymore, you coward," she screamed at him. "Why don't you pick on someone your own age? If you bother her one more time, you'll have to deal with me. Do you hear me, you chicken shit!"

I was stunned to see the furor coming out of Josée. The next thing I knew they were both on the ground, and people were separating them. Josée stood up, shook her dress, and came back to me. She had a scratch on her right cheek. She grabbed her things with one hand and held my hand with the other.

"Let's go," she said. "I'll tell Papa. He knows that empty barrel's parents."

When we got home, Josée explained to Papa what had happened and how I'd been teased to tears by that boy and his friends. Papa was obviously upset. After all, Josée usually didn't get involved in such trouble. Now if it had been me, that would have been another story. He took both of us to see Claude's parents, whom he knew very well. Claude's father called in his son as we all sat in their living room. He then asked Josée and me to explain what had happened. He quickly became furious with his son and demanded that he apologize to us.

"You bring me shame with *Monsieur* Benoit's family. We are like family with them, don't you know that? These two girls are like your own sisters, and you must treat them accordingly. You must be the one protecting them, not doing what you've just done. Look at her face! Go to your room, I will talk with you later."

He must have had a serious talk with his son, because, after that day, Claude was always very nice to us. The other boys in that housing complex continued to tease me, but it didn't bother me so much any more. I just did what Josée had told me to do, however hard it was in the beginning: I ignored them completely. And in next to no time, they got bored and gave up.

CHAPTER 17

No Longer
a Fairy Tale

At the age of twelve, I was a lot wiser than I had been before. I began to see and hear things I hadn't seen or paid attention to when I was younger. And I understood so much more of what I saw and heard. I knew that things were not going well once again between Mama Apoline and Papa. Mama Apoline announced that she needed to take Gilbert to stay with his father in E'ville, Papa disagreed, and they argued terribly. Finally, they came to an agreement. She would take Gilbert to E'ville and come back by herself in two weeks or so.

But six weeks passed before she returned. I was happy to see her on the day she came back, but Papa told her that she had no business coming to his house. It was over, he said. Mama Apoline insisted that she needed to see Misère, who was then a little over two.

"You didn't mind leaving her behind, how come she matters so much now?" Papa said, grabbing the baby and sending Mama Apoline away.

Two days later, Mama Apoline and *kambo* Colette came to our house and waited for Papa to return from work. When he arrived, the three of them talked for a long time behind closed doors. Josée and

I put our ears next to the doors, but we couldn't hear a thing. Both Mama Apoline and *kambo* Colette slept over in our bedroom that night. In the morning, *kambo* went home, but Mama Apoline stayed. The next night she slept in Papa's room. Then things seemed to get better again between Papa and Mama Apoline. And the funny thing was that Gilbert came back to stay with *kambo* after only a couple of months with his father. He said he didn't feel comfortable with his father's wife, after all.

One night, a few months after their latest reconciliation, Josée and I heard Papa and Mama Apoline talking about her being pregnant. Josée told me later that Papa wasn't the father of the baby, that the real father was none other than *muyomba* Kalenga, whom we called "Uncle" because he was muTabwa like Maman Thérèse. Kalenga was the head of the water company in Kongolo and was supposed to be a good friend of Papa's.

Muyomba Kalenga used to come and visit us—or rather Mama Apoline—very often, especially when Papa was out of town on business trips. Mature enough this time to put two and two together, it made me sick to my stomach. *Kambo* Colette begged Papa to let Mama Apoline stay until she delivered the baby.

"You must never kick a pregnant woman out of the house where she got pregnant," she said. "After she gives birth, then the man and woman can decide what to do."

Papa let Mama Apoline stay. A few months later, Mama Apoline delivered a baby girl who was given the name Pascaline. She looked like *muyomba* Kalenga's children.

My closest friend in school was still Godeliève, or Godé, with whom we had picked rice and played naked in the stream during vacation. Besides being in the same class, we also were together in our local group of *Xavériennes,* the Congolese version of the Girl Scouts. One of our tasks to earn points as *Xavériennes* was to help clean the nuns' convent or the priests' rectory on Wednesdays and Saturdays. Godé was usually assigned to work at the rectory.

Godé must have done a really good job at the rectory, I thought, because the parish priest kept on asking for her to work there, even on days other than Wednesday and Saturday. As Godé started to spend more and more time at the parish, we hardly ever saw her except at school, and there she started to act strangely. She kept to herself a lot or hung out only with the parish priest's niece, who was also in our class. Then she stopped coming to school altogether. We thought that she might have been sick.

A little while later, Papa shocked us. "Godé will not be going to school ever again. She's pregnant." And even more shocking, was the news that the man who made thirteen-year-old Godé pregnant was none other than the parish priest himself! He, of course, denied it. Godé's father took the whole affair to the tribunal. Some nuns from the convent tried to talk him out of going public with his accusations. Maybe Godé had a boyfriend with whom she had sex, the nuns insinuated.

Unfortunately for the nuns and all those who wanted to save the reputation of this so-called man of God, Godé had been telling the truth. She didn't know anything about sex until the parish priest started, in her words, "going on top of her." The parish priest kept asking her to fix his bed, and then he followed her into the bedroom. He asked her to lay down, and when she started to panic, he told her that she had nothing to worry about. After all, she was in good hands: he was a priest, he wouldn't do her any harm. He liked her very much, in fact, he loved her.

The first time, she said, he touched her breasts, or rather the little bumps on her chest. He told her not to tell anybody, that it had to be a special thing between him and her. She was really a very good girl, he said, and nothing would happen to her if she didn't tell a soul. He was a man of God, so she must trust him completely. She started to think that something was wrong, but she kept on going to the rectory, because she was afraid that the parish priest would send her to hell if she disobeyed him. Finally, she couldn't keep the secret any longer, and she told her mother what was going on.

When it became clear to everyone that Godé was telling the

truth, the nuns changed their tack. They asked Godé's father how he could do such a thing to the Father who had done so much for the parish. The parish priest had perhaps made a mistake—he was human after all—but he shouldn't be dragged through the mud and disgraced. They would give Godé any help she needed with her pregnancy—if her father dropped his accusations at the tribunal. They needn't have wasted their time and energy. The tribunal refused to hear Godé's case.

Godé was expelled from school for being pregnant. She would never have a chance to further her education—the nuns wouldn't let anyone who got pregnant back in school. After all, it was a bad example for the other girls. She gave birth to a little boy, who was the spitting image of the parish priest. Less than two years later, at the age of fifteen, Godé married a man who accepted her son as his own.

One day, a few months after Mama Apoline's daughter Pascaline's birth, I was trailing far behind Josée on our way home from school. When I got to our house, I saw a group of people on our balcony, including Gilbert and Mama Apoline.

"Why are you walking like a tortoise?" Gilbert called out. "Come and tell us about your adventures at school."

I glared at them, without paying much attention. When I got upstairs, I went directly to our bedroom to put down my schoolbag. Near my bed I saw a suitcase and two bags.

"Looks like somebody is visiting," I said to myself. Not an unusual occurrence in our house. I started to guess. Was it *ma* Jeannette Feza, *papa* Daba's wife? Or *ma* Alua? As I was about to go to the kitchen, Mama Apoline called me.

"Georgette, come and say hello to one of my sisters who has come to visit me with her daughter."

I went out to the balcony and saw people sitting on mats on the floor and Gilbert sitting on a chair by the balcony railing. They suddenly hushed and stared at me. Josée was sitting next to the daughter of Mama Apoline's sister, who looked to be about five or six years old. Josée had a secretive twinkle in her eyes, but it looked as if she had been crying. I turned around and looked at Mama Apoline's sister. She was pretty, and her daughter was very cute. They looked familiar. I extended my hand to the lady, then to the little girl, and said, "*Hamjambo*" [hello]. Then I turned, went inside the house, and headed for the kitchen. I was hungry after a long day of school. Behind me, back on the balcony, I heard what sounded like someone crying.

"Georgette!" It was Mama Apoline. "Come back here this instant."

"What now? I'm hungry. I've already said hello to her sister," I grumbled.

When I got out to the balcony again, I saw Mama Apoline's "sister" crying.

"Georgette, don't you remember?" Mama Apoline said. "This is your Maman, your Maman Thérèse. And this is your little sister, Jeanne."

I felt like I did when the lightning knocked me off my chair in Samba. I ran to Maman and Jeanne, and Josée joined us in a big hug. We all started to cry and laugh together. Even Mama Apoline was wiping her eyes.

Maman Thérèse had finally returned. I was twelve years old, and I hadn't seen her since I was two. I looked at Josée, and she smiled at me, shaking her head up and down. I knew what she was thinking: *I told you that she would come one day, didn't I?*

I even forgot about my hunger and stared at her to make sure it was really her. Josée had never stopped talking about our real mother, the woman who carried me in her belly. I wanted to ask her so many things but felt shy. I went first to ask Josée. I only spoke to Maman after Josée refused to answer my questions and pushed me towards Maman.

"She's your mother, too," Josée said. "Why do you keep asking me first? Go ask her directly by yourself." I soon learned among other things that Maman was now divorced from Jeanne's father.

Although it seemed strange, in another way it seemed natural that for a few weeks, both of *Monsieur* Benoit's wives lived together amicably under the same roof. Then it was wife number two who moved out. It was as if Mama Apoline had only borrowed us from Maman; now she was giving back to Maman what was rightfully hers, her husband and her daughters. When Mama Apoline moved back to *kambo* Colette's house, she took baby Pascaline with her; Benjamin and Misère stayed with us. Mama Apoline never came back, though Josée and I visited her and Pascaline from time to time.

Maman left our bedroom and moved all her things into Papa's room. It seemed that Papa and Maman's old flame had never really died away. Being together after many years apart rekindled it again. Benjamin and Misère got used to Maman in no time, and Jeanne was very excited to be living with the two sisters she had heard so much about. Jeanne got along fine with Benjamin and Misère. She even got them into the habit of calling me *da* Geolo, instead of only Geolo. "You're our big sister," she said, "and we ought to use a sign of respect when addressing you." I liked that, I really liked it.

As for Josée, she was in heaven. Not only had her dream of Maman's return actually come true, but Maman and Papa were getting along so well. It had been a very long time since we had seen Papa so happy. They went out often and usually came home giggling like young lovers. My big sister, who had spent so much of her childhood rejecting Mama Apoline's maternal advances, now at last had the mother of her dreams.

I was also delighted to have Maman with us. But no matter how much kindness and affection she showed me, I couldn't overcome the distance engendered by the ten years that we were apart. Unlike Josée, I had no treasure chest of early childhood memories of Maman, and I had never spent much time fantasizing about how beautiful things would be if she returned. Nevertheless, I was happy for Papa and happy for Josée. I was especially happy that Jeanne was with us and that the tensions introduced into our home by Mama Apoline were no longer there. I was happy that this kind and good woman lived with us and was taking care of us. But something was missing in my relationship with her. Though I no longer needed Josée's mediation to speak with my mother, I continued to turn to Josée and not my mother for comfort, advice, and maternal affection.

When Maman came to live with us, she brought with her a photograph of Josée and me that Papa had sent her just before the first war. I must have been four and Josée seven. It was a black and white photo; there were no color shots in those days. In the photo, we are standing side by side in front of a nondescript mud wall, Josée on the left a full head taller than me. We wore identical striped dresses with a collar and puffed shoulders, but Josée's dress flowed smoothly down her body while mine seemed to be creased in all the wrong places. We were posing as we'd seen older people pose for staged photographs. No broad smiles or "say cheese" for Congolese portraits at that time. The idea was to stare straight at the camera with a deadly serious expression, almost a scowl. We got that part down very well, but Josée also wanted to put make-up on, just like the grown-up ladies did. The closest thing we could find was baby powder, so she had patted some onto her face, a bit too much, for the white powder was still evident on her brown skin. Her feet were at shoulder's width apart, pointed straight at the camera. Her left arm lay straight at her side, while her right hand was placed on her waist with her elbow pointing out gracefully, forming a perfect triangle with her shoulder and waist. She stared straight ahead, with a regal look. Next to her I stood, a four-year-old whose head seemed far too large for her body. My feet were far apart and pointing to the left of the camera. My right arm didn't quite hang all the way down, and my left hand seemed to be tugging on my dress. My left elbow was bent but it was pointing behind me and was only a few inches from my side; the fingers of my left hand were halfway between my waist and belly button. There was only a hint of a triangle. My dark face was spotted with white powder, and my eyes were squinting.

How much I wanted to be like Josée! My sister was everything a big sister usually is and then some. She took advantage of being older, teasing me, bossing me around, and forcing me to do her work for her. She even pretended she didn't know me when her friends were around, trying to discourage me from playing with them. Every now and then she threatened to tell Papa about what I had done with Gilbert in Samba. She even told me, one day, that she was a virgin, but I was no longer a virgin because of the incident with Gilbert. From then on, whenever I got on her nerves, she would turn slowly toward me and simply say, "*Deja!*" [already]. I knew what she meant: I'd already lost my virginity. Some days, I told her to go ahead and tell Papa. She was there when that incident happened, wasn't she? Everyone was there. I told her that I would tell Papa that she and everyone else let him do that to me. But deep inside I was still afraid of what Papa might do to me if he found out. I never told him.

But she was my sister, and she was always there. Although sometimes she didn't want me hanging around, we wound up spending hour after hour playing together. We'd invent new games, give old ones new twists, and share secret after secret. She seemed to know when I needed loving attention, and she gave it to me. When Papa traveled, it was Josée who kept an eye on *Monsieur* Benoit's mischievous second daughter. She encouraged me to behave in class; she gave me advice on how to get along with my friends. She was born not quite three years before me, but she seemed so much older and wiser than me. She was, in many ways, my real mother.

I often had the same teachers that Josée had had two years earlier. They liked the way I did my school work, and they all thought I was very intelligent. But they often asked why I couldn't behave like Josée. I had to learn not to interrupt a teacher for questions all the time. I had to learn to discipline myself and not to talk to my classmates during lessons. I had to learn to be like Josée. She was a model student in every way, they never tired to remind me.

Realizing how much I loved to talk, my teachers usually gave me good roles in school plays and dance and choir performances. I even got to make solo presentations. Everyone told me I was very good at performing. But Josée, she was the real star.

"Besides being beautiful, she has tremendous natural talent, that young lady," I heard many people say about Josée.

But I never got jealous of her. I felt like she was part of me and

I part of her, and all her successes somehow brought me glory, too. I was so proud of my big sister's accomplishments. How much I wanted to be like her.

Josée graduated from elementary school in 1967, a very impressive accomplishment for a girl in a small town such as Kongolo. Most girls never made it that far. Those who did usually got married as soon as they finished elementary school. Formal education was not a high priority for most girls. "The less they know, the better housewives they are," went a local saying. A small minority of girls would continue their school careers, typically following the three-year course of study for a degree in home economics or a four-year course of study to prepare themselves for teaching elementary school.

But, with Papa encouraging her, Josée applied for and was accepted into the prestigious, six-year Liebermann High School, which was largely populated by boys. The few girls studying there usually came from outside of Kongolo and were attracted by Liebermann's excellent reputation and the high success rate of its students on the State Exams. Two years later I followed my sister's example and enrolled in the best high school in town.

It took only a few months for new tensions to surface in our home. The trouble started with Jeanne and me and soon led to conflict between our two great protectors. When Jeanne and I argued, Maman always seemed to take Jeanne's side and dole out punishment to me. Josée started to get annoyed by Maman's bias; I imagine it reminded her too much of our problems with Mama Apoline. One day she lost her temper and lashed out at Maman.

"Why do you have to defend Jeanne all the time at the expense of Geolo? Just because she's younger doesn't mean that she should be able to get away with murder and give Geolo the blame for everything."

"What do you mean?" Maman replied, shocked by the tone in her daughter's voice. "You know yourself how wild Geolo can be at times. I'm teaching them how to get along."

"Yes, she can be wild at times, but that doesn't mean she's

always at fault. Besides, Jeanne often behaves like a spoiled brat; so why should Geolo have to put up with that all the time?"

"Don't talk to me like that, young lady. I am the mother of both of those girls, and I treat them both fairly."

"Maman, you always take Jeanne's side. Yes, you are Geolo's mother, but I know her better than you do. She's also a child, you know!"

"I'll speak with your father when he comes home. If he's raised you to talk back and be impolite to your own mother, that's got to change. I can't put up with this nonsense."

The conversation ended right there. Maman soon forgave Josée for her impudence, and Josée gave Maman another chance to be fair. But somehow the euphoria over Maman's return had begun to dissipate. Even Papa's joy seemed like it was starting to fade. They stopped going out as much as they had in the beginning, and they started spending more and more time apart. They didn't argue much, as Papa had done with Mama Apoline, in fact, they seemed to agree on most things. But something was missing.

The distance betweeen them grew. After awhile, they didn't really act like husband and wife. I began to wonder if they were just staying together for our sake. Two years into their second go-around, they decided that they couldn't pretend any longer; they both needed to go their own ways. There was no anger, no yelling, no fighting. "We are friends," they told us, "and will remain friends." They would always write to each other. Papa promised Maman that Josée and I would visit her during vacations.

Maman and Jeanne went to live in E'ville for a short while and then they moved to Albertville. But thanks to those two years together and those vacations, she had become at last my flesh-and-blood mother. She was no longer a fairy tale.

CHAPTER 18

FLYING

By the late 1960s the Congolese economy was performing reasonably well, and people grew confident that the wars were finally over for good. The new prosperity led to a change of address for my family. Many new businesses came into Kongolo, and their managers needed housing. Papa fixed up and rented out all of TRANGEN's properties, and soon he had to rent out even the house in which we lived. So, it was back to Kangoy neighborhood on the outskirts of town for us. We liked the new house Papa bought for us in Kangoy, but it was far away from Liebermann High School. Because he felt our education was so important, Papa decided that Josée and I should go live in the dormitory near the school.

Although we visited every weekend and our living at school was his idea, Papa was greatly saddened by our departure from home. Through all his marital turmoil, we were the constant presence around which he built his life. Not to mention that, with Maman gone, we also were the ones doing the bulk of the housework. But Liebermann was the best secondary school in town, and there was no way he was going to make the slightest compromise in the quality of our education.

"Education is the most important thing in your lives," he'd tell us over and over. "It will open all the doors in the world for you. Education is your future."

We missed Papa terribly, but we were also excited about being on our own and getting to spend so much more time with our friends in the dormitory. And, of course, Josée and I had each other.

There were three dormitories, each with about thirty girls living in them. For the first time we were surrounded by other girls for whom education was a top priority. They came from many different areas: Kasongo, Lodja, Kindu, Kabalo, and Albertville. Due to the excellent reputation of the Parish's schools, a few girls came from as far away as E'ville and even Léopoldville. When they first arrived, the boarders tended to form cliques based on their home area. But those ethnic ties didn't seem to matter so much after a few months of living and working together. Or so it seemed, when times were good.

Each and every one of us in the dormitory had chores to do in the morning before we went to school. Our assigned responsibilities were rotated at the beginning of every trimester. As a seventh grader, my tasks typically involved things like bringing logs of wood to the kitchen, cleaning up the bathrooms, and working in the vegetable garden. Some responsibilities were largely reserved for girls who were deemed to be "mature." Only serious, highly disciplined girls got to be the dormitory chief. The chief's role was to maintain order in the dormitory; her main tool was a little notebook in which she wrote down the names of all students who broke dormitory rules, such as making noise after the lights were turned off at night. Never in my wildest dreams did I believe that mischievous little me would ever be given such a weighty responsibility. Of course, Josée was repeatedly selected to serve as our chief.

At the end of each trimester, the Belgian and Italian nuns who ran the dormitories gave out prizes to residents. The prizes were distributed according to how many bad points, or demerits, one accumulated by the end of the trimester. Students who accumulated a lot of bad points got warnings sent home and risked eventual expulsion from school. Offenses that were subject to immediate expulsion included going out of the dormitory and allowing males into the dormitory without permission.

Naturally, I never won first or second prizes, and, just as naturally, Josée was a regular winner. It seemed that I was always earning bad points, either for talking in the dormitory during study hours or for climbing trees to get mangoes without permission. Sister Juliette Monard, the nun in charge of all the dormitories, punished me by making me clean rooms or weed the garden in the back of the convent. I always did a first class job on these punishments, actually doing more work than my sentence mandated. Soon the nuns realized that I didn't really mind doing these punishment chores. I liked to work hard. The only thing that bothered me was not having anyone to talk to while I worked.

On the rare occasions when Josée got in trouble, it always seemed to be my fault. Once I almost got her expelled from school for pulling on a nun's habit. I was in eighth grade at the time, and I was just recovering from a nasty flu that had left me weak. During study hour, Josée sat far away from me, because it was hard for me to stop talking if I sat next to her. Sister Thérèse had already given me a couple of warnings that day about talking during study hours. But then I read something that I absolutely had to share with Josée. When I saw that Sister Thérèse was looking in the other direction, I sneaked out of my chair, got down on my hands and knees, and crawled toward Josée's chair. Before I arrived, Sister Thérèse was at my heels. Burning with anger, she grabbed me by both shoulders and started to shake me back and forth.

Josée stood up and flashed me a dirty look for causing trouble. But as the nun kept on shaking me, Josée came to my rescue pulling me away from Sister Thérèse's grasp. She had that fighting look in her eyes.

"I know she's done a dumb thing, she deserves to be scolded. But you have no right to shake her like that, especially after she's been so sick," Josée shouted at the nun.

The two of them squared off like boxers waiting for the bell to ring so they could go at each other. All the girls fixed their eyes on the unlikely combatants, not wanting to miss a moment of what could have been one of the most memorable study hours in the history of the dormitory.

By this time, Sister Thérèse had grabbed hold of me again, and Josée had, in turn, grabbed hold of the nun's habit around the chest. Fortunately, for all of us, Mama Alphonsine, the adult supervisor of our dormitory, heard the noise and rushed in from the kitchen.

"Josée, please, let go," she pleaded. "It's bad luck to strike a nun. Please let go!"

Josée backed off, but not before pulling me out of the nun's clutches.

"All right, Josée," Mama Alphonsine said with great authority. "You need to apologize this instant to Sister Thérèse for pulling her robe."

Josée stunned the study hall by refusing. "What if she had broken Geolo's arm? Geolo has been sick. How can she shake the girl like that? Does she want to kill her? There's no way that I'm going to apologize to her. If I have to be expelled from the dormitory, so be it. She ought to apologize to my sister."

While we were waiting to meet with Sister Juliette, the director of the dormitories, Josée understandably turned her wrath on me.

"How many times have I told you to stay quiet during study hour? And Sister Thérèse even warned you before, didn't she? You're going to have to apologize to her. You know you're not a child any more. I shouldn't have to remind you all the time about following the rules."

Even though in private she had chastised me, in public she was my supporter. When Sister Juliette called us in, I quickly apologized to Sister Thérèse, who, in turn, apologized for shaking me. Josée didn't apologize to anyone—and she managed to escape without punishment.

After returning from a business trip to Albertville, Papa told us that he had seen Maman and brought us letters from her.

"I promised her that you two are going to spend your vacation with her this summer," Papa said. "She and Jeanne are looking forward to seeing you."

I was so excited that I could barely sleep that night. I was fourteen years old, and this would be my first vacation. Not only would I get to see Maman and Jeanne and beautiful Lake Tanganyika that Josée had told me so much about, but, finally, I was going to fly.

"Wait till you see the lake," Josée kept telling me. "The water is so clear that you can even see little fish swimming in it. It's not like the muddy old Lualaba. And, Geolo, the lake is so big that you can't even see the other side of it. It's so big that it looks like it goes on and on until it meets the sky. And there are waves, Geolo. Wait till you feel the water pounding against your legs."

About a month before the end of the school year, Papa told us that he had our plane tickets to Albertville. I started counting down the weeks, the days, the hours to our departure.

Finally, the moment came. All my things had been packed for a week. I was ready, was I ever ready. Our plane was an antique, propeller-driven Fokker with only twenty-four passenger seats, but it looked like a jumbo jet to me. I sat by the window to take in the whole show.

The take-off was thrilling, everything I had always dreamed it would be. But all of Josée's warnings couldn't prepare me for the gut-wrenching, periodic drops in altitude we experienced as the old Fokker battled the wind. I tightened my seat belt, but that didn't help much.

"Do you feel like throwing up?" Josée asked when she saw the look of anguish on my face.

"No," I whispered, as I squeezed the arms of my seat. Soon enough, the plane stabilized and I could go back to enjoying the view. After only forty-five minutes, the captain announced that we were flying over the Lukuga River. Out the window I could see a magnificent blue-green glistening body of water beyond the Lukuga.

"That's Lake Tanganyika," Josée said excitedly.

I couldn't say a thing, I was stunned by the awesome beauty of the majestic lake. As the plane started landing, it looked as if we were headed right into the lake. I clapped my hand over my mouth so I wouldn't cry out. Then the plane turned and I saw another miraculous sight: a landing strip made of black asphalt that put Kongolo's dirt strip runway to shame. When we got off the plane, I told Josée, "I can hear the waves of the lake welcoming us." She just smiled.

The first one to greet us was Jeanne, who jumped on top of us with such excitement that she nearly knocked us to the ground. With her was Aunt Anne Joubert, Maman's cousin. Maman had stayed at Aunt Anne's house to prepare food and drink for a great party in honor of her two young visitors. On the car ride to Aunt Anne's house, my eyes widened as I saw, for the first time in my life, paved roads and street lights. The road ran parallel to a pretty sandy beach along Lake Tanganyika, which was as clear and beautiful as Josée had described. Most of the stores in downtown Albertville were located along the lake, and most, Aunt Anne told us, were flooded from time to time. There were a lot more houses than in Kongolo or Samba, and quite a few of them were two stories high; there were even some three-story buildings! The town, like the lake, seemed to go on forever. Maman, who had been anxiously waiting for us by the patio, came running out to us as the car pulled in. Josée and I raced to her—Josée got there first, of course—and when I reached Maman, we hugged and laughed and cried.

We spent many afternoons on the beach. Neither Josée nor I had the courage to try to learn how to swim, but we frolicked in the shallow water and lazed on the sand. The weeks passed quickly, and soon it was time for us to return to Papa and tiny, little Kongolo. I had quickly grown used to the asphalt and lampposts of Albertville. After that vacation, I began to dream of some day living in an even larger city, such as E'ville, or maybe even Léopoldville, our nation's capital. By the following summer, Maman and Jeanne had moved to E'ville, and Josée and I joined them there for our vacation. E'ville was much bigger even than Albertville. For the first time, I heard the chimes of an ice cream truck cruising through a city neighborhood and the subsequent roars of delight from mobs of children. It was in E'ville during that vacation that I took my first ride on an elevator.

Later, looking back, we would remember the late '60s and early '70s as the best of times for our country. There were still many terrible problems in the Congo: the great majority of the people remained desperately poor and Mobutu was brutally suppressing all those opposed to his rule as he accumulated more and more dictatorial power. But at least we were at peace. In 1967 Mobutu had banned all political parties—except for his. One nation, one party. Like it or not, every single Zairian became a member of Mobutu's Popular Revolutionary Movement, known by its French acronym *MPR*. All of us students earned the privilege of being drafted into the *JMPR*, the youth wing of the party.

Mobutu let us have a presidential election in 1970, but it wasn't much of an election: there were no other candidates besides Mobutu. He won with more than 98% of the vote. Then, starting in 1971, he made many changes in the government and in the way we lived. First, he changed the name of our country: the Democrat Republic of Congo went out of business and was replaced by the Republic of Zaire. Then, Mobutu changed the names that the Belgians had given to many of our cities: Albertville became Kalemie, Elisabethville became Lubumbashi, Jadotville became Likasi, Léopoldville became Kinshasa, Paulis became Isiro, and Stanleyville became Kisangani. The name of our school was changed from Liebermann High School to *Institut Mwamba* [Mwamba Institute].

Mobutu announced that we had to become culturally independent; so he adopted a policy that he called "authenticity." Only that which was authentically African was good, all that we inherited from the Europeans had to be discarded. The first thing to go was our given names, for they were Christian, European names. Zairians had to be named after their African ancestors and not Christian saints. On all our legal documents and in school, I was no longer called Suruba Marie-Georgette Bernadette, my sister was no longer Kanero Marie-Joséphine. We all had to choose "authentic" African names to replace our Christian names. That was not hard for us because Papa had already given us several 100 percent authentic African names: I became Suruba Ibumando, taking my legal second name from Papa's grandmother, while Josée became Kanero Suruba. Everybody still called us by our Christian names, except at school where I was called Suruba and Josée was called Kanero.

And the changes kept on coming. Women were no longer allowed to wear wigs, pants or short skirts; men were forbidden to wear ties. Women were encouraged to wear *pagnes*, and men were told that, to look good, they needed to wear an *abacost*, a type of jacket worn with all its buttons closed. Any organization that did not fit within the *MPR* or *JMPR* was banned. This included the Boy Scouts and the *Xavériennes*, the scouting organization for girls.

Before school began every day, we had to gather in the court-yard to dance and sing songs of praise for our "Great Helmsman," Mobutu, who took the "authentic" name of Mobutu Sese Seko Kuku Ngbendu Wa Za Banga, which, loosely translated, means "He who goes, invincible, from victory to victory leaving fire in his wake." Many of the songs were Christian hymns in which words of praise for Mobutu were substituted for words of praise for God.

Josée and I and our friends in the dormitory thought all the name changes, and the singing and dancing to honor Mobutu, were pretty silly.

"What will come with all these name changes, that's the important question?" one of our friends asked at lunch one day.

"More dancing, I guess," said another, and we all burst out laughing.

"I'd take dancing over war any day," Josée said to a chorus of amens. Mobutu had brought peace, and we were willing to give him the benefit of the doubt, as long as he kept the peace.

But soon even the dancing and singing were no longer funny. Students chosen as *JMPR* leaders, or "animators" as they were called, were responsible for overseeing "patriotic" activities within the school, such as the daily ritual of dancing and singing the praises of the Great Helmsman. Ever anxious to ingratiate themselves with party officials, the *JMPR* animators became zealots, consumed with ambition and a ferocious desire to detect any traitors in their midst. Students, and especially teachers, soon learned that expressing their opinions about anything going on in the country would inevitably lead to accusations, police interrogations, and even arrest.

One day, the Commissioner of the Zone of Kongolo, the top governmental leader in the area, came to our campus to give a speech to the school's students and its mostly expatriate teaching staff. The theme of his talk was the importance of not giving students any subversive ideas about their country. Apparently, he had received some reports from *JMPR* animators about European teachers criticizing President Mobutu's policies.

"If I hear such a thing is still going on here, those individual teachers responsible will be deported from our nation immediately," he proclaimed in front of all the classes. "This country is giving you the opportunity that you didn't have or find in your own country. You are welcome here. But if you act against our country, we will throw you out, without the slightest hesitation. You must learn, once and for all, that the colonial era is finished!" He went on to congratulate his nameless "compatriots" for their good work in bringing to his attention what the "enemies" of the country were doing.

We were not at war, to be sure, but it seemed that we were no longer really living in peace. When I was alone with her one day, Josée cautioned me.

"You have to be very careful who you talk with and what you say, Geolo. It's like what our history book said life was like in the Soviet Union after their revolution. There are spies everywhere. You can't trust anyone. Even your dearest old friend can turn out to be an informant."

At the beginning of the second trimester of my freshman year, in early 1973, the unbelievable happened. It was announced that the new dormitory chief for the trimester would be none other than Suruba Ibumando!

"Sister Juliette," I said with a confused look on my face. "Are you sure there hasn't been a big mistake?"

"Yes, it is you. No mistake about that. I know you'll do a good job."

Josée, who was in her senior year, couldn't believe it, and neither could our friends.

"Geolo in charge of the dormitory?" they said. "Well, we'll see how she'll quiet herself."

I had always been among the ringleaders who started the whispering going in our dormitory when it was forbidden to talk. I couldn't imagine why the nuns had made me the chief. Was it some new type of punishment? How could I start whispering when I was the one who was in charge of stopping any talking in the dormitory? I decided to step up to the challenge. If they were trying to see if I was capable of assuming that responsibility, then I'd show them I could do it—and with style.

My first night on the job, everyone looked at me to see how serious I was about my new duties. Even Josée chuckled a little when I entered the dormitory after our study hour. I put on a painfully serious face and remained unusually calm. The dormitory was quiet, very quiet. Deep inside I wished someone else would start talking so that I could have an excuse to talk, even if it was just to remind the others to keep quiet. But it seemed as if everyone else wanted to stay in line and help me do my job. A month went by like this. Our dormitory had no life any more. Going to sleep had become miserably dull.

One night, after lights were turned off, I couldn't take it any more. I reached out to the bed of my best friend, Tabu, and I pinched her toes. Tabu started, but before she could sit up, I slid right back into my bed.

"Who pulled my toes?" Tabu whispered loudly. She turned to the usual culprit and said, "Stop it, Geolo!"

"Tabu, don't you start making noise and using me as an excuse," I responded, all innocence and indignation.

I gave her a lecture on how she, especially, should keep quiet and be an example to the rest. After a few moments of calm, someone pulled my hair.

"Tabu, stop it. I'll put your name in the notebook. I'm not bluffing!"

Then our "brawl" started a commotion that spread throughout the dormitory.

Yes, I told myself gleefully, *life is back in our dormitory again!* Stepping up to my duties, I warned the others loudly, "Don't talk too loud, please. If *ma* Alphonsine hears the noise, we'll all be in big trouble!" The situation in the dorm soon got out of hand, and *ma* Alphonsine came hurrying in with a flashlight. She scolded everyone for causing poor Geolo such headaches!

When my term as dormitory chief expired, the nuns congratulated me for my excellent work. In the following years, they picked me again and again to be the dormitory chief.

Papa talked to us a lot about how we shouldn't gossip or say bad things about people behind their backs. He told us not to fall for all the ignorant superstitions that led people in our country to blame their misfortunes on evil spells that they accused other people of casting upon them. This happened a lot in Kongolo. Whenever something went wrong, people blamed it on witchcraft and rushed to accuse anyone against whom they held a grudge. Papa also told us, "It's important to give every individual a chance, and not to judge people or treat them differently because of their tribe." Sometimes it seemed we survived by the grace of Papa's wisdom.

In our dormitory, high school students Bibiane and Godeliève were practically inseparable. Bibiane, who was from the town of Kasongo, was one of the most popular girls. Godeliève was much quieter than Bibiane, but she was also well liked. Bibiane often said that, "If *bi* Godé was a man, we'd get married. I love her so much."

There were rumors that they were more than best friends, that they were lovers. I paid no attention to such idle talk. It sounded like something someone made up just to sound interesting. Many girls had best friends whom they loved very much. Did that make them lovers? How could two women be lovers anyway?

Bibiane had a much more serious problem to deal with than such silly gossip. A number of mornings, just as the sun was rising, she had been found standing like a zombie outside the dormitory entrance with her blanket wrapped around her pajama-clad body. The noise of people opening the door sometimes startled her, and she snapped out of the daze she'd been in. When asked what she was doing outside in the cold so early in the morning, she said, "I have no idea how I got there in the first place."

"Have you been walking in your sleep again?" Godelième asked.

"I don't know, I had a dream. In the dream I left my bed and went outside. That's all I can remember," Bibiane replied.

Bibiane's school had recently hired a professor from the Luba tribe in Kasai Province whose wife could barely speak kiSwahili; she only spoke tshiLuba and a little French. She befriended only people from her own tribe and seemed to be very superstitious. She heard about Bibiane's sleepwalking, and she began telling people that, where she came from, sleepwalkers were considered to be *balozi* [witches].

"They go around at night to do their witch work," the teacher's wife said. "But they get stopped in a daze when they run out of the gasoline that moves them along—human blood. That's why Bibiane can't get back inside to her bed. She runs out of the blood she has taken from others."

At first, no one really paid attention to this nonsense. Then tensions arose between some of the Luba girls and some of the girls from Kasongo. The Luba girls began to repeat the horrible rumors that the teacher's wife had started about Bibiane. Bibiane began to get depressed, but her close friends told her to ignore the rumor mongers.

"They're just a bunch of ignorant village peasants. Can they tell you who you have killed if you're a witch?" they said to Bibiane. But Bibiane couldn't shake the feeling that there was something wrong, something bad about her.

Tensions between the Luba girls and those from Kasongo began to escalate, and Bibiane's sleepwalking gave them something to argue about. I thought we had overcome all those stupid prejudices, but I must have been naive. One nasty incident followed another. One day, *ma* Alphonsine called a meeting to try to ease the tensions. She and the nuns talked about how important it was for all of us to get along and how it didn't matter where everyone came from.

"You are all here to get an education," Sister Juliette said. "This education doesn't only mean being smart in school, but also being smart in other things in life. You have to cast aside ignorant prejudices and learn how to get along with each other."

These meetings seemed to ease the tensions, and, for a brief time, Bibiane was her happy old self. Then one day she passed the Luba teacher's wife and her two little girls on the street. The woman started to point fingers at Bibiane and say things in tshiLuba that could be understood even by those who didn't speak that language. To Bibiane's horror, the little girls imitated their mother and ridiculed her in public.

After that, Bibiane refused to go anywhere outside of the school campus. She grew gloomier and gloomier with each passing day.

"Maybe I am a witch without knowing it," she told her friends, sobbing. "How come I don't know how or when I get outside at night? Maybe I've been given witchcraft by some members of my extended family back home. I don't want it. I don't want to live if I really am *mulozi!*"

A few days later, Bibiane found herself outside in the morning again, and she became even more miserable. Bibiane was no longer the happy-go-lucky girl who made everyone laugh. It seemed like she was crying all the time. Her friends did their best to cheer her up and, just when it seemed like she was snapping out of her depression, she ran into the teacher's wife once again in the courtyard.

"You can fool all the other people, but you can't fool me," the teacher's wife said to her in broken French. "My daughters have seen you at night. I, myself, have seen you in my sleep, threatening my family. You have eaten other people, but, as for my family, you'll be in big trouble if you dare to try!"

Bibiane burst into tears and fled to her dormitory bed. When Godeliève came back from school, she was distraught to find her best friend in such a terrible state. Bibiane threatened to kill herself, so Godeliève stayed by her side all night long.

"*Bi* Godé," Bibiane said, "You can't be with me every second to protect me from myself. I don't want to live anymore."

By the morning, everyone in the dormitory thought that Bibiane had gotten over this latest crisis. But shortly after waking, Bibiane collapsed to the floor while on her way to the outhouse. She pulled herself up and started to stumble like a drunk. Then she fell down in the grass and lost consciousness. We learned that she had tried to take a lot of painkiller pills the night before, but Godeliève managed to hide them. Somehow Bibiane found them in the morning when Godeliève was getting ready to go to school. *Ma* Alphonsine and some of the girls lifted Bibiane and carried her to the porch of our dormitory entrance. They laid her down on the floor. She was moving a little and moaning. Sister Antonio, a nurse, came to check on her, and they took Bibiane to an infirmary outside of the dormitory compound.

The nuns told us all to go to school, but none of us paid attention to the lessons that day. A little before noon, we heard a shriek and a long scream. People seemed to be wailing all over the campus. We knew what it meant: Bibiane never woke up.

All classes were canceled. I couldn't grasp that she was really dead. I had just seen her in the morning. Why hadn't I thought of something to say to help her, something to make her want to live? But I hadn't, and now I never could. Her body stayed in the infirmary while the nuns cabled her family, and the priests looked for a car to take her body on the day-long trip home to Kasongo.

Godeliève was out of her mind with grief. She didn't let go of Bibiane's body. In the infirmary, Godeliève kissed Bibiane's face all over and even sucked her lips! Maybe they really were lovers.

Godeliève grabbed a *mtwangio*, a wooden stick about the size of a baseball bat that is used as a pestle, and ran like a madwoman to the home of the Luba teacher. She shouted at the house, "Murderers, assassins! Are you happy now that she's dead?"

She ran around the house looking for the teacher or his wife, all the time swinging the wooden stick over her head. She tried to get in the house, but all openings were tightly shut. The teacher and his family were there all right, they had barricaded themselves inside the house as soon as they learned about Bibiane's suicide. The nuns and older students were able to restrain Godeliève and brought her back to the dormitory.

A short mass was conducted at the parish. Everyone was crying, even some of the Luba girls. Many of the students, including me, felt guilty. Why hadn't we done more, why hadn't we stopped the madness, why hadn't we saved that sweet girl?

Later that day, two of Bibiane's close friends from Kasongo, Hélène and Martha Kilima, accompanied the body to Kasongo. Two days later, Hélène and Martha came back with another version of Bibiane's death. Bibiane's parents and close family members believed that Bibiane hadn't killed herself, but was, in fact, killed from Kasongo. Bibiane, they said, was killed by witchcraft from some family members who were jealous of the girl's success in school.

"You really show off about your daughter doing well in school. We will see," the jealous relatives had said during a recent family squabble.

They killed her; she didn't kill herself. I was confused. Bibiane had been on campus the whole time, she took those pills on campus, and she died on campus. We had seen her body. How could she be killed from Kasongo?

"Well, it's black magic, witchcraft," I was told. "You can't explain it logically."

CHAPTER 19

BLASPHEMY

With Jeanne and Marie gone, and Josée and I living in the dormitory, Benjamin and Misère were the only children still living full-time with Papa. But that didn't mean our home was any less crowded than it used to be. Papa had a habit of taking in stray people. We never met any of Papa's biological family, but it seemed he had a million and one relatives. Anyone who came from his home village was a relative. Anyone who came from a village near his home village was a relative. Anyone who came from a village in his home province was a relative. Anyone who served with him in the military was a relative. Anyone who had gone hunting with him was a relative. In fact, it seemed sometimes that anyone who had ever had a beer with him was a relative. And Papa couldn't do enough for his relatives.

Often, we shared our home with our relatives' children. Whenever Papa saw that his relatives were having trouble taking care of their children, or didn't have enough money to send them to school, he took their children to live with us. Josée and I said that our house wasn't a home, it was a boarding school! Papa was faithful to a fault to many of his friends, and maybe that was why he inspired so much loyalty and respect.

"True friends who can see you through thick and thin are a precious gift on this earth," Papa would say. "Such friends are related to you not necessarily by blood, but by a greater force, the love of God. True friendship: treasure it, girls."

Sometimes Papa would hire someone to do the cooking for the household, and sometimes he just did it himself. It was very unusual to see a man cooking in those days; after all, cooking was women's work, everyone said. But Papa was never one to pay attention to what everyone said. He had learned how to cook in the army—he was very good at it—and he enjoyed doing it from time to time. He wasn't going to let social prejudices keep him from doing something he enjoyed.

When Josée and I were home on weekends and vacations, we took over most of the household chores, including cooking and shopping. Although we were fine cooks, we hadn't inherited Papa's organizational skills. It was hard for us to take care of the kitchen when Papa was away on a business trip. It seemed like we were always cooking for a large crowd, and we weren't very good yet at figuring out how much to cook or how much to buy from the market. Some days we ran out of food: either there wasn't enough coming off the stove, or the cupboard was bare and it was too late to replenish it from the market. On those days, Josée knew who would save the day: out of the cracks and crevices of my bed, desk, and closet, I would pull out enough dry or canned food to get us through the evening. When food was in abundance, I compulsively squirreled it away in my little hiding places. It had become almost instinctual with me. Perhaps it came from the scavenging we had to do during the war or the specter of Gilbert and his giant hand scooping out from our common bowl a monster-size portion for himself and two-thirds of my serving to boot. Perhaps it was just a symptom of my voracious appetite and my passion to never go hungry again.

Although Papa talked to us a lot about the importance of being a good friend, he always returned to the importance of getting a good education.

"Many people, when they have girls, only think of their future in terms of getting a dowry, or how their daughters will spend time in the kitchen, or make babies. I don't see your future that way. I see you making your own decisions about how to lead your own lives. And the best way to have your own lives is to get an education. That's your weapon," he always said. Sometimes Josée and I completed the words even before he finished his standard lecture.

Many of Papa's friends thought he was out of his mind to insist that girls should finish secondary school and even go on to the university level. But Papa said that his girls were as good as any boys.

"My girls can do anything they want with their lives," he said. "They're not going to be limited to just getting married and becoming a man's appendix!"

Many of our friends at school were engaged to be married even before they finished primary school. They said they wouldn't get married until after they graduated from high school, but many wound up getting pregnant and most dropped out long before then. Papa said he didn't want to hear a word about fiancés at this stage of our lives.

"If anyone presents himself as your fiancé," he told us point blank, "I will shoot him right through the heart. And I'm not joking," he added, his face dead serious. Josée and I never doubted him for a moment.

At different times, some of his friends asked him about matching their sons with his daughters.

"You have done a good job with your girls, *Monsieur* Benoit. They are very good girls. I don't know of any father in Kongolo who wouldn't like them to be part of his family. Josée is getting big now. And my son has already finished high school. How about arranging their engagement? She's bound to bring you a considerable dowry!"

"If you want to stay friends with me," Papa responded with a glare, "drop that subject immediately. My girls are not for sale. They will choose their own lives after they finish their education."

Our prospective fathers-in-laws quickly dropped the subject. But we knew what they were thinking: *Monsieur Benoit is surely out of his mind! What kinds of ideas are those? Do they have any traditions*

*at all where he comes from? Let his daughters decide what they want to
be for themselves? What lunacy!*

Late one afternoon Papa took Josée and me to a bar owned by
a friend of his. He had a beer, while we gulped down soft drinks. As it
got darker, the bar started getting crowded. Many of the customers
were single women who were looking to find a man who would pay to
sleep with them. Many, many women did this, probably because they
could find no other way to support themselves.

"Look very well at those women," Papa said softly. "They
seem like they're happy and having fun. But most, probably all of
them, wish their lives could have been very different. Theirs is a life of
degradation in every possible way. They don't respect their bodies. I
don't want either of you to ever live that kind of life or, for even one
moment, to envy it. Always remember that wherever you are. That's
why I want you to put your education above everything else."

Papa reminded us again and again about our many friends
who had dropped out of school because they'd gotten pregnant.
"Remember what's truly important, girls. Boys and babies can wait.
The most important thing in your life now is your education."

Papa laid down the law for us, but at the same time he was
thoroughly reasonable. He was not at all the stereotypical father who'd
bring out a shotgun at the sight of a male approaching one of his daughters. He encouraged us to have male friends, and he insisted that we
bring them home to visit.

"You're going to a mixed school," he said. "You're bound to
have many friends who are boys. That's fine. Just stay alert, so you can
find out who is truly seeking your friendship and who is being friendly
only to take advantage of you." He made perfectly clear what was
important to him, but at the same time he showed us that he had complete confidence in our ability to live up to his expectations.

Josée clearly deserved Papa's confidence. She was as disciplined
outside of school as she was in the classroom. In high school, while most
of her friends were dropping out to get married or have babies, she
avoided entanglements with boys. Very pretty and charming, she

attracted a great deal of attention. But she knew how to say no. And she knew to keep her focus on her education, the thing that mattered the most to her and to Papa. Nothing was going to sidetrack her from getting the education that she deserved. Along with Papa, she helped me to believe that I, too, could do anything I wanted to do with my life.

Papa's emphasis on independent thinking and intellectual curiosity left us, at times, ill-suited for our courses in religion. I drove poor Sister Thérèse crazy with my "blasphemous" questions.

"Don't you think, Sister, that original sin is unfair?"

"Well, Adam and Eve did what they were forbidden to do in the Garden of Eden, and, since we are their descendants, we have inherited that sin."

"But that's like condemning someone for mistakes their grandmother made just because they're related. That's not fair."

"That's enough, young lady," Sister Thérèse, a Belgian in her late fifties, would say angrily and then move on to another topic. Unbowed, I'd try to ask other questions, but she'd refuse to acknowledge my raised hand.

Around Easter, we learned all about Judah's treachery, the death of Jesus, and His resurrection. I couldn't quite grasp the point of it all, and Sister Thérèse made the mistake of calling on me.

"Sister Thérèse, how did Jesus save us?"

"Well, He died on the cross for us."

"Why did He have to die to save us?"

"Because it was His Father's wish," she said, clearly irritated at my persistence.

"Why would a father want his son to die? Wasn't He mad at His father when He found out that His father was going to let Him die? I would be very angry at my father if..."

"You don't talk about God like that, young lady. That's blasphemous, and that's the end of this discussion!" She turned toward the crucifix in the front of the classroom, closed her eyes, made the sign of the cross, and moved her lips, apparently in prayer. The inspiration she received was to punish me by making me write one hundred times, "I shall stop asking blasphemous questions in religion class."

"Sometimes you just need to keep quiet, Geolo," Josée said when I complained about my hand hurting from writing the same sentence over and over.

"I didn't mean to be blasphemous," I told Josée. "I didn't understand the lesson, that's why I asked."

"Well, now you know how things work here," she replied with an air of maturity and wisdom. "Don't ask them those types of questions any more. You're not going to get any good answers, so what's the point?"

But how could I not question that which made no sense to me? "That's what having faith is all about," the nuns said. Papa had told us many times that God was loving and kind, that God was the source of all that is and all we have, that God is everywhere, in everything. But the God I was learning about seemed to be more of a tyrant than a loving, caring father.

I always felt that there was some horrible injustice in the way God treated His children. Why had He singled out one of His sons to be His "only" son? What about the rest of His sons and daughters? What about me? And why were they trying to get us to picture God as an old white man with a long white beard? Who had ever seen Him to make a picture of Him? Why did they have all these pictures and statues of God and Jesus and Mary? What was that if not idolatry, the same type of idolatry that they said had to be destroyed if it was a question of Africans making statues of African ancestors?

Blasphemous, indeed, were my questions, my doubts to all the priests and nuns. All but one, that is. Father Albert, a French priest who taught at my school, accepted my doubts, encouraged my questions, and acknowledged openly the difficulties of reconciling faith with an active mind. He taught me more about the beauty of Christianity than all the other priests and nuns put together. He became like an uncle to me, as he struggled to keep my battered faith alive.

CHAPTER 20

AGAINST
THE ODDS

In June 1973, at the end of her senior year, Josée took the rigorous State Examinations, a week-long marathon of test-taking that completely determined one's educational future. It was the final leg of a brutal triage that sharply limited educational opportunities. Only by passing the State Examinations could you earn a State Diploma, and without that document you couldn't go on to higher education. Although precise numbers were hard to come by, perhaps half of the students who enrolled in first grade in Zaire made it to the end of primary school. Even most of the boys dropped out because their families couldn't afford to continue paying school fees. The Zairian educational system was exactly the opposite of the American educational system in that parents had to pay fees to enroll their children in primary and secondary school, but there were no fees for university tuition. Indeed, university students received not only free tuition but also scholarship money to help pay for their living expenses. The fees for primary and secondary school were, for the most part, fairly modest, but, with Zaire having one of the lowest per capita incomes in the world, even a modest fee was beyond the means of a great many families.

Maybe half of those who started secondary school finished their final year of courses and took the dreaded State Examinations. Maybe half of this group passed the tests and received the coveted State Diploma. For girls, the percentage succeeding at each level was even smaller. However, in the early 1970s, Mwamba Institute tended to have more than 70% of its seniors earn State Diplomas.

Taking the tests was hard enough, but then you had to wait weeks and, in distant towns like Kongolo, even months to get the results. You could take the State Examinations more than once, and many students did so, sometimes with better luck on repeated tries. However, with so many families unable to pay to continue sending their children to school, students often had, in reality, but one crack at success. Learning that you hadn't passed the State Examinations was one of the most devastating things any student could experience.

Nevertheless, we were all confident that Josée would succeed on her State Examinations. After all, she had been such an excellent student for her entire primary and secondary school career. And, when the newspapers with the results listed finally arrived in Kongolo in August, 1973, there was Kanero Suruba, her beautiful, authentically African name, listed as one of those who passed. My sister had a State Diploma! Papa was so very proud of her. I was very proud of her too, but I was terrified at the same time. She had succeeded, but that meant that it was time for her to move on. One of my two guiding stars was escaping from my orbit.

There were no universities in Kongolo, so Josée had to continue her studies elsewhere. She decided that she wanted to learn how to help people improve their lives, so she chose social work and development as her major. She applied to the *Institut Superieur d'Etudes Sociales* [University of Social Work] in Bukavu, which was the capital city of Kivu Province in the easternmost part of Zaire. Fortunately for me, I got a reprieve from the dreaded separation. Josée's application couldn't get to Bukavu until after the start of the school year, and, as a graduate of the high school pedagogy program, she was obliged to teach for two years before going on to higher education. She got a job at *Ecole Normale* in Kongolo, the four-year secondary school that trained girls to be primary school teachers. The nuns were delighted to have Josée teach on their staff. They said she had been a model student, both at school and in the dormitory.

Since it was a long trip from our house in Kangoy to *Ecole Normale*, the nuns arranged for Josée to live at a big house within the boarding school compound with *ma* Alphonsine. I was in heaven! Not only was Josée still in town, but she lived right next to my dormitory. Not a single day passed without me dropping by to see her. On Sundays, we both went home together after mass. It felt as if she were still at the boarding school with me.

But Josée didn't get along well with *ma* Alphonsine, so later in the year she bought herself a bicycle and moved back home with Papa. Soon after, she learned that she had been accepted at the university in Bukavu and that she was excused from doing her second year of teaching at *Ecole Normale*. So, during the summer of 1974 Josée prepared for her move to Bukavu and thereby didn't share with me the most exciting voyage of my young life—my first trip to Kinshasa, the nation's capital and great metropolis.

Earlier that year we had received an invitation to vacation in Kinshasa from our brother René, Maman's oldest child and only son, who was at the time a captain in the Zairian Armed Forces based in the capital. And what an exciting time it was to be heading for Kinshasa. The whole world's attention was focused on our capital city, because it was to be the site of the world heavyweight championship boxing match between the two great American champions, George Foreman and Muhammad Ali. Even in remote Kongolo, we had heard about the "Fight of the Century" from the radio and visitors coming from Lubumbashi and Kinshasa. People talked about little else during the months leading up to the bout. And, as was the case throughout the nation, the population of Kongolo was solidly in the corner of our great hero, Muhammad Ali. After all, Ali was a black man, a descendent of Africans, while Foreman, we all knew, was white.

I spent a week with Maman in Lubumbashi before taking the two-hour flight to Kinshasa. And what a flight it was, so fitting for such a glorious occasion. No tiny, propeller-driven Fokker this time. Hundreds of fellow passengers joined me on a huge jet, a DC-10. When the plane changed altitude, I hardly felt a thing. The flight was so luxurious that they even served us a full meal.

What a scene I saw when we landed at Kinshasa's Ndjili Airport. There were lights everywhere, and all of the many runways were paved! At any one moment, there must have been fifteen to twenty planes on the ground and at least half that many taking off or landing. Trucks carrying luggage and mini-buses carrying passengers to and from the planes and the terminal were zooming all around us. All the commotion drove me dizzy, and I loved it, but I couldn't imagine how they managed to keep the planes from crashing into each other.

René was inside the terminal waiting for me. He could barely get me to leave the building, I was so fascinated by the paintings on the walls, the sculptures on the tables, and the ornamental plants all about. Not one to waste time, René drove me straight from the airport to downtown Kinshasa for some instant sightseeing. We took major thoroughfares to get downtown, all of which were paved and lit. Some even had gorgeous rows of brightly colored flowers down the middle separating the lanes. Then we turned onto the capital's main street, the legendary *Boulevard du 30 Juin* [June 30th Boulevard], which had been named after our day of independence. It was a magnificently wide four lane road, with buildings on each side, some more than twenty stories high. "Surely the *Champs d'Elysée* couldn't be any more glamorous than this!" I said. Beyond the Boulevard and the great buildings was the Zaire River, and across the River we saw the lights of our neighboring city, Brazzaville, capital of the former French colony that had kept the name Congo. René, who was quite a man about town, took me to the hottest dining spot in town. It was called "Wimpy's," and it served the largest sandwiches I'd ever seen. From there we dropped in at the classiest bar in town at the Kinshasa Intercontinental Hotel.

When we finally got to René's home, we were greeted by his wife Jeannette, their five children, and my little sister Jeanne, who was living with René and going to school in Kinshasa. In their living room I saw for the first time in my life, at the age of eighteen, television. There was no television in Kongolo, of course; some people in Lubumbashi had televisions, but I never got an opportunity to watch. In Kinshasa, it seemed all the citizens had televisions, and everyone kept them on all the time.

We watched Zairian comedy shows and, of course, concerts featuring Zaire's great musical artists, the greatest musicians in all Africa, stars like Luambo Makiadi, Tabu Ley, Zaiko Langa Langa, and Pépé Kalé. There were educational programs for children and adults, French movies, and American shows such as *Perry Mason*, dubbed in French. There were, regrettably, the hideously dull *MPR* propaganda shows that grew more and more shrill and took up more and more air time as the *MPR* grew more and more unpopular. The news shows basically told us what President Mobutu was doing and why we were so blessed to have him as our leader. Each newscast began and ended with a small dot in a blue sky that grew larger and larger until it was recognizable as—surprise—President Mobutu wearing his trademark leopard-skin hat. As a Luba song traditionally sung to praise ancestors and gods played in the background, the President's picture continued to grow until it filled the entire screen. The whole commercial took about a minute to complete and, even with the sound on mute, created an impression of power.

The talk of the town, however, not surprisingly was the forthcoming Fight of the Century. I was astonished, though, to find out that George Foreman wasn't white, he was a black man, with much darker skin than Muhammad Ali. If I hadn't seen his picture on television, I might never have believed it. But the people called Foreman *mondele* [white man], because his aloofness and fondness for German shepherd dogs reminded them of the Belgian colonialists. He seemed miserable about being in Zaire, and in Africa. Ali, on the other hand, seemed to be having the time of his life, here in the very heart of Africa. He mingled with everyone, young and old, rich and poor, black and white. His efforts to speak some French and Lingala were pathetic, but he tried at least. He had style and charisma, and he was beautiful. No one dared to admit that they were pulling for Foreman, we all lusted for a great victory by the people's champion, Ali.

The two boxers came to Zaire with some of the greatest black musicians from their country. Of course, the greatest of them all was the incomparable James Brown. People who went to his concerts said they had never seen a more exciting show. Everyone in Kinshasa went out and bought James Brown records; when they saw him performing on television, young and old stopped what they were doing and watched. All the young people tried to imitate James Brown's inimitable dancing style.

Unfortunately, Foreman got hurt while practicing and the bout had to be postponed until after my return to Kongolo. We woke up in the middle of the night to listen to the event on the radio; it was scheduled for around four o'clock when the temperature was still cool. Along with the millions of Kinois watching at the stadium and in their homes, and the millions of Zairians like us following the fight on the radio, we all shouted our lungs out with the great chant of the moment: "*Ali, boma ye! Ali, boma ye!*" [Kill him, Ali! Kill him!]

And so he did. Confounding all the boxing experts, Muhammad Ali pulled off one of the greatest upsets in sports history to knock out the seemingly invincible Foreman. What a celebration his victory set off! The whole nation felt they had won something much more important than a boxing match, it felt as if we had somehow been liberated once again from the Belgians and all those who had colonized and humiliated Africa. It was the high point of life in Mobutu's Zaire. Soon after, all began to fall apart.

The seeds of disaster had been planted in 1973 when Mobutu had taken a trip to Beijing and had seen what a good deal Mao had. Mobutu decided that if Maoism could reign in China, well then Zaire would have its own official ideology that he ever so modestly dubbed

"Mobutism." We could no longer call men and women *Monsieur* and *Madame;* instead we had to call them *Citoyen* and *Citoyenne*, Citizen. *Citoyen* Benoit instead of *Monsieur* Benoit? It sounded absurd, but we didn't have a choice in the matter. Our leading citizen had decided for us.

Then Mobutu decided that we also needed economic independence. He took control of many of the small to medium-sized businesses in the country that were owned by foreigners and turned them over to Zairians who, he assured us, were fully competent to run the businesses. Even religious enterprises, such as schools and hospitals, were to be taken over by "competent" Zairians who were not affiliated with the Church. Mobutu called this process zairianization. The new owners and managers were, for the most part, political cronies of Mobutu.

Not surprisingly, almost all turned out to be colossally incompetent businessmen. Within a matter of months, most of the companies were bankrupt, store inventories were totally depleted, and the economy was in shambles. Add to that steep global increases in oil prices and declines in the price of Zaire's chief export, copper, and it can be understood why Zaire's economy started a precipitous spiral downward that, to this day, continues out of control.

I returned to Kongolo with gifts for everyone from the great metropolis. For Josée's going away present, I bought a pair of platform shoes that were the rage in Kinshasa. The Kinois called them "Goodyear" because of all the rubber used to make those giant heels. Papa didn't approve, but Josée loved them.

In September 1974, she headed for Bukavu. The extra year had helped me ease into accepting the reality of her departure. I thought of Josée all the time and missed sharing every joy and disappointment with her. But she had helped make me a strong person, and I carried on. I wrote to her often and devoured every letter she sent back.

During Josée's first year away, I had to deal with a lot more than the loneliness of not being with her. First of all, I had a tough workload at school. I had decided during my freshman year to make Math-Physics my high school major. Everyone said this was the hardest major, certainly not something for a girl to try. In fact, only five of the twenty-eight students in my freshman class were girls. Papa and Josée said they weren't surprised by my choice, they knew what a daredevil I had been from a very young age.

Second, the advent of zairianization had devastated the living environment in the dormitory. As part of the zairianization process, the church was put under a great deal of pressure to turn control of its various social enterprises over to secular Zairians. A Zairian man was put in charge of the dormitory, and things changed overnight. No one encouraged the students to study anymore, and no one maintained discipline. The food served became monotonous and, eventually, meagre. After a while, a whole dinner was reduced to only tea with milk and half of a *baguette.*

The new director confiscated the government subsidies and applied them to what he apparently considered much more important priorities. Within a few weeks he had bought himself a fancy *Yamaha* motorcycle and ornate furniture for his house, for which he engaged an entire staff of servants. A nice life for him, while the dormitory fell apart. He bent the rules to get the girlfriends of his cronies admitted to the dormitory. Men no longer needed special permission to enter the dormitory compound. "Everyone who has family or friends in Kongolo," he said, "must go home on Saturdays after school; they cannot stay in the dormitory on weekends anymore." Those who had nowhere to go in town had to fend for themselves. Many girls' parents took their children out of the dormitory altogether. I couldn't take it anymore, so, despite the long commute from Kangoy to school, I left this corruption and went back to living at home.

Soon enough summer arrived, and we knew that Josée would

be coming home for vacation. In fact, she'd be doing a summer internship at Kongolo General Hospital. Of course, we didn't know precisely when she'd be arriving. There was one flight a week from Bukavu to Kalemie and then from Kalemie to Kongolo. We didn't have a telephone—there were only a handful of working telephones in the whole town—so Josée couldn't call us. Letters took weeks to arrive, and even telegrams often got lost before arrival. Josée had no way of telling us exactly when she was scheduled to arrive at the Kongolo Airport. Even if she did get the information to us, there was little possibility she'd arrive at the scheduled time. *Air Zaire*, the national airline, had recently been zairianized, so flights were canceled frequently, often over-booked, and hopelessly unreliable; people started calling it *Air Peut-être* [Air Maybe].

Benjamin, Misère, and I had to go wait for Josée at the airport every week after the first week in July. Finally, on our third week of waiting, after being crushed by her failure to descend from the plane the two previous weeks, we saw her stepping down the plane steps. We raced to Josée on the tarmac to hug her, and hold her and cherish her very presence. We asked her all about Bukavu and the university, and she kept us up late that night and the one after with tales of her adventures.

Of course, Josée did a magnificent job at the hospital. Her role was to make sure the women patients, mostly prostitutes, who had sexually transmitted diseases, completed their entire course of antibiotic therapy and didn't stop taking medication as soon as their symptoms disappeared. This was a critically important task, because the partially cured infections would most likely flare up again, leading to potentially severe damage to the women's health; this habit of not completing one's treatment also contributed greatly to the serious public health problem of microbial resistance to antibiotics. Josée was appalled to find that most of the medical staff were unbelievably rude to the venereal disease patients.

"They talk to them as if these women were garbage," she told me. "Who would want to come back to the hospital for care after being insulted like that?"

Josée treated the patients with great kindness and respect and no condescension whatsoever. Not surprisingly, they began to flock to her and pay attention to her advice. The doctor couldn't praise Josée enough.

"Oh, if only I had more staff like you, Josée," he told her. "What a difference we could make." He even forced some of the nurses to observe how compassionately the young university student was doing her job, so they could learn from her example.

When Josée departed, I, of course, became the senior child in *Monsieur* Benoit's home. I had grown up a lot during my years in the dormitory, though I was still probably the youngest looking 19 year-old in town. People often thought I was in my early teens. Not only did I look like a prepubescent adolescent, but I was still playing children's games: climbing on trees, kicking the soccer ball, making little trucks and cars with wires or empty food cans. I still thought of myself as that wild "tomboy" who was always getting into trouble. But the truth was I was getting into less and less trouble. I had finally learned not to ask every question that came into my mind and when it was time to stay quiet. For all the things that really mattered, I was finally starting to grow up.

I matured more, however, with the events surrounding the death of our dog, Shitikoti. Papa was out of town on a business trip, Josée was back in Bukavu, and Benjamin, Misère, and I were home alone. It was Spring vacation. One night, we heard a group of dogs barking in the distance. Then the barking got closer and closer to our neighborhood. Shitikoti, who had been laying outside near the front door started barking back and, soon enough, we heard the dogs barking right outside our house. For a few brief moments, the barking and wailing was furious, and it was clear that a great battle was under way.

"*Da* Geolo, let's go get Shitikoti. They're going to kill him," said my younger brother Benjamin, who loved the dog more than any of us.

"We can't right now, Benjamin," I said. "Those dogs sound crazed. They might attack us if we go out now. Besides, it's too dark to risk going out there."

I got really scared when we could no longer hear Shitikoti barking. He seemed to be whimpering instead. We raced through the living room to the door leading to the balcony and starting banging and shouting to try to scare the invading dogs away. We didn't dare go out on the balcony, because it had steps leading to the ground floor that the dogs could have mounted. Finally, our noisemaking worked, and the attackers fled. When all was quiet, we could clearly hear Shitikoti moaning in agony. We grabbed a flashlight, opened the door, and descended the balcony steps to find Shitikoti in a pool of blood. We took him inside, and Benjamin stayed by his side all night.

In the morning light, Shitikoti looked worse than he had just after the attack. He had wounds everywhere, which Benjamin nobly tried to heal with ointment. He tried to get the dog to eat, but Shitikoti wouldn't touch his food and started to act oddly. Then, in the early afternoon, as Benjamin tried to put more salve on the dog's wounds, Shitikoti bit him hard on his left hand. Benjamin shrieked and let go of the dog, whose teeth had almost gone through Benjamin's limb. I helped clean and bandage Benjamin's wound.

"I don't think you should touch him now," I told my little brother. "I'm afraid something's really wrong with him. Maybe those dogs gave him rabies or something." I had no idea that dogs could transmit rabies, a fatal disease, to people.

We kept our distance and stared at Shitikoti. Soon after, he stood up and tried to walk toward the door, but he collapsed after only a few steps. As he lied there, breathing heavily, moaning loudly, he started furiously biting himself. We continued to stay away and, by the late afternoon, we saw that some kind of whitish foam was coming out of his mouth. He soon stopped moaning and, in the early evening, he stopped breathing. When we were sure that he was truly dead, we buried Benjamin's beloved pet by the vegetable garden next to the Kangoy River.

Early the next morning, Benjamin started feeling ill. I helped him clean his wound again, but that night he was in such terrible pain that he started crying. I decided I would take him to the hospital the next day. He felt somewhat better in the morning and repeatedly said that he didn't want to go to the hospital. Benjamin hated injections and never wanted to see a doctor. But I insisted, and I was in charge, so to the hospital we went. When the doctor, the hospital's only physician, saw that we were Josée's siblings, he moved us ahead of the other patients waiting for service.

"You did the right thing by bringing your brother here," the doctor said. "There is a possibility that he might be infected with rabies, which is extremely dangerous, even deadly, for people as well as dogs."

He immediately started Benjamin on a ten-day treatment regimen that featured daily injections into his abdomen.

"He doesn't need to stay in the hospital," the doctor told me. "But you must make sure he comes here every day for his shots. He mustn't miss any day. Do you understand, Georgette? If he doesn't get the proper treatment, and he really has rabies, he could die."

"We will be here every single day," I assured the physician. When I left his office, I started crying just at the thought of Benjamin dying.

For each of the first three days of treatment I took Benjamin to the hospital to make sure that he arrived in time for his shots; I didn't trust him to do what had to be done on his own. In fact, each day he tried to talk me out of making him go to the hospital. Unfortunately, the doctor only had enough medicine for the first three days of treatment. Despite being tremendously overworked as the hospital's only physician, he went out of his way to send repeated emergency messages to a hospital in Kabalo begging for a fast delivery of additional medicine. The medicine got to us just in time to continue Benjamin's treatment without missing a day. Who knows if the doctor would have made the time to take such good care of us had he not been so fond of Josée? By the fourth day, Papa had returned and started taking Benjamin to the hospital. I needed to see this thing through to the end, so I went with them.

Papa thanked the doctor profusely for saving his boy's life.

"Oh, it was nothing," the doctor said. "I just did my job. But you should be very proud of Georgette. She's the one who really helped Benjamin by bringing him here and making sure he kept coming. She is quite a remarkable young woman."

Papa beamed with pride. I stood there, stunned. Nobody had ever called me a woman before.

In 1975, we had a new woman in the house. Papa had a new wife, ma Feza. About ten years younger than Papa, she was a very soft spoken woman with a sweet disposition. She had little formal education and no children of her own. It must have been quite daunting for her to take charge of a household with three large children, but ma Feza completely disarmed us with her modesty and generosity. She was always very kind to all of us, and we quickly grew very fond of her. I often brought my friends from school home for the weekend, and she made me proud by treating them as if they were members of the family.

Our most frequent guest from my school was my best friend, Tabu. She had no family in Kongolo, so I brought her home with me just about every weekend. Tabu's primary guardian was her older brother, who lived in Kalemie. He had let her become engaged at a young age to a man named Bebebe, a student at the university in Kisangani. But Tabu's brother insisted that she finish her education before getting married. He expected her to finish high school and even go on to university. Her fiancé, Tabu's brother said, would have to wait until she got her State Diploma before he could marry her. After that, Tabu could always go on to the university as a married student.

Tabu and I talked often about our dreams of going to the university. She seemed just as committed as I was, and I thought she wanted the same things I wanted. But in our junior year, in 1975, Tabu announced some dismaying news to me.

"Geolo, I love you very much. You are more than a friend to me, you've become like a sister. I feel welcomed at your home where I am treated as a true member of the family. I know what I'm going to tell you now will upset you. I'm sorry, and I apologize already for letting you down. But I'd rather have you hear it from me first than from any other source."

I guess I knew what she was going to say, I'd heard it before from so many friends. But I never believed I would hear it from Tabu.

"I'm pregnant from Bebebe. It happened during this past vacation in Kalemie."

"How could you do it?" I asked her, already on the verge of tears.

"It was only once, honest. Bebebe said that it was okay even if it's before we're married. People do that these days, they don't wait until they're married."

"But how do you know that you're pregnant? Your stomach isn't big at all!" I was hoping that she would burst out laughing and say that she had been joking. When I realized how serious she was, I got very upset.

"What happened to all our dreams about the university? You didn't think about that, did you? To hell with being engaged and Bebebe. If he were a good guy, he would have waited!"

When Tabu started to cry, I felt sorry for her. She showed me the letter Bebebe had written her after she told him that she had missed her period. Had I ever told her, I wondered, that, just from his letters, I never really liked Bebebe to begin with? She would have been better off being engaged to somebody who would have been patient about sleeping with her. Just the idea of having my best friend, this beautiful, intelligent, young woman, join all those other girls who had been expelled from school for getting pregnant—it tore my heart out.

Then I realized that, even if it was her own doing, Tabu was the one having a hard time. How was she going to face her brother?

"I'm still your best friend, Tabu. You can always count on me," I told her as I hugged her tight.

"I'm going to get my diploma, I swear I will, Geolo. I'm going to go back to school after the baby is born."

"Of course, you will. Of course, you will."

Two days later, when Tabu told the nuns that she was pregnant, they didn't believe her. They'd never had a case before where the girl herself volunteered that she was pregnant.

"Are you joking? Because if you are, it's not funny," Sister Juliette said to her.

"No," Tabu said. "I have been very irresponsible, and now I have to face the consequences."

Sister Antonio, a nurse, tested Tabu and confirmed the news: Tabu was about three months pregnant. The nuns told her that she would have to leave in less than two weeks—before she started showing. They didn't want the other girls to learn from her example.

I gave Tabu two sets of *pagnes* that Maman had given me during vacation. She would need them when her belly got bigger. I couldn't stop asking Tabu to show me her belly. She was getting a little chubby all right, and she was hungry all the time. Tabu left exactly two weeks later. The nuns took her to the train station and let me go along.

"I'll write to you soon, Geolo," Tabu said on the ride to the station. "Don't look so sad! I'll write to *da* Josée too. When you write to her, tell her how sorry I am that I let you both down. But I'll go back to school in Kisangani after the baby is born, I swear I will."

A few weeks later, I got a long letter from Tabu telling me how very disappointed her brother was to hear the news. She said that Bebebe would be coming to get her at the end of that month, they would get married, and then pass through Kongolo by train on the way to Kisangani. When their train arrived in Kongolo, I caught a glimpse of Tabu and her husband at the window of a second class compartment and ran toward her.

"Geoloooooo," Tabu shouted.

I couldn't believe the changes in Tabu: her stomach was round and popping out. Finally, I had the opportunity to meet the person who had done this to her. I was not very impressed. Well, as Tabu herself had told me before, Bebebe wasn't extraordinary. He seemed eager to meet me, though.

"Tabu has told me so much about you. I'm so glad to finally meet you," he said as he shook my hand.

I don't remember exactly what I said to him, but it definitely wasn't "glad to meet you." The train soon pulled out, and Tabu and I cried as we waved goodbye.

I lost touch with Tabu soon after. More than ten years later in 1986, Josée ran into her in Kalemie and learned that Tabu had never returned to school. She had had three children with Bebebe, and then they got divorced. When Josée saw her, she was the mistress, probably one of many mistresses, of a wealthy businessman.

"*Da* Josée," Tabu said, "it's the only way my children and I can survive."

In June 1976, I was twenty years old and it was my turn to go for it all. This was my chance to pass the State Examinations. My whole class had to take the train all the way to Kalemie, 195 miles away, to take the big tests. Security was tight for the State Examinations, so they only offered it in large urban centers. Although I had confidence in my abilities, I couldn't help but be nervous.

"I know you'll do fine," Papa said. "You'll pass the exam. Just get down to your studies as soon as you get there."

The next morning he left for his farm on the other side of the Lualaba River. Misère, who was twelve years old, and Benjamin, age seventeen, came with me to the train station. When we were about to leave, Misère started to cry. She was very close to me and dreaded the idea of me moving away, as Josée had done.

"I'll be back before you know it," I reassured her. "Just wish me luck that I get my diploma."

I got a token of luck on the train ride. In the luggage rack above my seat, someone had put some "live" baggage. There were duck feet above my head!

"Now aren't people supposed to put livestock underneath their seat instead of up there, on top of people's heads?" I asked myself. Before I could decide whether to give up my seat and stand the length of the trip, the luggage deposited a warm, mushy dose of duck shit on my blouse. The owner silently stood up, took his duck down, and gave me a piece of cloth to get rid of the smelly gook.

The woman sitting across from me smiled. "Well, since you are going to do your State Exams, that's a good sign. Your trip will be successful. You'll see," the woman said.

"Yes," I said to myself, "but in the meantime I smell like shit! Thank you very much."

I took the exam and did my best, praying that my best was good enough.

More than a month passed. We were waiting for the newspapers to arrive from Lubumbashi with the results. One day Papa came home and again told me not to worry myself so much.

"Someone from Kalemie just told me that he has seen your name in the newspapers," Papa said. "The train from Kalemie arrives tomorrow afternoon. Why don't you go to the train station and see if you can get a copy?"

I got very excited. Had I really passed? I needed to see it for myself. The next day I went to the train station long before the train arrived. When it pulled into the station, a horde of students was waiting with me to get the newspapers that would be sold momentarily.

One classmate of mine got a copy of the *Salongo* newspaper before the rest of us.

"Hey, Georgette, your name is here! Look, here!"

I grabbed the paper, and there, in black and white, under the heading of "Section Scientifique, Math-Physique, Institut Mwamba, Kongolo," I saw the most beautiful sight in the world: SURUBA IBU-MANDO!

I did it! I gave back the newspaper and took off like an eagle to go tell Papa the news. I got home in no time. Before I told Papa, he began to smile. He knew already just by looking at me. The celebration began: *Fanta* and *Coca-Cola* for everyone.

"I knew you'd pass," said my beaming Papa."There wasn't a doubt in my mind. Congratulations, *kambo* Ibumando." Papa called me "Grandma Ibumando" when he was very proud of me.

"What are you going to do next?" he asked. "Are you going to teach for a year like your sister did or are you thinking of going directly to the university?"

I told him that I hoped to go directly to the university in Kinshasa. We talked about the different majors I might take, and Papa concluded by saying, "Whatever you choose, you'll do fine."

Later that summer I decided that I would try to study medicine, which started at the undergraduate level in Zaire. Because the results of the State Examinations had come to Kongolo so late, I couldn't register for an academic program by mail; I would have to register in person in September. But first I would go to Lubumbashi to visit with Maman and my half-sisters.

Naturally, I had mixed feelings about my trip. I was very excited to further my education, and, as much as I loved life in Kongolo, I was dying to live in a large city and have so many new experiences. But at the same time, I worried about how Misère would cope without her two older sisters. Would she be able to manage when Papa went away on his trips to the other side of the Lualaba River? I was comforted by the fact that her mother, Mama Apoline, still lived on

Avenue Kindu with *kambo* Colette, and they would be there to help take care of Misère.

I also worried about how I would manage being so far away from my beloved home and the person to whom I owed everything. But Papa had made me strong, he had shaped me to be ready for this separation. Living away from home at the dormitory had helped, as had being separated from Josée and going to spend summer vacations with Maman in Lubumbashi for the past six years. In many ways, I realized I was ready to go out on my own. It was time. And, besides, Maman's oldest child, René, lived in Kinshasa, along with many cousins who could help me through any difficulties that might arise.

On the day of my departure, Misère, Benjamin, and Papa took me to the train station. Papa reminded me that if I didn't get admitted to the university that year, I could always come back to Kongolo and wait for the next year. He gave me pocket money for the trip.

When the train started to pull away, I stood by the window and stared back at them. I looked at my Papa and whispered, "You did it, *Monsieur* Benoit, you did it. They laughed at you when you said your girls could do as well as any boys. But here I am, off to join Josée in the ranks of university students. We made it through high school, graduating with honors, and no fiancés, no pregnancies. We are indeed going to choose our own lives. I hope you're proud of us, Papa. We are so very proud of you." Tears flowed down my cheeks, sliding past my grin of excitement.

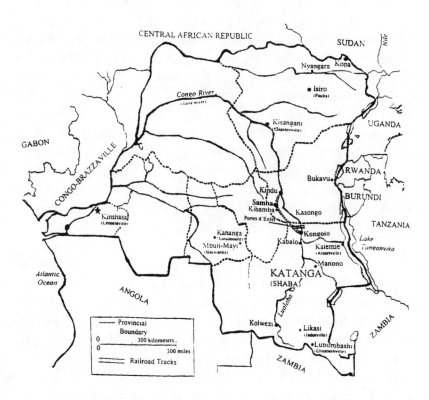

The Democratic Republic of Congo (Zaire) is the third largest country in Africa. It shares borders with nine other countries. (Former city names are in parentheses)

Josée, age 7 and Georgette, age 4, in matching dresses and poses.

Georgette, age 10 (far left) and Josée, age 13 (far right) with their younger half-siblings, Benjamin, age 7 and Misère, age 4.

Josée, age 16 and Georgette, age 13.

College students,
Georgette
and Josée relax at
the Hôtel Karavina
in Lubumbashi.

Georgette visiting Josée
at her college in Bukavu.

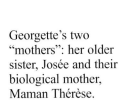

Georgette's two
"mothers": her older
sister, Josée and their
biological mother,
Maman Thérèse.

Josée, age 26

Georgette, age 36

Benoit, age 50

Josée and Alex view
the Statue of Liberty
during Josée's trip to
America.

Georgette and her family
(clockwise from top right);
Bob, Alex, Tatiana,
Georgette, Howell,
Sandra and Rocky.

CHAPTER 21

KINSHASA
MATATA

Life in the nation's great metropolis was not as glorious as this small town girl had expected it to be. When I arrived in Kinshasa, I was told that it was too late to get into the medical studies program. Not wanting to waste my first year, I searched around for any academic program that would take a latecomer from the countryside. That's how I wound up majoring in geography at the National University of Zaire's *Institut Supérieur Pédagogique de la Gombe* [Gombe Advanced Pedagogical Institute], known by its French acronym of ISP/Gombe. The mission of the advanced pedagogical institutes was to train teachers for secondary schools. Now I had never wanted to be a teacher—a doctor or maybe even an airplane pilot, but never a teacher. However, that's the discipline where there was an opening, so that's what I decided to study. After a few weeks, I realized that I didn't find geography all that interesting. When an opening popped up in ISP/Gombe's biochemistry department, I transferred to that program.

Meanwhile, since the campus dormitory was already booked to capacity, my application to live there was rejected. All I got was a spot at the end of a long waiting list for housing. My older brother René, who was at the time a major in the Zairian Armed Forces, let me stay at his home in the Bandiandingi military camp. His household reminded me, to some extent, of home with Papa in Kongolo: it was always packed with people. René and his wife had five children, and also living there when I arrived were our kid sister Jeanne, a nephew, and a sister-in-law. And, of course, there were always visitors spending the night. That was how the extended family worked in our country. Successful members of the family, such as René, were expected to take in the children of their siblings and cousins as if they were their own. René took his family responsibilities seriously and treated us all with great kindness. Despite that, his home never really felt like my home; I always felt like I was imposing. What's more, he lived far from the Gombe campus. I had to wake up around 5:30 A.M. and ride for close to two hours, sometimes more, and take three different buses to get to class.

At least I didn't have serious financial worries. All students who had passed the State Examinations with honors, as I had done, received scholarship money from the government. We had no tuition charges, and the scholarship money covered my transportation and other living expenses.

Fortunately, in February 1977, a spot opened up in the campus dormitory, and I moved in. Life became a great deal easier, now that I wasn't spending three to four hours a day commuting to and from school. Housing and meals in the dormitory were free, and, although my scholarship money was reduced considerably now that I was living in the dormitory, I still had enough coming in to pay for school supplies, toiletries, and other essentials. I even managed to save some money.

ISP/Gombe was an all-girl campus, a fact that comforted me considerably. I wasn't ready yet to deal with the smooth-talking, ultra-aggressive men of Kinshasa. The gates of the dormitory were closed at 10:00 P.M. on weekdays and 11:00 P.M. on weekends. Students who were caught spending the night out without permission during weekdays were expelled from the dormitory; I imagine that was how I moved so quickly up the waiting list. Despite the school's efforts to protect the girls, many of my classmates had boyfriends and active social lives. I was tempted to go out with them, but I hadn't really made any friends in whom I felt I could place my trust. Part of me also rebelled at the thought of belonging to somebody. And another part of me was just waiting for something magical to happen, for a knight in shining armor, *mon chevalier*, to carry me off in love-at-first-sight, fairy tale bliss. Needless to say, it didn't happen. I spent nearly all my free time studying or visiting family.

I missed home terribly. I kept in close touch with Josée and Maman through letters, but Josée and I hardly ever heard from Papa, no matter how many letters we sent him. Papa never liked to write. However, when one of us wrote about serious difficulties we faced or being sick, he would finally put pen to paper. And, of course, his rare letters were always full of advice about how to overcome obstacles, make the most of our opportunities, and, most of all, stay positive and happy.

The ISP/Gombe campus featured three long, three-story academic buildings with classrooms on each floor, a large auditorium, a biochemistry laboratory, an English laboratory, and a geology laboratory, plus two dormitory buildings, each housing about sixty students. Undergraduate studies in Zaire lasted three years, and those students who survived to the third year usually had their own private rooms; first and second year students shared living accommodations, two in each room. Residents shared a common bathroom on each floor and a cafeteria and television lounge in each dormitory. My favorite spot on campus was the basketball court. I made the school team and even started at center.

In the first year biochemistry program, you had to pass fourteen different courses in topics such as psychology, pedagogy, mathematics, biology, chemistry, physics, zoology, and botany. Everyone took the same courses; there was no such thing as an elective course in the Zairian university. Classes started at 7:30 A.M. and continued, with a short lunch break, until 3:00 P.M. You had to pass every course—passing grade was 50%—to move on to the next year's studies. Students who failed a course got a chance to pass a comprehensive examination on the subject during the summer. If they still didn't pass they'd have to repeat the entire first year, all fourteen courses, and they'd lose their scholarship money during any year they were repeating. I did just fine in twelve of my courses, but, to my utter dismay, I wound up failing zoology and botany.

While we struggled with our coursework on campus, life in Kinshasa was deteriorating all around us. It was no longer the beautiful city that had enchanted me earlier; it had become Kinshasa *matata* [problems]. Mobutu's zairianization debacle and ongoing mismanagement of the economy had led to an unprecedented inflationary spiral in prices. Many previously comfortable families now struggled to cover their rent and food bills, while the impoverished majority of the population could barely scrape together enough money for one meal a day. The extended family system, so strong in African tradition and society, took a blow, as strapped wage earners had difficulty covering their nuclear family needs, let alone those of their cousins' children. We began to see something we had never seen before: large numbers of non-disabled children out on the streets begging for money. Before, this would have been considered shameful for the entire extended family; someone, somewhere, even if it was just a person who came from the same village, would have provided for these children and their mothers. Along with the rise in begging came, quite naturally, a dramatic increase in robberies. Hordes of pickpockets and con artists roamed the streets of the capital, while homes were plagued by an epidemic of nighttime break-ins.

The infrastructure of the capital began to crumble. As the government could no longer afford to maintain its fleet of buses, public transportation became difficult and expensive. One often had to literally fight for a spot on the bus. Many people risked their lives by hanging onto the outside and rear of overcrowded buses, and quite a few paid for it dearly. It was no longer possible to get a taxi without others joining in; drivers would fill all seats and drop people off in sequence at their various destinations. The roads were no longer maintained, potholes grew larger and larger, and the old cars and taxis were torn apart by them. Many streetlights and just about all the public telephones no longer functioned.

As people became desperate to keep up with the galloping inflation, the entire concept of public service fell apart. Of course, you had always had to pay bribes to get any kind of service in Zaire, whether it was installing electricity or water service, enrolling your child in a school, or getting a license to operate a business. But now, you couldn't even get a question answered without paying a stiff bribe. You could no longer see just one person to get something done, now you had to pass through a gauntlet of bribe takers. Every office became an obstacle course and, at each leg of the course, you had to pay to get to the next level. Top government officials, who had always taken some off the top of any accounts they managed, soon began diverting all of the top, and much of the middle as well, to their own private use.

The corruption got so bad that the President felt compelled to call a meeting of top civil servants to lay down the law. Did the Great Helmsman scowl with anger and threaten to fire, even imprison any official who betrayed the public trust and stole from the public treasury? Not exactly. In words that will forever epitomize the depravity to which his administration had sunk, President Mobutu told his civil servants: *"Soki boyibi, boyibaka na mayele"* [If you're going to steal, steal wisely]. I guess he thought a yellow light was better than a green light, but all the officials in attendance and all their colleagues who heard about it afterwards interpreted the President's words as a blessing upon their corrupt heads. Of course, it would have been the foulest of hypocrisy for Mobutu to condemn corruption, since he himself was diverting millions of dollars from the public treasury into his own Swiss bank accounts—not to mention the giant cut he was getting from just about every business that he let operate in his nation. He never could explain how a fellow with such a modest salary could wind up on everyone's list of the world's richest men.

While the corruption in high places was devastating the country's future, nothing caused more pain in people's daily lives than the
terrorism inflicted upon us by Mobutu's soldiers. We had no police
force; the army was supposed to protect us from internal as well as
external dangers. With their salaries almost meaningless in the face of
hyper-inflation, and what little they did receive often coming three,
four, even six months late, more and more soldiers turned to other
means of feeding their families. The easiest and most common way for
them to supplement their income was to arrest *citoyens* and *citoyennes*
for being on the street without their identification cards. Since colonial
times, everyone had to carry identification papers with them at all
times.

This gave the soldiers a pretext for stopping anyone and everyone. Even if you had your identification card, they'd come up with one
excuse or another to detain you—until you lost patience and turned
over some cash to them. Even this was too subtle for some soldiers,
who started working hand-in-glove with the city's burgeoning population of thieves.

Meanwhile, across the country in my home region, Mobutu
faced the greatest crisis of his presidency. Soldiers from the old
Katangese army, who had been living in exile in Angola, crossed the
border and occupied a large swath of territory in Katanga, which
Mobutu had come to call Shaba Province. Fortunately, there was no
fighting anywhere near Kongolo and Lubumbashi, where Papa and
Maman lived. Mobutu's hopelessly corrupt army was of no use, but the
Guide of the Nation was able to blame the invasion on the supposedly
communist government of Angola and its Cuban allies. This enabled
him to obtain major support from the Western powers, as well as
direct military intervention from the army of his good friend, the King
of Morocco. The Moroccan soldiers turned the tide and sent the
invaders scurrying back to Angola.

The Clairvoyant One couldn't acknowledge his own errors
that allowed a ragtag crew of rebels to whip his army. So he had to
find treason in others. He arrested and sentenced to death his own

minister of foreign affairs, Nguza Karl I Bond, who, at the time, was highly respected by the Western powers; they pressured Mobutu to be merciful, and the Great Helmsman complied by commuting Nguza's punishment to life in prison. Nguza would later be released from prison and return to government service, first as foreign minister again and then as prime minister. Others, equally innocent, lacked the powerful friends Nguza had and were executed. Mobutu began a general purge of military officers that continued well into 1978.

There was an air of uneasiness and fear. I had two months before I had to take my re-tests in zoology and botany, and I was desperate to go home. Unfortunately, the little money that I was saving from my scholarship wasn't enough to pay for airfare to Lubumbashi. I felt uncomfortable asking René for money, because he already had a large family of his own to support. Papa would have sent me money for airfare, but, outside of personal delivery, he had no reliable and trustworthy way to send funds across the country.

So, when the dormitory closed for the summer, I went to stay at the Kinshasa home of my Aunt Titi, Maman's younger sister. Her oldest son, Auguy, who treated me like a sister, was an officer in a military commando unit stationed in Kota Koli, in the far north of the country. He made monthly visits to Kinshasa and, on his July visit, he invited me to visit his family in Kota Koli. He arranged for me to fly on a military plane and even gave me some spending money. The plane took me to the village of Gbadolite, a two-hour ride away from Kota Koli. Fortunately, I got to spend a day and a half in Gbadolite, which was the most famous village in all of Zaire. It was, after all, the home village of the nation's Great Helmsman.

Arriving in Gbadolite was like stepping into another world. While the rest of the country was falling apart, this tiny village in the heart of the equatorial rain forest was booming. Glittering buildings and spanking new highways leading to nowhere were under construction. The village's main boulevard was immaculate with blooming flowers dividing the lanes. It led directly to the presidential palace, a giant mansion that looked something like the Magic Kingdom. The palace's floors were built with Italian marble and covered with priceless antique furniture imported from several continents. Outside was a spectacular garden with a breathtaking assortment of tropical flowers. Magnificent rows of white houses lined the great boulevard, houses that had been built free of charge for a lucky handful of villagers who benefitted from the President's largesse. Even more spectacular than all the luxury blooming incongruously in the jungle was the cost of living. Mobutu subsidized all aspects of life for his favorite village, so most goods cost half as much, or even less, than we paid for them in Kinshasa. It was said that the President himself maintained strict control over who was allowed to live in Gbadolite.

I had a lovely two-week stay with *ya* [brother] Auguy and his family in Kota Koli. Then, in an extraordinary act of generosity that was so typical of his kind nature, *ya* Auguy gave me enough money to buy myself airplane tickets to Lubumbashi, Kongolo, and back to Kinshasa.

"Don't hesitate to tell me when you need anything," he told me when I was leaving. "Don't be shy with me. I'd rather have you ask me to help you financially than see you do what so many girls are doing in Kinshasa. You're my sister, and I'm very proud to see you work so hard at your studies."

I met up with Josée in Lubumbashi and, after visiting Maman for two weeks, we took the train together to Kongolo.

We found many changes in our hometown. A few months after I had left for Kinshasa, Papa sold his transportation business. He had decided to get out of this business before the effects of the deteriorating economy could be felt. He preferred being self-sufficient anyway, so he became a farmer. He was able to obtain some choice farmland for a nominal fee from a good friend who was a Hemba village chief on the other side of the Lualaba River. Misère and Benjamin stayed with Mama Apoline and *kambo* Colette on *Avenue Kindu* during the week so they could continue at school; they would join Papa and *ma* Feza on the farm for the weekends. Unfortunately, Mama Apoline wasn't as firm as Papa about their education, and the children didn't stick with it. Benjamin quit school and started hanging out with a bad crowd. Misère, my baby sister, had gotten pregnant at the age of thirteen and was forced to drop out of school. Her baby died soon after birth. We asked Misère to come with us to Papa's farm, but she refused.

"I can't come," she said. "Papa doesn't want to see me since I dropped out of school."

When word reached Papa that we had arrived, he came to town to take us back to his farm. While crossing the Lualaba River in a taxi canoe, I saw camped on a sandbar in the middle of the river downstream a half dozen or so lazing hippopotamuses. They were barely moving, so it was hard to even tell they were alive. The sight didn't faze me—I knew Papa wouldn't take us anywhere dangerous—but I prayed that Josée didn't see them. I knew she'd be terrified by the thought of being so close to wild animals, and I feared that she'd start rocking the boat. I tried to distract her by talking on and on about the view upstream, but my conversation must not have been compelling enough; she turned her head downstream and then did a double take.

"What are those things over there? Are those birds on rocks?" she asked Papa, who was calm and relaxed, as if we were on dry land.

"Please don't tell her, Papa. Please don't tell her," I murmured to myself while crossing my fingers.

"What? Those?" Papa said, pointing to our left. "Those aren't rocks, Josée. Those are hippopotamuses. What looks like birds are actually their ears. Those hippos are always hanging around that part of the river."

Just at that moment, as if they knew we were talking about them, a couple of the hippos opened their pink mouths wide, bellowed, and spit out gushes of water. A flash of terror swept over Josée's face. Being so close to the huge animals even gave me the creeps and I shivered.

"Papa, let's get out of here," said Josée, clearly on the verge of panic.

Papa shook his head and said, "Don't worry, Josée. Those hippos won't hurt us—as long as we don't bother them." Josée and I managed to keep calm, and soon enough we reached the other side of the river.

Then, after a brief rest, the real journey began. No automobiles ever went past this village in the direction of Papa's farm. We walked on a narrow, winding dirt path for over an hour. Weary and dusty, we finally caught sight of the vast farm. The farm was surrounded by woods. There wasn't another farm or compound in sight. Great fields of corn, manioc, and vegetables stretched out for acres. At the center of it all were two two-room, brick houses and a two-story log cabin that Papa had built. The first floor of the log cabin was a storehouse for farm products, and Papa and *ma* Feza occupied the second floor. *Ba* Olenga, an old friend of Papa's from the military, lived with his wife in one of the brick houses and helped Papa work the farm. Dozens of chickens and ducks waddled unfettered around the houses. Papa also had two sheep that he was hoping would breed a flock of lambs. His other source of meat was the forest, where he'd hunt for gazelles and wild birds.

After warm greetings and a delicious feast, Papa said, "You two are going to spend your nights up there." He pointed to the second floor of the log cabin. "*Ma* Feza and I will sleep in this house. We sometimes have visitors at night that might disturb your sleep. We're used to them." The visitors included anteaters, porcupines, and gazelles.

We spent close to two weeks at the farm and had a great time. Josée and I frolicked like little girls. When it was time for us to leave, Papa gave us, as always, pocket money and insisted that we continue writing and giving him our news.

"Why don't you answer us when we write?" pleaded Josée. "We get tired of writing and not getting any reply from you. You don't only have to respond when one of us has problems or is sick."

"All right, all right. Your old Papa will try do a little better. But you just make sure you write to me." He paused and said softly, "And take good care of yourselves." And, of course, before we left, Papa asked us to give his regards to his dear friend, *bibi* Thérèse.

While in Lubumbashi on my way back to Kinshasa, I began getting severe headaches. Several weeks of medical treatment didn't make me feel better. One smart physician finally figured out that I didn't need pills or injections, I needed glasses! After getting my first set of prescription eyewear, my headaches quickly vanished. With the glasses, I was physically ready to challenge the university once again. After spending time with Papa, Josée, and Maman, I was emotionally recharged and ready to take a fresh crack at life in the capital. Connecting again with those dearest to me had somehow liberated me from my anxieties and made me fully ready, as I guess I hadn't been before, to live on my own.

By the time I got back to Kinshasa, though, it was November—too late to take the re-tests in Botany and Zoology. I went back to living at Rene's house and tried to find some kind of office work to keep me busy and help pay for my expenses. Without the proper connections, however, I had no luck. So I passed the time taking courses in secretarial skills and accounting at a French-owned business school.

Meanwhile, Mobutu's purge of military officers continued. One leading officer after another was arrested. The nation's attention was riveted by televised show trials, in which dozens of high-ranking officers were tried and convicted for treason. One of those convicted was Kalonda Katalayi, one of René's best friends, who lived next door to us and had spent many an evening over at our house. Kalonda was sentenced to twenty years in prison. Then one day, René's turn came; he didn't return home from work in the evening, and we had no word from him all the next day. On René's second day of absence, Kalonda was escorted home by military police to pick up some personal items before returning to prison. He told René's wife that René had, in fact, been arrested but was in good condition. René had asked him to tell her that he was safe and that she shouldn't worry. We knew that René wasn't involved in any coup conspiracies, and he certainly wasn't guilty of any other high crimes, but we were frightened nevertheless. Even though the reason for his arrest was perfectly clear to us: he was a native of Shaba, whose people had revolted against Mobutu.

We were even more alarmed one month later when Kalonda and twelve other officers were executed by firing squad. No one ever explained why his sentence had been changed. His body was thrown into the Zaire River. Then our own fears were realized. René was tried for conspiracy, convicted, and sentenced to ten years in prison.

All the arrested officers lost their military camp housing privileges, and their families were evicted immediately. René's wife and children moved into the already overcrowded home of a relative. I was blessed to have *ya* Auguy to take care of me; he gave me enough money to rent a room in a building near the ISP/Gombe campus.

Mobutu's show trials and his public declaration that Shaba would never be attacked again didn't faze the Katangese rebels one bit. They invaded again in May 1978 and easily took over the important mining town of Kolwezi. Naturally, once again, the Zairian army was useless. Since there were many expatriates trapped in Kolwezi, Mobutu was able to appeal for help to his friends in Paris. A week after the fall of Kolwezi, 700 French legionnaires attacked and drove the rebels back to Angola. Hundreds of people died in the fighting. But Mobutu was once again saved by his foreign friends.

CHAPTER 22

BACK ON TRACK

In June 1978 Josée completed her studies and earned a university degree. She had maintained her discipline and accomplished our father's first dream for his daughters. Now it was up to me to get my university career started again. I had decided that I wasn't cut out for biochemistry or any other science program. My new plan was to major in English and African Culture at ISP/Gombe. African culture was interesting, but what really attracted me was the opportunity to learn how to speak English. I had always excelled at languages; besides French and kiSwahili, I also spoke Lingala and a little bit of tshiLuba, kiKongo, and kiHemba. Not to mention the Greek words I had learned from Mr. and Mrs. Constantinides. And what language could be more interesting than the language of James Brown and Muhammad Ali, the language of worldwide business? I had a feeling that I would be good at it.

In the Zairian university system, switching majors meant starting all over again, so all my work during that first year in biochemistry went for naught. But I enjoyed my new field of study so much that I didn't mind this setback. In addition to African culture, we studied English grammar, conversational English, and Anglo-American literature. How thrilling it was to read the adventures of *The Canterbury Tales, Ivanhoe,* and, my favorite, Shakespeare's *Macbeth!* I liked English so much that I joined the school's English Club and soon was elected President. We sponsored public readings from English-language classics that packed the school auditorium. My friend Betty would wow the crowd with her rendition of Hamlet's Soliloquy, but I topped her with my passionate reading of Edgar Allen Poe's *Annabel Lee.* I passed all my courses that year with honors!

With academic success came social success. This time around I made many good friends at school and started enjoying the exciting nightclubs of Kinshasa. And I finally decided it was time to think about a boyfriend.

"Don't worry about me," I wrote to Josée. "I know I'm not ready to settle down. I feel that I'm ready for a relationship, but I still have my head on my shoulders. My studies are still the most important thing to me."

Despite my successes, there was one area of my life with which I was not yet at ease. Even though I occasionally went to church on Sundays, I always felt that something was lacking, that the Church wasn't giving me what I needed from religion, it wasn't bringing me closer to God. I needed something else. But what?

I tried out a few Protestant prayer groups on campus but didn't feel at home in any of them. I even tried the Mahikari religious sect, of Japanese origin, in which the leaders prayed with hands over the members' heads to help chase away bad thoughts or spirits, so that we could reach harmony with God. I had a few moments of serenity there, but, after a while, their prayers above my head brought me close only to discomfort and skepticism.

Then I heard of another Asian religious group that intrigued me. Three of my classmates had joined. My suspicions grew, however, when I learned that most members lived communally in the group's headquarters and spent most of their time on the streets of Kinshasa selling goods to raise funds for the movement.

"Why do you have to move there? Is this some kind of cult where they take advantage of you?" I asked Sankilila, one of my classmates who had joined.

"No, Suruba, this is a serious religion," she replied with great calm. "We pray to the Living God. Moving to their headquarters makes it easy to observe regular prayer times. Besides, the group takes care of our daily needs. It has been very good to us."

"So why do you have to sell things all the time and turn over all the money to them?"

"This selling work won't last for very long. It's part of the first stage of membership. When we reach the second stage, we won't be doing this any more. Instead, we'll concentrate on praying and helping new members in their obligations. And, eventually, they'll send us to Europe and America to help spread the word there."

They seemed absolutely convinced that they had found the Living God, and they certainly acted like the happiest people I had ever seen. Nothing ever seemed to get them down. I was almost ready to tell them I'd come with them to their prayer meetings when a good friend of mine, Marie, announced that she was going to check it out. I figured I'd let her get some more information for me.

"The leaders of the group greeted me very nicely," Marie said on her return from her first session. "But I don't know what this Living God is that they're praying to. Near the end of the prayer session, we were told to bow our heads down and keep them down while the curtains in front were pulled open. Only members who have reached the third stage are allowed to look up. I found that pretty strange. But, on the other hand, I felt so comfortable there. The people seemed to really care about us."

"Well, Marie, when you get to that third stage, maybe I'll join you," I said in all earnestness. It sounded good, but I was so tired of hopping from one spiritual quest to another. I knew that I believed in the loving and caring Power that we call God, but I had failed in all my efforts to find a path that would bring me closer to Him.

"I'm tired of running after God," I decided. "I think I'll just wait and let Him come to me."

A few weeks passed, and Marie came back from a prayer session with astonishing news.

"You won't believe what I found out yesterday at the prayer session. During the bow-down part, I asked myself, 'Marie, what if you're praying to Satan?' I couldn't stop myself, I had to look up to see what was behind the open curtains, I had to see the face of the Living God. Guess what I saw?"

"It must have been Mobutu," one girl joked.

"No, it had to be Mao," said another.

"Stop joking, this is serious," Marie said. "I'm not going back there. Behind the curtains was a big picture of a round-faced man. He looked something like Buddha, but he was wearing a business suit. He must have been either Chinese or Korean. That's the Living God we were praying and bowing down to."

Soon after, one of my three classmates who had joined the group quit and moved back home. The two who remained started to miss school regularly. When they did show up for classes, they no longer had the glow they radiated when they first joined the movement. In fact, they looked as if they hadn't slept for days. They would usually sit in the back of the classroom and doze off. After failing one test after another, they dropped out of school altogether. It was only later that we came to call them *moonistes*. The name of the man in the picture behind the curtains, the Living God, was Reverend Sun Myung Moon.

During my second year studying English, René's sentence was commuted, and he was freed after having served more than a year in a remote military prison. He was given a dishonorable discharge from the military, but, thanks to his engineering experience, he was able to get a job with the country's electric power utility company. Later in 1979, Josée came to visit Kinshasa and wound up living with René and his family after finding a job with the Department of Education. It was then that she told me that she thought she had found the man for her. His name was Lolo; she had met him in Lubumbashi, where he was studying in the mining engineering program. They had even gone so far as to introduce each other to their respective families. Nothing was final yet—they hadn't discussed marriage—but she said it felt like they were getting close to doing so.

I began almost immediately to fantasize about their wedding. How beautiful Josée would look in a flowing white gown! How proud Papa would be marching her down the church aisle! And me, of course, I would be the maid of honor. I knew that Josée was probably having the same fantasy, we had talked about it often enough as children.

After a few months Josée managed to get transferred to the Department of Education's Lubumbashi office, where she could be close to her sweetheart. In Lubumbashi she lived with Maman. She had finally gotten to live full-time with the mother she had longed for throughout her childhood.

After Josée's move to Lubumbashi, Lolo came to Kinshasa for a visit, and I got to meet my sister's heartthrob. He seemed to be, indeed, everything Josée had told me: charming, intelligent, and very much in love with my big sister. I was very happy for both of them.

With each passing year, the economy plummeted to unprecedented depths of despair, and Mobutu's unpopularity soared. But somehow he always managed to brutally crush or cagily divide the opposition and con other countries into saving his dictatorial regime. Every time he disappeared from public view for awhile, rumors began circulating that he was gravely ill, that he was suffering from leukemia, that his days were numbered. Every time he would resurface looking hale and hearty, a powerful and seemingly invincible figure.

He survived the two rebel attacks in Katanga, and he survived the demonetization crisis of 1979. The money crisis came when the government announced that the nation's currency was going to be changed, and all the old bills in circulation would become worthless.

The goals of this scheme were to get a handle on the inflation the government had caused by letting the money printing presses run wild and to coerce people into keeping their money in the government banking system, where it could be used to help pay off the massive debt Mobutu's regime had accumulated with Western banks. Money on deposit in banks would be automatically changed to the new, devalued currency, but many people didn't keep any money in banks: bank accounts exposed them to taxation, gave next to no interest, and there were no guarantees that you could withdraw your money when you wanted to. If you had old bills outside of a bank account, the government announced, you could change them for new bills at your neighborhood bank.

There was one slight catch to the deal: you only had three days to make the change. Most people in Zaire lived in rural areas and could not physically get to a bank in time. For those of us living in large cities, it wasn't much better. On each of the anointed days, I got to the bank at the crack of dawn only to find huge lines already formed. Most of us never even got close to the inside of the bank during those three days; when the bank closed on the third day all our cash instantly became as worthless as dust. Many people pushed and scratched their way to the front of the line and managed to reach a teller in time, only to find out that the bank had run out of the new currency. Well, that's one way to fight inflation. Fortunately for me, my savings from my scholarship grants didn't amount to much. But many previously well-to-do people became instant paupers, and more than a few businessmen killed themselves. Of course, all of Mobutu's cronies managed to change their money with no problem, and they didn't even have to wait on line. His government's legendary corruption—this was the government for which the term "kleptocracy," government of thieves, was coined—soon fueled a new megainflation. Despite one economic and political crisis after another for the nation, life went on for its *citoyens* and *citoyennes*.

However, nothing, not even Mobutu's tyranny, it seemed, could stand in the way of love. Josée could not wait any longer: she had found her man, and she was ready, finally ready to become a wife and a mother. She was twenty-seven years old, and there weren't many other women in the entire country who had held out that long. Still, I was shocked when I got the news after the event. Josée and Lolo had exchanged vows before a magistrate in the county government office. They were married. No church ceremony, no wedding gown, no Papa, no maid of honor.

"It doesn't make any difference, wedding gown or not," Josée told me later. "We just wanted to be together."

Before the quick wedding, in fine Zairian tradition, Lolo's family members had met several times with our family members—Maman's family, that is—to discuss the union of their children. When they all decided that there was no reason to oppose the marriage, one of Lolo's uncles gave one of Maman's brothers a token payment of cash as dowry and asked for Josée's hand on behalf of his nephew. When the proposal was accepted, the families got together for a huge party, with music, beer, dancing, beer, food, beer, and more beer—all paid for by the groom's family. As the music began for the first dance, the bride and the groom were symbolically presented to each other by their respective uncles. Papa, in faraway Kongolo, unreachable by phone and slow to reach by the increasingly unreliable Zairian Post Office, did not even learn of Josée's marriage until weeks after the event.

I was very disappointed that Josée had abandoned our childhood dreams of a formal wedding. And I was angry at her for not involving Papa at all. I began to think that, perhaps, she had fallen a bit too much under Maman's influence. But I believed that she was happy; so I made peace with her decisions and welcomed Lolo into our family.

On the day after Christmas 1980, my big sister became the mother of a baby girl, Sandra. "I am the happiest wife and mother on earth," she wrote me. "People say that Sandra looks just like you. When she's big enough, I'll be sending her to spend vacations with you."

Early in 1981, Josée went back to work. She left the Department of Education and found a job with Catholic Relief Services (CRS), an American aid agency, as a nutrition specialist. She continued to support the family, while the recently graduated Lolo looked for work. With her modest salary and Zaire's inflation rate ever rising, they lived from paycheck to paycheck. Luckily, she lived within walking distance of Maman, who watched baby Sandra every work day.

Later that year, I completed my undergraduate degree, graduating with honors. I knew exactly what I wanted to do: study some more. I applied for the masters degree program in English and African Literature at *Institut Pedagogique National* [National Pedagogical Institute] and was accepted. I also got a spot in the dormitory, for what it was worth. As economic conditions deteriorated around the country, conditions for university students also worsened. The cafeteria didn't function regularly anymore, buildings were no longer maintained as before, water on the campus became a rare commodity, and dormitories were seriously overcrowded. I wound up sleeping on the floor in a room with three other roommates but only two beds.

The Guide of the Nation himself threw fuel on the fire when, during a 1981 trip to the United States, he responded to a journalist's question by painting a rosy picture of the university student's life in Zaire. This infuriated the students and, when he returned home, they started staging protest rallies in Kinshasa against their living conditions. The government cracked down harshly, violently breaking up rallies and ordering the closing of the universities for an entire year.

Only a month into my career as a graduate student, I suddenly found myself on a year's sabbatical. With my scholarship money cut off, I was penniless. I went to live with *ya* Auguy's family. Bored and frustrated at the latest turn of events, I remembered one of the pieces of advice that Papa had given us so often.

"A big part of life is trouble, and the secret to survival is courage, courage to start over and carry on," he would tell us. I had witnessed my father's courage to start over from ground zero after the war. He had built up financial security only to see it ripped from him. He built it all back again, lost it all again due to the second war, and then quietly went back to work and became successful once more. He had done this without any hint of resentment.

"There are always a thousand and one excuses for giving up when bad things happen," he said. "All that you need is to find a single good reason to turn the misfortune into a lesson, then pick yourself up, and do the right thing."

I wrote Josée about my situation, and she asked her boss to write a letter of recommendation for me to the CRS office in Kinshasa. I could speak English relatively well and had learned some secretarial skills; so Josée thought I might find a job with CRS. That would surely help tide me over while I waited for the university to reopen.

Sure enough, I got an interview with the officials in CRS' Kinshasa office and was hired as a Project Assistant. I started work in May 1982 with a salary of roughly 580 Zaires per month, the equivalent at that time of approximately $60 U.S. It was a small salary, but it was a lot higher than the national average. I finally was able to chip in to help cover the cost of food and other necessities at home. I also decided to invest some of my salary. *Ya* Auguy's younger brother, Ghislain, and his family, also lived at Auguy's house. Ghislain's wife was a flight attendant for *Air Zaire* and made many trips to Europe. I gave her money to buy cosmetics and other small items for women that I could sell in Kinshasa for a small profit. She herself had been doing that kind of business for some time. Her help enabled me to earn a nice sum of money, since I didn't have to pay for any of the costs of business beyond the price of the merchandise.

At CRS I was in charge of various refugee relief and community development programs. Most of the refugees had fled the civil war in Angola, while others came from the turmoil in Ethiopia. For the refugees who needed temporary support while they awaited relocation to other countries, we distributed clothing and food and helped them find temporary housing. Other refugees were settled in Zaire, and we provided them with assistance for farming, animal husbandry, and crafts. I also worked with community programs such as centers for the handicapped and the aged. I enjoyed every minute of my work, particularly since I was able to help people in need. The refugees' plight reminded me of my own family's situation during the war years, so I was anxious to help them as much as possible.

It was while working at CRS that I made a friend who became like a sister to me and changed the course of my life. An attractive blond with blue eyes, Robin Waite was a young American working on nutrition projects for CRS. She had spent some time in the Lubumbashi office and become quite friendly with Josée. I knew, from the first day I met her, that she was one of the most remarkable persons I would ever meet. So many expatriates, even those working on development projects, came to work in Zaire primarily to make money. Even if they had idealistic motives, they tended to enjoy and take advantage of the special privileges they received because of their white skin. Very few really took the time to get to know Zairians. Oh, but Robin did, did she ever. Extraordinarily sincere and compassionate, Robin clearly came to Zaire to help people. She was always doing kind things for others, and everyone thought she was wonderful. We began hanging out together a lot after work and became very close friends.

One day at the office, Robin showed us a ring and announced that she and her boyfriend Brian, who worked for the United States Peace Corps in Kinshasa, had just become engaged. Their wedding was scheduled for August 1983 in the small town of Perkasie, north of Philadelphia, in the state of Pennsylvania in the United States of America. She wanted me to come to her wedding.

I was already excited about her wedding, because I was going to help her make her wedding dress and find Zairian craftwork to adorn the wedding tables. Now, she was suggesting that I might actually see this beautiful event. And see the United States of America to boot! I knew that getting the airplane ticket would eat up all the money I'd made from my cosmetics sales. But, never one to shy away from adventure, I decided to go for it.

Before leaving for the United States, I took a vacation home to Shaba. This gave me my first chance to see Sandra and Josée's second child, Bob, a boy born in June 1982. Lolo had found work as a high school teacher, but his salary was negligible, and, even with two salaries, they could barely keep up with inflation. Things were tough for them until 1983 when Lolo got a high-paying job as an engineer with *GECAMINES*, the giant Zairian mining company, in the copper mines of Kolwezi. Josée was then able to quit her job and become a full-time homemaker. She was already pregnant with their third child when I helped them move to Kolwezi in the summer of 1983. There they lived comfortably and even managed to save money. They were also only a four-hour ride from Lubumbashi, so Maman was able to visit on a regular basis.

From Kolwezi, I went on to visit Papa and *ma* Feza on their farm outside Kongolo. The farm was thriving, and Papa had added pigs and goats to his menagerie. Papa rarely went into town, and I could understand why. He was completely self-sufficient on the farm. All he needed from town were salt, batteries for his radio, and medicine. People from nearby villages came to buy products from his fields. He was now making more money from farming than he ever had from his transportation business. Ever the shrewd businessman, he used his profits to buy additional farmland.

Papa was almost sixty years old, but he was still working hard and taking care of himself. While many parents in Zaire counted on their grown-up children to provide for them, he always found ways to be productive and self-sufficient. Most parents with grown-up children in Zaire expect their children to buy them gifts and even openly insist on it. When I gave Papa shirts and pants as a present, he thought only of me.

"I know it's tough to live in a big city," he said. "You shouldn't spend money on me like this. I have enough clothes. I wish I had a way of helping you. Thank you, my *kambo*."

In Kongolo I visited Mama Apoline, who had never remarried and continued to live on *Avenue Kindu* with *kambo* and Pascaline. And I saw Misère, who had married a tailor and had a baby girl. She and her family stayed in Kongolo, and they frequently went to visit Papa and *ma* Feza; Papa had eventually forgiven her for not finishing her education. Misère remained the sweet baby sister she had been when we were growing up together. She made a living by selling vegetables and spices at the market near the Lualaba River. I did not get to see Benjamin. He was living near the Zambian border, apparently making money from illegal activities. He had lost all contact with his family.

CHAPTER 23

MILK FROM
THE FAUCETS

The United States of America.

The land of cowboys and astronauts, the United Nations and the Statue of Liberty.

The land of Hollywood and Harlem, Al Capone, gangsters, and *Shee-kah-go*.

The land of *Dallas* and J.R. Ewing, and Steve Austin, the six-million-dollar man.

The land of George Washington, Abraham Lincoln, JFK, and the great and good Martin Luther King.

The land of Edgar Allen Poe and *Uncle Tom's Cabin*, the book that made Josée sob out loud as she read it by candlelight after lights were supposed to be out in the dormitory.

The land of James Brown, *la musique funky*, and, of course, Muhammad Ali.

The land where unemployed people were paid by the government and even the people who cleaned the streets had fancy new cars.

The land where milk came out of the faucets.

I arrived at John F. Kennedy International Airport in New York City in the middle of August. The first thing that amazed me was seeing the sun still shining at 7:30 P.M. Because Zaire straddled the Equator, throughout the year the sun would rise right around 6:00 A.M. and set right around 6:00 P.M. I had read all about the long summer days farther away from the Equator, but it was a jolt to see it in person. Obviously, I was greatly impressed by the tremendous size of the airport and the automated equipment that made everything move so quickly and efficiently. But, perhaps, the thing that most amazed me was that there were no soldiers in sight. At Ndjili Airport in Kinshasa, you couldn't turn around without bumping into a rifle-toting soldier.

Brian's mother, who lived on Long Island, met me at the exit from Customs and put me in a limousine headed for Pennsylvania. Then the real show began as I marveled at the hundreds and hundreds of giant buildings in the city, the highways stretching on as far as the eye could see, the breathtaking bridges and tunnels, the magnificent rolling hills in the countryside, the signs everywhere announcing where you were, and the colorful billboards selling everything an American ought to have. And no soldiers stopping the car to ask for our identification papers!

The limousine dropped me in the town of New Hope, where I was met by Robin's older sister Diane, whose photograph I had seen in Robin's Kinshasa apartment. I was fatigued, a little nervous, and anxious to see Robin. But after a few minutes alone with Diane, I felt like she was my sister, too. She made me feel so very welcome, so much a part of the family—and there was absolutely no pretense about her, she was as genuine as any person I had ever met. But then I could say the same about all of the Waites: Robin's brothers Randy and Cam and her mother, Bea. From the first warm hug Bea gave me, I felt a surge of maternal affection. The Waites had a great deal of experience with foreigners, since they had welcomed foreign exchange students into their home for many years, and both Robin and Diane had studied overseas while in high school. That helped explain how quickly they set me at ease and made me feel at home. For me, meeting the Waites was definitely love at first sight, a love that just grew deeper and deeper as each hour passed. They adopted me as their sister, their daughter. They became my "American family." How honored and blessed I was to belong to such a loving family.

At Bea's house that night, I fell asleep as soon as my head hit the pillow and didn't wake up until the next afternoon. By then there were dozens of busy people preparing the yard for the next day's party. The large grassy yard stood on top of a tall hill behind the beautiful two-story brick family home. Robin had brought home a number of Zairian touches for her wedding. For one thing, there was me: I wore a typical Zairian outfit consisting of two colorful *pagnes* wrapped around my waist and a blouse made from the same material. The bridesmaids wore two-piece outfits that Robin had had made in Kinshasa, and the seeds with which the guests pelted the bride and groom after the ceremony were distributed in little baskets made at one of the centers for disabled people supported by CRS in Kinshasa.

And then the day of the wedding dawned. Robin was, of course, beautiful in her white, mostly lace gown. After the ceremony at the Presbyterian Church, we returned to Bea's house for a joyous party. I met Robin's entire family and many of her friends. Everyone seemed so impressed by the fact that I had come so far all by myself to be with Robin on her special day. Everything—my trip, the wedding, the party, the new friends I'd made—was all that I had dreamed it would be. I was so glad that I had decided to make the trip. These would be, I told myself, memories that I would cherish for the rest of my life in Zaire.

A couple of days after the wedding, Robin took me sightseeing around Perkasie. At one shopping center we saw a geyser fountain with many coins in the water and people were tossing more coins in. "Why are people throwing money in the water?" I asked Robin perplexed.

"People believe that if they make a wish while they throw coins into the water, their wish will come true. We call it a wishing well. You turn your back to the well and throw coins in, like this," Robin explained as she demonstrated proper wishing well technique. "After you've made your wish, you don't tell anyone what it was or your wish won't come true," she added with a grin.

I decided to try, just for the fun of it. It couldn't hurt, could it? I took a penny, turned my back to the well, closed my eyes, and wished: "I wish that I can one day come back and visit again this land where I don't have to show my identification card all the time, where I don't have to be harassed for not dancing in honor of the president, where I won't get arrested for criticizing a government official." I flipped the coin into the well behind me and cheered when I saw that it had landed in the water.

I had almost two weeks left before my scheduled return flight to Kinshasa. I knew that I had to go back and visit New York City. In Kinshasa, a friend of mine from the university, Symphorose, had asked me to hand deliver some letters to her sister, Marie-Claire, who lived in New York City and was married to a Zairian diplomat working at the United Nations. Another friend had asked me to hand deliver a letter from a Guinean friend to his cousin in New York. The Zairian Post Office was so notoriously unreliable that people couldn't pass up a sure opportunity to get a letter delivered. Even without the letters to deliver, I just couldn't have come this far and not visited the greatest city in the whole world.

The newlyweds were headed to Long Island on their way to a honeymoon in the Dominican Republic; so I tagged along with them. On the way there I marveled at the quality of the roads and asked how they were so well maintained.

"Tolls and taxes, everyone has to pay them," Brian said, with a tone of complaint in his voice.

"Everyone, even the big shots?" I asked.

"Yup, even the big shots."

What a country! I thought. In Zaire, the big shots have everything set up so they avoid paying what everyone else has to pay. How much better off my country would be, I thought, if only the big shots paid their fair share.

We spent the night in Long Island, and, before leaving for Santo Domingo, Robin and Brian gave me $100 for my stay in New York City. I was excited, but more than a little afraid as I took the Long Island

Railroad into New York City's Pennsylvania Station. After all, this was New York City I was entering, the biggest, meanest city in the world. The city in which Kojak, the lollipop-sucking, bald detective, had to solve so many crimes. The city of skyscrapers above and thousands of murders every day on the streets below. I gathered up all my courage and stepped out of the train station onto the streets of Manhattan.

Not wanting to take any chances with public transportation on my first day in the great city, I decided I had better take a taxi to the home of Marie-Claire, Symphorose's sister. As I looked around for a taxi, a disheveled looking man wearing an overcoat came towards me. Strange, I thought, to be wearing an overcoat on a hot day like this. The man smiled at me. I smiled back. Then he opened his coat and revealed his naked body to me. I shuddered, turned, and fled down the block where, fortunately, I quickly found a taxi. This was New York City? My goodness, I thought, how could people put up with such horrors?

Marie-Claire laughed when I told her my Penn Station story. She assured me that such an event didn't happen every day; in fact it had never happened to her. She took me on the amazing New York City subway to the East Village, where I was to deliver my second letter to Mr. Touré, the Guinean. Like my brother René and my cousin Auguy, Mr. Touré truly lived the ideal of the African extended family. He had several nephews and nieces staying in his two-bedroom apartment, but he invited me to stay there too during my New York visit. I spent my days exploring the crowded streets of Manhattan with Mr. Touré's nephews and nieces; I couldn't believe how many stores there were and how many different things you could find in them.

Marie Claire invited me to a party at her house that same week. At the party, her husband, Kabeya, asked me what I had studied at the university. When I told him I had majored in English, he said that the Zairian Mission to the United Nations had just lost its receptionist and was looking for a new one.

"With your qualifications," he said, "you're an excellent candidate for the job. I can put in a good word for you with the diplomat in charge of local hiring."

"Who is the diplomat in charge of local hiring?" I asked.

"Oh, a very nice fellow named Kabeya," he said with a smile that spread quickly to my face as well.

The offer was exciting, but I told him that I needed time to think about it. After all, I had a job in Kinshasa and was planning to go back to work on my graduate degree the next year. Mr. Touré, who was a university instructor, thought I was crazy.

"How can you pass up such an opportunity? Don't you know that thousands of Africans would kill for a chance to live and work in the United States?"

"But I've got to go back to graduate school in Kinshasa," I replied.

"My dear, they have some fine universities right here in New York City where you can get a much more useful graduate degree. You can work during the day and study in the evening. And, believe me, the government here is not going to shut down the universities like your President Mobutu does."

His logic was impeccable, and the thought of studying in New York City was much too alluring. I applied for the job and got it. One week before my scheduled return to Kinshasa, I started work at the Zairian Mission to the United Nations. I never used my return ticket.

There were plenty of times when I wasn't sure I had made the right decision. Every time I saw a man in an overcoat my heart rate would accelerate and I'd hold my breath—until I got past him without being shown all that lied underneath his coat. And every day the newspapers and television news reported one grisly killing after another.

And there was another problem—new to me. When walking down the streets or through the parks of the East Village, I'd be approached by one young person after another, some whispering, others shouting, but all saying the same mysterious word: Smoke, smoke, smoke! The first time this happened, I turned around and searched in vain for a fire. After it happened a second and third time, I asked Mr. Touré about it, and he explained that they were selling marijuana. I

couldn't believe that the American police would let people sell drugs
so openly, right on the streets of Manhattan.

And then, of course, in the East Village we had the world's
most colorful collection of punks. Green hair, purple hair, spiked hair,
Mohawk hair. A half dozen earrings through the ears and a couple
more through the nose, mouth, and navel. Wild clothes and wild
behavior, right there on the streets in front of you. Every time I saw one
coming down the street—which was quite frequent at that time in that
place—I'd cross to the other side. I didn't know what to make of them,
but they scared me. As the weeks passed, I learned that they meant me
no harm, and I started to get used to them.

But I never could get used to the sight of all the beggars on the
streets of the biggest city in the richest country in the world. Here people spent more in one night out than most of the people in my country made in an entire year—and, yet, there were more beggars in
Manhattan than I'd ever seen in the worst of times in Kinshasa. Didn't
people here have any shame? Didn't they have any families to take
care of them? I felt so sorry for the American beggars that I always gave
them whatever change I had—until Mr. Touré told me that most of
them would just use it to buy drugs.

But, as troubling as America's social ills were to me, my doubts
never overcame my awe for all the things that made this country so
great. The extraordinary mix of people of all colors, cultures, languages,
and religions. The plethora of economic and educational opportunities.
So much creative genius, from architecture to tap dancing to the best
basketball playing in the world. The rows and rows of stores with everything you could possibly ever want—in 101 different varieties. The
crowds and energy on the streets that seemed to holler to me: You can
make your dreams come true here! And, most of all, freedom of
speech. Turn on the television, and you wouldn't see a deified image of
Ronald Reagan descending from the heavens to guide the nation. No,
you'd see opposition politicians and journalists and ordinary citizens
openly criticizing President Reagan or Governor Cuomo or Mayor

Koch. Walk the streets and you wouldn't see people being forced to dance in honor of a President they despised. No, you'd see ordinary people on the street making speeches criticizing government officials and even the Constitution of the United States. And the police would walk by and just take it all in, without arresting, torturing, or executing those who dared to criticize the leaders of the government. My dear America, do you have any idea how much it meant to me to experience this new phenomenon, freedom of speech? Do you have any idea how lucky you are, Americans? How could I not love this country?

And so I stayed. While I saved money and looked for a place of my own, Mr. Touré was kind enough to let me stay at his place for over five months. How much I wanted to speak to Papa and Josée to let them know all the exciting developments in my life! But there was, of course, still no telephone connection to Kongolo and, since Zaire was in arrears on paying its international telecommunication bills, it was now next to impossible to place a call to Josée in Kolwezi. So I sent them my news by mail, but, in the Zaire of 1983, even that was a difficult proposition. Letters typically took more than a month, and sometimes two or three months to arrive in or from Zaire; more than a few letters would simply get lost.

After a few months, I did get my family's reaction to my staying in America. "Knowing the daredevil you are, I wasn't all that surprised," wrote Josée. "I was a bit concerned about your living in such a big city, about which you hear so many bad things. But from what you write in your letters, it sounds like you will do just fine."

My news was momentous enough to even prompt a rare letter from Papa. As always, he expressed his confidence in me. "I know and trust that you are doing the right thing for you," wrote Papa. "Make sure you concentrate on your education, don't let all the distractions of a big city sidetrack you. Keep on writing to me. And remember that the Almighty and your ancestors are with you."

CHAPTER 24

MON CHEVALIER

At the Zairian Mission to the United Nations, I started as a receptionist and later became a bilingual secretary. The Ambassador at that time, Umba di Lutete, was an extraordinarily decent man. The government in Kinshasa was often months behind in sending funds to cover staff salaries, but Ambassador Umba advanced us our paychecks with his own money.

December came along, and I experienced, for the first time in my life, winter. And not just any old winter. The winter of 1983-84 was one of the coldest winters the Northeast had seen in many years. I had planned to visit Robin's family in Pennsylvania for the holidays, but I caught cold and felt too sick to go. By New Year's Eve, I felt better, so I went to a holiday party at Marie-Claire and Kabeya's apartment.

Shortly before the clock struck midnight and we kissed 1983 goodbye, a man arrived at the party. He was not like any white American I had met in the United States. His name was Howell Wechsler, and he spoke Lingala, the language of Kinshasa and northern Zaire, Papa's native language, just like a Zairian. Everyone called him *semeki* [in-law], because he was a friend of a returned Peace

Corps Volunteer who had married a Zairian woman. He was over six feet tall, trim but muscular, with dark hair and a well-groomed beard and mustache. He had a long, thin face with distinctive features, most notably large brown eyes and a long, Roman nose. Without his mustache, he might have easily been confused for Abraham Lincoln. Right after he greeted everyone in Lingala, I expected him to switch immediately into English. But I was wrong, he kept on speaking Lingala as if he were a native speaker. I had lived in Kinshasa for a number of years, but his Lingala was clearly a lot better than mine! I learned that he had only recently returned from a three-year stint as a Peace Corps Volunteer in a Lingala-speaking area of Zaire. It was a fun party, and every time I looked up, *semeki* was at my side. We danced some, spoke a lot, and flirted even more. He was very charming, our *semeki.*

It was a pleasant interlude, but when I left the party I did not expect to hear from him again. A few days later, I got a call at work. "Hello, may I speak with Suruba, please?" a male voice said in French.

"This is she. Who's this?" I asked.

"Hi there. This is Howell, we met at Kabeya's New Year's Eve party, remember?"

My mind went blank for a moment, then he said in Lingala, "I can't believe you've forgotten me already."

A big smile crossed my face as I realized who it was. "*Semeki*, it's you. How are you?" I said, giggling.

"Yes, it's me," he said. Then, with great seriousness, he added, "But I'm not your *semeki.* My name is Howell, and I'm calling to see if we can go out to dinner sometime after work."

I got his message loud and clear. Calling him *semeki* meant he was family. You couldn't find romance with family. What an interesting way of making his intentions known to me. I was intrigued. Of course, I said yes. He took me out for dinner, a lovely first date. He was, at the same time, one of the funniest and most serious persons I'd ever met. He knew how to make a story interesting, and he had no shame about acting silly. But it was clear that he had a sense of mission about his life, that he felt he was put here to do things that would help make life better for other people. During his Peace Corps service he had done remarkable work: he created an immunization program that had saved the lives of countless children and, not only did he learn to speak Lingala beautifully, he also co-wrote the first public health text-book in that language. Here in New York he was working for a pro-gram that helped community organizations organize health fairs to teach people how to improve their health. Howell had the same American genuineness and lack of pretense that I had found so beau-tiful in the Waite family. We went out again and again and, by the end of January, we were pretty much going steady. A native New Yorker, Howell shared his love of the city with me, and his guided tours helped me fall under its spell.

During one of our early conversations, Howell mentioned to me that he was Jewish. "But I'm not very observant," he quickly added. I didn't think much about it. In fact, when I told him that I was Catholic, I quickly added, "But I'm not very observant." I didn't know if I had ever met a Jew before. There was a synagogue in Lubumbashi that had thrived during the colonial era, but, particularly after zairian-ization, few Jewish people remained and I certainly hadn't met one. Of course, we had studied the Old Testament in school. Some of the priests and nuns said the Jews were the people who had killed Jesus, but Father Albert said that wasn't a fair or good thing to say. I knew the Jews believed in One God; they were the people who came up with the whole idea. And I knew that they didn't accept Jesus as the Messiah. But then I wasn't sure that I did either. I knew that the Jews were among the greatest fighters in the world: look at what little Israel had done to survive among all those larger countries intent on destroying it. I thought of Howell as Howell and didn't think much at all about him being Jewish.

But other people thought of little else when they heard me talk about Howell. Some of my African friends warned me that I was in for a big disappointment.

"Not only are you from a different culture," they said, "but you are also from a different race and a different religion. You're wasting your time. His Jewish parents would never let him marry a non-Jew, let alone an African. He'll just have a good time with you and then dump you when he's had enough. He'll never bring you home to his parents. You're a beautiful woman, find yourself someone else."

It was as if they were talking about someone I'd never met before, a complete opposite of the man I was slowly getting to know—and to love. He was genuine, the real thing, I was sure of it. He took me to so many different places and introduced me to so many of his long time friends. This was a man who obviously cared deeply about his family and was absolutely devoted to his friends. He wanted to know about me, to really know me. And he let me know him. Unlike all the other boyfriends I had had, he never pretended to be something other than what he was. He was comfortable being himself. And I liked that a lot. He reminded me, in many ways, of my father: he was a man who knew how to adapt to different cultures, who got along well with people from all different cultural and economic backgrounds, who made friends for life, who tried his best to live by the highest moral values. And he was a man who cherished education.

After we had been seeing each other for five months, Howell made an announcement to me: "I'd like you to meet my parents. They're pretty anxious to meet you. I've spoken with them, and they've invited us for dinner Friday night."

It was clear from his tone that this was a big deal. I liked the sign: it seemed to indicate that he was really serious about me. On the way to his parents' Bronx apartment, Howell seemed a bit nervous, as if he wasn't quite sure this was such a good idea after all. I couldn't help being nervous myself, considering all the things my friends had said about Jewish parents. But, from the very start, Howell's parents made me feel welcome. They insisted that I call them by their first names, Marilyn and Herb. Conversation came easily; I think they were surprised by how well I spoke English. It was *Shabbat* dinner, celebrating the start of the Sabbath day that is sacred to Jews. It was, of course, my first *Shabbat* dinner, and I was naturally curious about all the prayers and rituals. Marilyn and Herb seemed very pleased by my curiosity, and they took great joy in explaining everything in detail.

We talked a lot about my life in Zaire and my impressions of America. I told them how my father had served in the military, and Herb entertained us with stories of his service in the United States Army during World War II. We talked about technology and computers. When I mentioned that I had never used a computer before, Herb took me to use his and helped me write a letter on it to Papa. During the conversation, I happened to mention that one of my favorite hobbies was stamp collecting. Howell's jaw dropped—he had never heard me mention that before—while Herb's eyes lit up. Little had I known that Herb was an avid stamp collector who had won numerous prizes at philatelic exhibitions. What a wonderful time we both had as he showed me just a small portion of his collection. Herb and Marilyn and I were having such a pleasant conversation that we barely realized Howell was there!

After we left their apartment, I turned to Howell and asked, "So, how'd I do?"

He smiled and said, in his best Ralph Kramden imitation, "Baby, you're the greatest! You did great!"

My African friends were certainly wrong about one thing: the color of my skin and the fact that I was from Africa didn't seem to matter in the slightest to Howell's parents or the other members of his family whom I met in the months to follow: his older sister Barbara and her family in the Philadelphia area, his older brother Michael and his family in Minnesota, and his Aunt Arlene and Uncle Al, who lived near Mr. Touré in Manhattan's East Village. His parents and his sister, however, were very actively religious, and my impression was that they were more concerned about me being Christian. But Judaism, I would soon learn, was very open to conversions, so perhaps they held out hope that, if our relationship was to get more serious, I might consider that option.

I learned a great deal more about Judaism from our visits to Howell's sister Barbara's home outside of Philadelphia. Her husband, Jack, was a rabbi and a professor at the Reconstructionist Rabbinical College. At their home I would participate in *Shabbat* dinner; celebrations of Jewish holidays, such as Passover and Sukkot; and the *brit b'not Yisrael* [ceremony to celebrate the birth of a daughter] for their third child, Hana Beth. I found the Jewish rituals and observances quite interesting. However, it didn't seem like anything that would ever truly touch a spiritual chord within me. Nevertheless, I started urging Howell to learn more about his religion.

After spending a few months living in Queens, I moved to an apartment on the Bronx's Grand Concourse, not far from Howell's apartment. Ironically, it was right down the block from a small museum that commemorated one of my literary heroes, Edgar Allan Poe, who had lived in that area. With Howell's help, I began my quest for an American education. I enrolled in a few courses at Baruch College, City University of New York, in 1985, while waiting for my official transcripts to be sent from the university in Kinshasa. The wait took more than a year, a sign of how poor communication was between the United States and Zaire. The City University authorities decided I had to re-take quite a few of the courses that I had successfully completed in Zaire, a sign of how American universities don't appreciate the hard work done in universities overseas. Despite my undergraduate diploma from Zaire, they insisted that I earn an American bachelors degree. So I enrolled in Baruch's Bachelor of Business Administration program.

During the summer of 1985, after we'd been dating for more than a year, Howell and I decided to take a vacation together. We traveled to Chicago for a wedding, and I saw beautiful Lake Michigan and the campus of Howell's alma mater, Northwestern University. We visited San Francisco to see a friend of Robin's whom I had met at her wedding, and I crossed the Golden Gate Bridge and ran my fingers through the Pacific Ocean. Best of all, we spent a week in Squamish,

British Columbia, with Jacquis Peeters and her family. *Da* Jacquis grew up near Kongolo and was Josée's best friend during our years in the dormitory. They had maintained contact all through the years, and Jacquis was like another older sister to me. She had married a Belgian and moved to the Pacific Northwest in the mid-1970s.

Somehow spending all this time together on our vacation changed the dynamics of my relationship with Howell. After going out with him for over a year, I had come to the conclusion that he was the one for me and that, with my thirtieth birthday approaching in January, I was more than ready to make such a commitment. Howell, three years younger than me, was, like many men, somewhat slow in making up his mind. But our vacation together helped him get over the precipice of indecision. Soon after we returned to New York, he asked me to move into his apartment.

We began having delicate discussions, negotiations you might say, about a future together and what our family life might be. The biggest issue was religion. Though I was very impressed with all the Jewish experiences I had had since meeting Howell, I had no interest in converting to Judaism. Howell said he would never pressure me to make such a profound spiritual decision just to please him and his family. But, since we had first met, he had started to think more about his religion and its importance in his life. "I've decided that it is extremely important to me that my children be raised as Jews."

"That would be fine with me," I replied.

I understood that meant that my children couldn't be raised as Christians, but that didn't bother me much. I wasn't sure any more how much of Christianity I believed in, so why should I impose it on my children? I wanted to make sure they grew up with some meaningful religious experience, in which they could learn to cherish God and live by the highest moral precepts. From what I had learned, Judaism could do that for them as well as anything else.

On January 18, 1986, my thirtieth birthday, Howell took me to a Broadway show and dinner at a French restaurant. When we got home, he sat me down on our bed and said, "Stay here. Don't move. I'll be right back." When he returned, he had both hands behind his back. He asked me to choose one hand.

"This one," I said, touching his right shoulder.

He pulled his right hand out from behind his back and in it was a beautiful, long-stemmed red rose. Then I tapped the left shoulder, and his left hand surfaced. In it was a small, velvet box. My heart jumped.

"Open the box," he said. I did and saw a sparkling diamond ring. I was speechless.

"Do you know what this means?" he asked.

"I think so," I said cautiously. He got down on his knees, took my hands in his, and said, "Suruba Ibumando Georgette, will you marry me?"

My head bounced up and down as my heart went wild with joy. I grabbed him and made it quite clear that, with all my heart, my answer was, "Yes."

Something was rotten at the Zairian Mission to the United Nations, and it started at the top. A new ambassador had arrived, and we had expected him to be a compassionate boss, just like Ambassador Umba. He had visited the United Nations several times before and made a very good impression on the Mission staff. But it soon became apparent that he had no enthusiasm for his work and no appreciation whatsoever of his staff. He took possession of the keys to the office kitchen and the men's room, so that only he could use them; all the male diplomats had to share the women's bathroom.

A week or two after his arrival, he called me into his office. "Why don't you come to my home after work today," he said with a vigorous smile.

"I'd be honored to," I said, naively thinking that he wanted to introduce me to his family. Even though I had a class that evening, I figured I could drop by to greet his wife and children on my way to school. When I rang the bell to his apartment, I was surprised to see the ambassador himself open the door. He cheerfully invited me in. I looked past him, expecting to see other people there, but he was alone. Suddenly, I figured out what this was all about.

"Beer or wine?" he asked.

"I'll have a glass of water, if you don't mind," I said, calmly resisting the urge to stand up and leave.

"Well, a beer or a glass of wine can't hurt, why not have one?"

"I've got to go to school in a little while," I said, trying ever so hard to be polite. "So it's not appropriate for me."

He then asked me what I was studying and talked about his own plans to go back to school for a higher degree.

"You're not only smart, but you are also a very pretty woman," he said. "Why don't you stay a little longer, so that we can get to know each other better. Missing one day of school won't really make any difference."

"I'm sorry, I don't think I can afford to miss my class," I said, as I put the glass of water on the coffee table. "I'm already late, and I have to leave now."

"Well, another day then, when you don't have school," he said, as I rose.

"Yes, another day," I said, while swearing to myself that I'd never enter his apartment again.

The following day he called me into his office. After he gave me documents to type, he reminded me again of his invitation to visit his apartment.

"Since your father is from my home region, you are my sister," he said. "That's why we should know each other better. You'll be like my right hand here. Open your eyes, look around, and report to me when someone falls out of line."

I left his office without saying anything but went immediately to speak to Kapya, one of the Mission's secretaries who had become my best friend there.

"Can you believe it? He wants me to spy on people under the pretense that we're brother and sister since we share the same home region. I feel like going back and telling him I'm a secretary, not a spy, certainly not his spy."

"Don't tell him that, Suruba," Kapya wisely advised me. "Just ignore it and do your job. You know, many of them have worked with girls who are all too willing to do that kind of thing, so they assume every girl is the same."

After a few weeks, the ambassador came to realize that I was not going to spy on my colleagues for him and I certainly wasn't going to stop off at his apartment again. I had since learned that he was actually renting that apartment for his mistress, who was to arrive shortly from Zaire. His wife and children were to stay in a house in Westchester. Needless to say, I soon became one of his least favorite employees. His favorite way to get back at me was to deny me permission to leave on time to get to my classes.

"Who does she think she is?" he would say to the other secretaries. "She talks to me as if I wasn't the boss here. She's impolite and full of herself, just because she's studying at an American university. She should watch her step, or I'll send her out on the street."

Kapya would always speak up on my behalf, concocting some story or other to excuse my impertinence. He eased off on me a little bit, when he started an affair with one of the other secretaries.

When his "official" mistress was in town, he'd saunter into the office around noon—and demand that we work until 11:00 P.M. or later, even though we'd been there since nine o'clock in the morning. There was no question of giving us overtime pay, we weren't even getting our regular pay on time. Although we were supposed to be paid weekly, the funds for our salaries would usually arrive from Zaire two to three months late. When the money did come, the Ambassador would take a large portion of our salary money for his own personal use. He even had the nerve to tell us that we shouldn't complain because we were getting paid a lot of money compared to our compatriots back in Zaire; he didn't acknowledge, of course, that the cost of living was astronomically higher in the United States.

Whenever President Mobutu came to visit the United Nations, we'd work late into the evening every night and all day Saturday and Sunday as well. The Ambassador gave us a bonus for this hard work—but then deducted the bonus from our next regular paycheck. He was even taking money from the salary of the secretary who was sleeping with him! She got so fed up that she left and got a job at another United Nations mission. Most of the office staff, however, did not have visas that allowed them to switch jobs, so they were stuck at the Zairian Mission. To replace her, he brought a secretary over from Zaire. She could barely type, was an awful speller, and spoke little English. But, as far as the Ambassador was concerned, she did her job to perfection. She would report to him everything that staff members did or said around the office. When he would hear that diplomats were complaining about him, he would maneuver to transfer them out of New York. All of us at the office were miserable. Our only hope was that he would soon be replaced, which seemed reasonably likely since other ambassadors hadn't lasted long in that position.

Fortunately, I got time off in the summer of 1986 to take a trip home. It was very important to me to see Papa and Josée before I got married. Everyone was awfully excited to see my engagement ring. They all assumed that Howell and I would be living in the United States after our marriage. We hadn't really discussed whether we would consider living in Zaire, but my visit convinced me that it would not be a good idea, as long as Mobutu remained in power. The economy had continued to deteriorate, and more and more children were going hungry. Crime was soaring, and the criminals were getting more and more violent—almost as violent as American criminals. The corruption was suffocating. At the airport, I had to pay bribes just to keep my passport, even though everything was in order. Petty harassment by soldiers checking identity cards was now completely out of control. After having experienced American freedom, I had little tolerance for the never-ending abuses of power one experienced in Mobutu's Zaire.

Papa was delighted to receive a letter from Howell, particularly since it was written in Lingala. While in Kongolo, I visited Mama Apoline and learned that *kambo* Colette, who had been born around the turn of the century and helped us to survive the horrors of the 1960s, had passed away in 1985. How sorry I was that she wasn't here to see her *kampulumayamba nyoka havala mukaba* engaged to be married. I also visited with Mama Apoline's daughter, Marie, who had married a Zambian and had had three children with him before getting divorced and moving back to Kongolo.

Back in New York for the Fall session of the United Nations, I learned that our despised boss had not been replaced. When he kept on insisting that I stay at work past the time that my classes started, I couldn't take it any more. I typed up a letter of resignation. One of the Ambassador's spies must have told him what was coming, because, as I handed him the letter, he announced that I was fired and I would lose all but two weeks of the many months of back pay that the Mission owed me. This infuriated me, so I did what would have been unthinkable for just about any Zairian: I wrote a letter in which I accused the Ambassador of illegally confiscating my salary. Then I mailed the letter to Zaire's Ministry of Human Rights, Ministry of Foreign Affairs, and several other ministries in Kinshasa. I knew full well that they'd never go after a corrupt official, but I just couldn't sit back and do nothing.

Naturally, I sent a copy of my *J'accuse* letter to the Ambassador. I was later told that, when he saw the letter with my return address on it, he said, "I see. Now she wants to come crawling back to me to beg for her job back. How arrogant she was, just because she had an American fiancé. I guess now she realizes that her so-called fiancé was keeping her because she had a job."

He went on and on in this vein as he opened the letter. But when he saw what it was, his face turned pale, he dropped the letter to the floor, and the veins in his head nearly exploded with fury. He immediately forbade all the staff members from ever mentioning my name again. Six months later, he received a faxed message from the Ministry of Foreign Affairs that commanded him to pay me the entirety of the back pay I had claimed was owed to me. Justice didn't exactly prevail in the end, however. Instead of paying me, he sent a fax to the Ministry in which he reported that I was extremely "unpatriotic" and didn't deserve anything at all. The Ministry never responded, and he never paid me. In fact, for seven months after my resignation, he kept my name on the Mission's account books and continued to receive my salary, which he promptly deposited in his own bank account.

Poorer but happier, I found some part-time work translating documents into French and busied myself with wedding preparations. Howell and I decided that, considering our religious differences, it would be inappropriate to have a religious ceremony. We would be married by a judge, but in a special ceremony that would involve many traditions from both the Jewish and Zairian cultures. We did not have the financial means to pay for Papa or Josée to come to the United States for the wedding, and it was certainly beyond their means as well. But we were able to have the ceremony and highlights of the party videotaped, so that we could send it to Zaire and, in that small way, share our big day with them. In addition to Howell's family, my American family, the Waites, and many of our friends, we had two very special guests: *da* Jacquis, Josée's childhood friend, came from Canada, and Robin came to the United States from Zaire for my wedding, as I had done for hers.

We held the wedding ceremony on July 25, 1987, in the beautiful New York Botanical Gardens, located in Howell's native Bronx. It was about the hottest, muggiest day of the year, and it had rained much of the day. But the skies cleared just in time for us to proceed with the outdoor ceremony we had planned. I wore the beautiful white wedding gown of which I had always dreamed. It hurt not to have Papa and Josée there, but I felt truly blessed to have *da* Jacquis represent my loved ones in Zaire and my wonderful, loving American mom, Bea Waite, there to walk me down the aisle to my groom.

The ceremony began with the groom's procession, featuring five pairs of Howell's dearest friends followed by Howell and his parents, marching down a long walkway flanked on both sides by gorgeous rows of flowers. As they marched, a tape recorder played, "Now I Have Everything," a beautiful song from *Fiddler on the Roof*. This was followed by the bride's procession, featuring five of my dearest friends dressed in colorful Zairian-style outfits that I had sewed for them, followed by my matron of honor, Robin. I walked arm in arm with Bea. As we marched, the tape recorder played "Yamba Ngai," a dreamy, upbeat Zairian song in which a woman sings of her joy on her wedding day and invites her groom to "Take me, take me in marriage."

When my procession arrived at the end of the walkway, Marilyn and Herb, Howell's parents, read in Hebrew and English the blessings that Jewish parents say for their children every Friday night. Then Marilyn said with a great big smile, "Go see your bride, Howell." Herb brought Howell over to me for the *bedeken* ceremony, in which the Jewish groom lifts the veil of his bride just before the wedding ceremony to verify that she is indeed the bride he has bargained for—and perhaps also to take one last romantic look into the eyes of the woman to whom he will soon be bound forever. This tradition goes back to the biblical story of Jacob, who worked seven years to earn the right to marry Rachel, but was tricked into marrying her older sister, Leah, instead. Satisfied with the beaming face he saw under the veil, Howell returned to his position opposite from me.

Then Howell's sister Barbara, her husband Jack, my American sister Diane and her husband Greg hoisted up between us the four poles connected to the *huppah*, the wedding canopy under which Jews are married. We had designed and embroidered the covering for our *huppah*. It featured four symbols: a pair of flowers and a pair of fish, both traditional symbols of fertility, and map outlines of Zaire and the Bronx, which almost fit together like adjoining pieces of a jigsaw puzzle. Howell and I slowly walked away from our respective families and came together under the canopy. Facing us were our mistress and master of ceremonies, *da* Jacquis and Howell's best friend, Jon Brooks. They began by reciting in English, then French, then Hebrew, then kiSwahili: "Blessed is the beauty of this lovely garden in which we gather to consecrate the beauty of your love."

Much of the ceremony that followed mirrored the traditional Jewish wedding ceremony, including blessings over two cups of wine and seven blessings in honor of the marriage. The first cup from which we drank was a traditional Jewish *kiddush* cup that Howell's sister and her family had given us; the second cup was a clay mug made from the soil of Katanga/Shaba, which Josée had given me in 1986. During the ceremony, Howell and I read our own personal statements of commitment. First, Howell spoke.

> Here in The Bronx, my life and dreams began. I dreamt for so long that I'd enter my wedding canopy with a beautiful woman. A strong and confident woman, comfortable with herself as she is. Secure enough to love without games of jealousy and suspicion, faithful to me as I'd be to her. An intelligent woman to fascinate me for a lifetime, hard working and ambitious for a successful career, anxious as I to experience other cultures. A kind, caring woman with a passion for political freedom and social justice, and the good sense to know when it's time to think of our own needs. A serious woman who can be outrageously silly when it's time to have fun, with enough joy and energy to dance all night long, who appreciates tap dancing, Frank Capra movies, and an occasional ball game at Shea. An affectionate and romantic woman who's delicious to hold, sweet enough to win the hearts of my family and friends, loving and wise enough to be a wonderful mommy. I thank you, my beloved Ibu, and I thank God for making my dream come true.

Then, it was my turn. I lifted up my veil and shared my feelings with the eighty or so people in attendance.

> I always wished to share my life with someone who'd love and respect me the way I'd love and respect him; who'd support me in my strengths and help me deal with my weaknesses; who would respect and encourage my ambitions, and be proud of my working toward a career; who is not jealous and possessive; who is mature and has confidence in himself; and whom I can always count on; who is social and concerned not only with our little world, but also other people's problems; who will be faithful and who will love children the way I do; who'll be part of me and yet understand that we are distinct individuals. Well, Howell is that special person I've been dreaming of. He is *mon chevalier* whom I love very much, in his strengths and weaknesses, and he is the person I wish to spend the rest of my life with. Thank you, Howell, for being you.

Then we read the following vows together:

> We are committed to building a warm and loving family life, enriched by the traditions of our peoples.
> We love each other and want to share our lives.
> We intend to honor and support each other, to care for one another in tenderness, with trust, understanding and compassion.
> We will aim to deepen our bond of love while continually renewing our respect for each other as distinct individuals.
> We will strive to translate our personal fulfillment and family joy into social blessing, for our peoples and for humankind.

After some final blessings, *da* Jacquis and Jon gave way to a New York State judge, the husband of one of Howell's work colleagues, who pronounced us man and wife. Howell's brother Michael placed by our feet a large napkin with a glass cup wrapped tightly inside. Howell and I crushed it with our feet, signaling the end of the ceremony. Hoops and hollers and cries of *Mazel Tov* rose from some onlookers, while *da* Jacquis made the joyful clicking sound of *bikelekele.* And, just as we crushed the glass, a loud peal of thunder roared from the menacing sky. The clouds let loose a torrent of rain upon our happy crowd, prompting Jon to say, "Even God couldn't hold back his tears of joy."

When Howell and I entered the hall in which the party was being held, the disc jockey played music for a *hora,* an Israeli dance, and, in traditional Jewish fashion for brides and grooms, they hoisted us into the air on two chairs. The men carrying us danced around the room, as all our guests clapped their hands, stamped their feet, and cried out in joy. High up in the air, I could see the happiness on the faces of all these wonderful people, I could feel the thrill of my dreams coming true. I was flying! Then when they set us down, my sister-in-law Barbara, the wife of a rabbi, was there waiting for me, as if to tell me: "Yes, we love you, and we are delighted to have you in our family." She grabbed my hands and pulled me on to the dance floor, where soon everyone joined us in a wild, pulsing, frenzied, spinning dance powered by pure love and joy.

Naturally, the menu for dinner was part Jewish, part Zairian: in addition to cold cuts from our favorite Jewish delicatessen, we had cassava leaves and fried plantain. Dinner was about the only time the dance floor was empty, as we danced on and on to a mighty mix of Motown and the best of Zairian music. As the party wound down, Howell and I recorded messages for my family back in Zaire. I looked into the camcorder and said in French, "*Da* Josée and all my family, how much I wish that you could have been here with us." Then Howell spoke in Lingala: "To all my in-laws in Zaire, I want you to know that I love this woman very much, and I promise to take good care of her."

A few months later we were able to send a copy of the videotape of our wedding to Josée through a colleague of Lolo's who was visiting Canada. We learned later that, over and over again, Josée, Lolo, and the children watched the video, showing it to all the relatives and friends in town. Maman also watched it many times.

"It was as if we were there for your wedding," Josée wrote. "Maman couldn't stop crying. Now, when are the babies coming?"

CHAPTER 25

THE NIGHTMARE BEGINS

I was never one to believe in magical or mystical experiences. But sometimes the connections between two people are so strong that things happen that simply cannot be described by the language of logic and science.

In the second half of 1988, one year after my marriage, I was the happiest person on earth. I was working full-time as a bilingual secretary and credit inquirer at a French bank and studying part-time at Baruch College. Howell was going to school full-time at Columbia University's School of Public Health, while working part-time on public health research projects. We were looking forward to starting a family. Then, the walls started caving in.

It began as a bad cold that lasted a long time. Then I started to hear a consistent, painful buzzing in my ears that wouldn't go away. This was followed by terrible, throbbing headaches and a rash covering my face that seemed incurable. I felt an awful sense of dread, as if something terrible were looming over me. Both at work and school, I couldn't concentrate, and it was a miracle that I even finished the semester. The doctors gave me every imaginable test, but they couldn't find out what was causing my pain.

I began to have nightmares in which I relived the horrors of the war years. In my dreams, I saw myself as a grown woman caught up in the fighting again: gunfire ringing in my ears; bodies dropping to the left and right of me; soldiers aiming their rifles straight at me, fingers cocked on the trigger; armless, legless, headless corpses, some with gaping, bloody holes in their chests rising from the ground and chasing after me. The slightest sounds on the Bronx streets outside our bedroom window would wake me from the terror. Unfortunately, the same sounds would startle me out of my rare periods of peaceful sleep. Why, after all these years, was I having such nightmares? Why, with all the good things in my life, was I so engulfed with fear?

I turned to the Church for comfort and, for the first time in years, started to attend Mass regularly. Howell sometimes even sat with me in church. But all my prayers brought me no peace. And the large, impersonal nature of the parish left me feeling cold.

"Maybe if you find a parish where you feel more comfortable, that might help," Howell told me. "You know all parishes aren't the same, you need to visit a few different ones and see which one meets your needs." But I knew, deep inside, that even the warmest, friendliest parish couldn't be my spiritual home. As far back as I could remember, I hadn't truly felt a sense of belonging in any church.

Howell and I decided that maybe a change of scenery would help me. So, after the end of the spring 1988 semester, I went to spend some time with Marilyn and Herb, Howell's parents, in their quiet and peaceful Florida home. They tried everything possible to help me relax and feel better. Despite their best efforts, I had nights when I'd wake up in terror, reach out for Howell to comfort me, and cry pitifully when I remembered that he was back in New York. I'd then go knock on Marilyn and Herb's bedroom door, like a small, frightened child, and ask my mother-in-law if she would stay with me. She'd sit by my side for hours until I fell asleep, then tiptoe silently back to her own bed. After a few nights like this, she started spending the entire night by my side, so that every time I woke up in horror she could reassure me that I was safe.

One day there was something about Zaire on the television news, and Marilyn asked if I had heard from my family lately. No, I said, I haven't received any letters lately. I guess we all thought that getting news from home would help lift my spirits.

"You're too young to suffer like this," Herb said.

"We don't want anything bad to happen to you," Marilyn said. "Howell will be devastated, and so will we."

Howell called every day to find out how I was doing. Then one evening he had some exciting news, we had received a letter from Zaire. He was desperate for something that might cheer me up, and he was sure this would do it. He knew how happy getting news from Josée or Papa always made me. The letter, he said, was from Josée. I felt overcome by pangs of fear, but I urged him to read me the letter right away. When he opened it, he noticed that it was written in kiSwahili, which was unusual because Josée usually wrote in French. Instantly, my heart sank.

"Who is dead, oh dear lord?" I mumbled to myself as I urged Howell to try to read the kiSwahili that he could not understand.

He began to awkwardly sound out the words. He stopped when he heard me gasp. When he asked what the problem was, I responded sharply, "Just read." He didn't understand but continued. He read until I dropped the phone. I shrieked, I wailed, I bent over and shook from the pain. Marilyn raced into the room and held me tight. And poor Howell on the other end had no idea what he had just read to me.

Josée's letter started by asking me how we were doing. She was concerned about how I was feeling since I had written to her about my illness. She wrote, "We are only passengers on this earth, everyone has a time to live and a time to die. Be courageous because if you of all people begin to panic, I will lose the little courage I have left. People here who know about the situation have told me not to tell you about it, because you will be devastated. But I couldn't keep such a thing from you, my oldest, dearest friend. I will tell you, and somehow you will find the strength to carry on."

Josée's letter talked about Mémé, her fifth child (she had had a fourth child, Jean-Marc, who died in infancy from unknown causes). Mémé appeared healthy at first but started getting sick around age five months. She would have a few weeks or months of good health, but then the illnesses would come back again and again. The doctors were baffled and decided to do a number of diagnostic tests. Finally, they found the cause of her recurrent illnesses. Mémé's infections were what doctors call opportunistic. "Her immune system wasn't functioning well. She is infected with HIV. She has AIDS. The doctors then tested the whole family. The other children are fine, but Lolo and I have tested positive." My beloved Josée was infected with HIV, a gift of her husband and his infidelities. She and Lolo were healthy— for now. But we knew all too well what awaited them. The nightmare had begun.

Suddenly, my pain was not so mysterious anymore. And my sweet and innocent life was gone forever. I was living my big sister's pain, my "mother's" pain. I started to see life in a very different way. I prayed for miracles. Oddly enough, after I got the news from Josée, the nightmares became less frequent, and I began to sleep better and have fewer headaches. I felt ready to return to my home and husband in New York. I wanted desperately to speak with Josée, but it was next to impossible to arrange a telephone connection with Kolwezi. When Josée wrote that they were headed to Kinshasa for experimental medical treatment, I managed to successfully place a call to the Kinshasa home of my cousin Emérence, where they were staying. I tried very much not to cry over the phone, I didn't want to disappoint Josée and make her feel that she needed to give me support. I wanted to be strong enough to give her the love and encouragement that she so desperately needed. She was thrilled to hear from me. As hard as I tried to boost her morale, I could tell that she was doing all she could to give me hope.

"So, when are you going to give me a grandchild?" Josée joked.

"Soon enough, *dada*. I'm still taking medicine for my headaches; so I'll have to wait till that's finished."

"Well, you tell Howell that we're anxious to see the heir to his throne. I can't wait to hold your baby in my arms."

I couldn't go on talking small talk. "*Dada*, please take care of yourself. You need to stay confident, just like Papa always told us during the wars. We made it through that, and we're going to make it through this. Don't you ever doubt it." I pleaded with her to always keep me posted on her news, not to hold anything back from me. After that call, I wrote often, and we sent them vitamins and the latest information from the United States on AIDS treatments.

With Howell's love and support, love from my American families, good medicine, and the knowledge that I had to be strong for Josée, I got better and fully recovered. I went back to school full-time to complete my bachelor's degree in business administration. Howell and I then decided that the time was right to start our family. Amazingly, we managed to conceive in our very first month of trying.

Josée was ecstatic. "Thank you so much," she wrote. "Now I will soon be a 'grandma.' I feel like I have done my job with you. You will soon be a mother, and no one in the world is happier for you than I am."

I wrote to her about every development of my pregnancy, hoping to give her something happy to think about. I even sent her our baby's first picture, the sonogram taken of my womb. Three months into my pregnancy, I was able to share with her more exciting news: I had just participated in the graduation ceremonies for Baruch College. Her little sister had a degree from an American university!

Since Howell and I had decided to raise our children Jewish, we knew that we both had to learn more about the religion, particularly because so much of Judaism is practiced in the home. During my pregnancy, we took a six-month class in basic Judaism at New York's 92nd Street Y. We learned a great deal about *Torah, Shabbat,* the Jewish holidays, and the ethical values of the Jewish people. We decided together that we would start celebrating *Shabbat* with a special dinner and prayers in our home every Friday night.

At the end of November, as I waddled around our apartment in my ninth month, a minor miracle occurred: for the first time, Josée was able to place a call to us from Kolwezi. She had tried dozens of times before without success.

"I want to know everything about your delivery," she told me. "I'm praying for you, Geolo." Before we hung up, she told me that her two girls, Sandra and Mémé, were hoping I'd have a girl, while Bob and Rocky, her sons, were definitely pulling for a boy.

Just two days later, on the second of December at 2:22 A.M., after a grueling forty-three hours of labor, our first child, a healthy nine-pound boy, was born. With great pride, we named him Alex after Howell's beloved Uncle Al, who had passed away the previous year. Uncle Al and Aunt Arlene had done many kind and generous things for me, and they had welcomed me into the family with great love and affection.

In a remarkable twist of fate, during the week of Alex's birth, Lolo was traveling to Tucson, Arizona, where the Zairian mining company had sent him for an intensive training program. Like Kolwezi, the Tucson area has some of the world's biggest copper mines. It was Lolo's first trip to North America. When he called from Tucson, we learned that his schedule was tight, but he did have one free day, which turned out to be the eighth day of our son's life. That was a very special day for all of us, because it is on the eighth day of life that Jewish boys go through the ritual of *brit milah*, the covenant of circumcision. Howell sent Lolo an airplane ticket for New York, and he got to be with us on that very special day; he was the first one from my family in Zaire to meet my husband and son. Lolo was tired from his travels, but he looked fit and healthy. We didn't talk about the virus or the medical treatments he, Josée, and Mémé were receiving. We talked, instead, of good times and, mostly, about Alex.

Lolo even got to participate in the ceremony: He held baby

Alex at the start of the prayers and, after the deed was done, he offered a toast to the baby and his parents on behalf of all the family members in Zaire. We had a beautiful ceremony in our home, with about twenty-five friends and family members in attendance. Some people thought that it would be difficult for me to witness this minor surgery performed on my baby, but it didn't really upset me. Just about every boy was circumcised in Zaire, and it seemed to me a perfectly normal thing to do. And the prayers and blessings brought beautiful meaning to the occasion. Lolo had to leave just three hours after the ceremony, but we were able to send with him photographs and a videotape of baby Alex, which Josée would treasure.

After Alex's birth, we began to observe *Shabbat* every Friday night and other Jewish holidays over the course of the year. "I'm happy to do this for my son and for my husband," I told myself. But, after a while, a funny thing happened: I started to look forward to every *Shabbat* and each of the holidays for me.

Two months after Alex's birth, I was getting a prescription filled in the pharmacy down the block from our apartment. Marilyn, who had come up from Florida to see her grandson, ran into the store to tell me that I had a telephone call from Zaire. Knowing how hard it was to establish telephone contact, I raced back to the apartment. As I picked up the phone, my heart was pounding from the physical exertion—and from a combination of excitement and fear. I felt immense relief when I heard the voice on the other end: it was Josée.

"Hello, *dada?* How are you?" I said.

"*Da* Geolo," Josée said, pausing a second to control herself. "Mémé is dead." Josée began to cry. After a moment of shock, I dropped the phone to the floor. I sat on the floor, grabbed my head with both hands, and rocked back and forth while crying loudly. When I came to my senses, I picked up the phone, but, by then, the connection had been cut. I dropped to the floor and began wailing again.

"Please, dear God, let her live, let her live," I repeated over and over again. "Don't let her die."

May her soul forgive me, but at that moment I was not praying for she who we had just lost. I'd only seen Mémé on one trip, when she was an infant. I didn't really know her or have lots of memories of her. I cried for the niece I would never know. I cried for the terrible pain her death was undoubtedly causing my family. But, most of all, I cried for my fear, my terror that I would soon lose my beloved Josée.

Soon, the phone rang. Josée had gotten through again.

"I'm sorry, *da* Geolo," she said. "I couldn't help it. I felt I needed to tell you right away. I knew I'd get some comfort after talking with you."

I did my best to give her that comfort. I thanked her for letting me know right away and reminded her that she should never keep any bad news from me. I told her again and again that she needed to focus on all the positive things remaining in her life, that she had to be strong to take care of her three beautiful children. We promised to write soon.

After Mémé's death, Josée grew deeply depressed. Lolo realized that she needed to get away. He managed to scrape together enough money to buy her a round trip airplane ticket to New York. We were expecting her sometime in June of 1990, but we didn't know the exact date of her arrival. One morning, as I got out of the shower, the phone rang.

"Hello," said a strange male voice. "There's a lady here who wants to talk with you."

"Allo, *da* Geolo?" My heart jumped as I recognized Josée's voice.

"*Dada*, where are you calling from?" I asked with excitement.

"I'm here, and I'm trying to get a taxi," she said.

"Are you in Kinshasa?" I asked, not really understanding.

"No, I'm here at JFK Airport. Didn't you receive the two letters I sent you in April?"

My heart soared. "Good heavens, she's here!" Knowing how taxi drivers can take advantage of foreigners who don't speak English, I told her to stay at the airport and went to pick her up. The letters she had sent informing us of her itinerary arrived three weeks after she did.

On the first night of her visit, Josée shared terrible news with me: she had recently heard that our younger brother Benjamin had been killed in a town near the Zambian border. The rumor was that he had been doing something illegal when he was killed. He was thirty years old. Neither Josée nor Papa nor I had seen him in over ten years. Despite the sad news, the rest of Josée's visit was all upbeat. I don't think Lolo could have imagined how much good this trip would do for his wife. Just the sight of her adoring little sister picked up her spirits enormously. She got to hold and cuddle and tickle and spoil her baby nephew. She got a chance to establish a deep, enduring friendship with her sister's husband. Plus, she got to meet all our friends, Howell's family, and my American family, the Waites. She even got to see, for the first time in nine years, Robin, her old buddy from CRS-Lubumbashi. Robin and her husband Brian had recently moved back to the United States and were expecting their first child. Josée got to see all the tourist attractions in New York City and plenty others in Washington, D.C. She celebrated Independence Day in grand style, as we watched together the spectacular fireworks display over New York's East River. In the middle of her stay, we bought her a plane ticket to British Columbia, where she was able to spend precious time with her dearest friend, *da* Jacquis, and her family.

Josée was scheduled to stay for one month, but we talked her into staying for two. When that period came to an end, I asked her to add another few weeks, but she said it was time to go. She had to get back to help the children prepare for school. How much stronger she looked on the day of her return compared to her arrival! She had an amazing adventure in North America, and her zest for life had been recharged. As we embraced to say goodbye at the airport, she started to cry. I tried to control myself, to be strong, but soon the tears fell down my cheeks as well.

"Don't worry," Josée whispered into my ear. "We'll grow old and start talking like this," she said, mimicking the voice of an old woman. We both laughed through our tears. As she passed through the doors leading to her plane and disappeared from our view, the tears poured down my face. Howell held me tight.

Five months after Josée's return to Zaire, I received a letter from her in which she told me that our baby sister Jeanne had passed away at the age of twenty-nine. She had lost a lot of weight and fallen ill repeatedly in her last months. I would later learn that her death was due to an AIDS-related illness.

After giving birth to our son, I worked as a part-time teller at a credit union near our home. By the summer of 1991, we were able to save enough money to plan a trip to Zaire. But before leaving, I had to take care of one very important piece of paperwork: my application for American citizenship. I had passed the probation period for aliens who married citizens and was finally eligible. I aced the civics test, and, on May 29, 1991, I swore an oath of allegiance to this amazing country, which had been so good to me. I felt great pride in becoming the latest in a long line of immigrants to find refuge in this beautiful land. I felt little sadness about losing my Zairian citizenship. How could I regret rejecting the duties and privileges of being a citizen in Mobutu-land? Of all his crimes and sins, perhaps the greatest was the degree to which he destroyed hope for a better day in our homeland. No, my only regret was that the rest of my family could not be by my side swearing allegiance to the United States of America.

CHAPTER 26

OUT
OF CONTROL

With each new year of the 1980s in Zaire, everyone said it was impossible. There was absolutely no way the economic situation could deteriorate further. But every year it did. While their president was consistently ranked among the richest men in the world, the people of this fabulously wealthy country had one of the lowest standards of living on the planet. There seemed to be little hope of improvement. To make matters worse, Zaire was the epicenter of the international AIDS epidemic, which had already claimed my young niece, my baby sister, and now threatened my big sister and thousands upon thousands of young people of every social strata.

Everyone hated Mobutu, but somehow he held on. Then the winds of change swept the world, and even Mobutu could not stay the course. The Soviet Union disintegrated and, with it, the Cold War and Mobutu's role as a bulwark against Communism. Dictators across the globe were being chased from power: Duvalier, Marcos, and, even Mobutu's dear friend, Ceausescu of Romania. A videotape of the rebel assassination of Ceausescu and his hated wife made the rounds of nearly every Kinshasa home with a VCR, and the people fantasized about a bloody but happy ending to their nightmare. But Mobutu was a genius at keeping power. He knew he had to bend, but he figured he was wily enough to figure out how not to break. So he opened the system up.

Howell and I had read about all the changes going on in Zaire before our 1991 trip, but we were shocked at what we saw from the moment we arrived at the Kinshasa airport. Every Zairian man seemed to be wearing a tie, and many women were wearing pants. People were calling each other by their Christian names in public and even on state television. Newspapers criticizing the president were being sold openly. A slew of new political parties were being formed, and plans for a convention to write a new constitution were being openly debated.

The Guide of the Nation could have bowed out at this time and turned power over to a new generation. Despite his murderous, thieving past, he might have received some shred of credit from the history books. Instead, he could not shake off his addiction to power. He believed only he could guide the nation, which he seemed to regard as his own personal property. He might some day be the late president, he once said, but he would never be the ex-president. And, damn him, he succeeded in dividing and manipulating the opposition and stalling all meaningful efforts at political and economic reform. Without being able to play the Communism card any more, he had little sway in Western capitals, and the great capitalist powers, repulsed by Mobutu's crudeness, quickly cut off all economic assistance to his beleaguered government. That only made things worse for the people, but Mobutu never cared about that.

At the airport in Lubumbashi, we anxiously awaited the opportunity to see Josée, Lolo, and their three children. But first we had to pass through Customs, where the officials pounced on us like a lion on its prey. They tried every trick in their long book of corruption to get us to pay a bribe for the privilege of exiting the airport. Through a combination of guile and pretend ignorance, we fended off all their maneuvers. Then, they pulled out their trump card: "But, *monsieur*, you have a camera and camcorder. How do we know that you did not buy these goods in Zaire without paying the appropriate taxes? That is a very serious offense."

Little did they know that they were dealing with a white man who had no interest in paying a bribe and enough experience in traveling through Zaire to outwit them. Howell calmly pulled from his pocket the original receipts for the camera and camcorder from the New York store where we had bought them. The customs thieves gave up and released us into the excited arms of Josée, Lolo, Sandra, Bob, and Rocky. We were delighted to see them all looking so well.

We spent three days in Lubumbashi at the home of *da* Louise, Maman's oldest daughter. Maman and her two other daughters in Lubumbashi came by to see me, their in-law from America, and, of course, the star of the show, baby Alex. Everyone was very happy that they could communicate with Howell in French and Lingala, because none of them spoke English.

On our second day in Lubumbashi, Lolo took us to visit the town's synagogue. The rabbi, a dapper-looking, white-haired man in his seventies, was happy to have visitors. He took us on a tour of the beautiful synagogue and the adjoining Chaim Weizmann Social Center. The rabbi was of Italian origin; he had come to the Belgian Congo in the 1930s after studying in Palestine. He charmed us with stories of the 1950s, the golden era of Katangese Jewry, when there were as many as 2,000 Jews in town. Just a few months prior to our visit, he told us, a Jewish family had moved to South Africa; there were now only about a dozen Jews left. "Though I no longer have much work to do," he said, "this has been my home for decades, and I wouldn't feel comfortable anywhere else."

"I don't have any regrets," the rabbi repeated over and over again with a charming smile. "I've had a wonderful, fulfilling life here."

Later that day, Josée and I tried to visit Mama Apoline, who had moved to Lubumbashi to live with Gilbert several years before. Josée told me that Gilbert had recently died from a mysterious illness.

We couldn't find Mama Apoline's house, and there had been many stories circulating about Mobutu's commandos killing people in the streets at night; so we decided to head back to *da* Louise's house. The next day, fortunately, we were visited by Pascaline, the child Mama Apoline had just before breaking up with Papa. I gave her presents that I had brought from America for Mama Apoline. As an adult and a mother, I had come to a greater appreciation of all the good things Mama Apoline had done for us during the war years and how we might not have survived without her courage.

A few days later, we left with Josée and her family for Kolwezi. After less than a half hour on the road, Lolo's car broke down. Like all car owners in Shaba, he had been reduced to buying gasoline from street vendors; business was too unreliable for a real gasoline company to serve the Lubumbashi market. Unfortunately, the street vendors often adulterated the gasoline with cheaper liquids. Whatever concoction they had sold Lolo had clogged his engine, and the car chugged to a stop. While Lolo went looking for a mechanic, we waited by the roadside. I started to take video pictures of the kids playing together. Then Josée reminded me that we were just across the street from the university campus where, only a few months before, Mobutu's commandos had massacred more than twenty student activists in their sleep. I put the camcorder back in its bag.

Fortunately, the mechanic was able to fix the car, and we arrived, two hours later, at my aunt Salome's house in the town of Likasi. My aunt and uncle threw a tremendous party for us, but the highlight of the day was when I presented my baby Alex to my grandmother *bibi* Marguerite, who lived with Mama Salome. *Bibi* Marguerite was in her mid-eighties—she had been born when Congo was the personal property of King Leopold—but her mind was as alert and vigorous as ever. *Bibi* Marguerite, Mama Salome, me, and baby Alex—four generations together for one brief moment. How much I regretted that Alex wasn't old enough that he would remember being held by his great-grandmother.

From Likasi we moved on to Kolwezi, where more parties awaited us. While there, Lolo took us way down under the ground to visit one of the copper mines that his company exploited, and then he showed us one of its massive open-pit mines. So much natural wealth in the land and so little of it being used for the benefit of the people. My disgust for Mobutu grew even greater.

We then took a two-week trip to Kinshasa to see family members and friends of mine, as well as some of Howell's friends from his Peace Corps days. The capital was all abuzz with political rhetoric, as the new parties jockeyed for position at the upcoming constitutional convention. Mobutu rarely showed his face now in public; he started spending most of his time on his luxurious yacht docked in the Zaire River. Rumors were spreading that he didn't feel comfortable being in the presidential palace, since the two leopards in his private park around the palace had died suddenly.

"Those two leopards had inside them his magical powers. Now they're dead, so his magical powers are also gone," people said.

The city that had once been called "petit Paris" was now a giant eyesore. The roads were chockful of potholes; more than a few were so deep that you, if you drove into them, you needed a tow truck to get your car out. Many more people seemed to be living on the streets, begging for a handout. Everyone was obsessed by fears of crimes like muggings and carjackings which, previously unheard of, were becoming increasingly common. I visited my school, ISP/Gombe, and found the buildings and grounds decaying. Worse yet, my beloved basketball court was gone, covered by a hideous looking building.

We came back to Kolwezi one week before Howell had to return to his job in New York; Alex and I were going to stay for another two months. At the end of the week, *da* Louise and her husband Martin, who were visiting in Kolwezi, gave us a ride in their Toyota back to Lubumbashi, where Howell would catch his flight. When we arrived in Lubumbashi late in the afternoon, we drove right into the tail end of a political rally that had gotten out of control.

Newly legalized political parties were jockeying for power and influence in whatever government came out of the constitutional convention. The *UFERI* party, headed by Mobutu's old aide and scapegoat, Nguza Karl I Bond, had quickly established itself as the dominant party in Shaba. *UFERI* tried to flex its muscles with public rallies, but many of the unemployed, unruly young males of Shaba saw the breakdown in authoritarianism and the call for public participation in politics as an opportunity to run wild. After *UFERI* rallies, young hooligans would linger on the streets, making a lot of noise and harassing all who got in their way.

Within a few blocks of *da* Louise's house, we tried to take an early turn down a side street to avoid the mob ahead of us. Suddenly, a group of at least a dozen menacing young men cut us off, standing in the road in front of and around the car, forcing Martin to stop moving. They tried to pry open the car doors, which Martin had locked shut. Then they started banging on the roof and rocking the car, back and forth as if it were a cradle. When the mob realized that there was a white man inside, more rushed to assault the car. In their minds, a white skin meant lots of money to share with them. Howell and I tried to stay calm, but with Alex in the car, we were clearly on the verge of panicking.

"Martin, please give them money fast," said *da* Louise in kiSwahili. "Give them whatever you have. Who knows what they might do with a foreigner in the car? The poor man came all this way to see us, we've got to get him home safely. Give them the money, get rid of them!"

Martin reached into his pocket and pulled out some cash. As soon as he rolled down the window and handed over the money, the rocking stopped. The punks gathered around their leader and shared their loot, while hooting and hollering over what a good time they'd just had. We got to *da* Louise's house, safe but shaken.

When we decided to visit Zaire, some journalists were reporting that the country was a powderkeg, ready to blow up at any moment and relive the horrors of the 1960s. But we had heard that sort of talk just about every year since the mid-1970s. We had both lived in Zaire and felt secure during years when journalists were predicting war. We were simply not going to let unsubstantiated rumors keep us from seeing my family and our friends. After the incident in the car, however, we began to feel more vulnerable. I'm sure Howell was terrified at the thought of leaving his wife and infant son in Zaire at a time of such turmoil. But there was no way I was going to leave without seeing Papa and spending more time with Josée. Though I barely believed it myself, I assured Howell that this had been an isolated incident and that, with a little Zairian street smarts, of which I had plenty, I could avoid more serious trouble.

We had hoped to travel together to Kongolo to see Papa, but the unpredictability of transportation in Zaire ruined our plans. There was only one flight a week from Lubumbashi to Kongolo, and there were many weeks when it was canceled. There were also rumors going around that the air service to Kongolo was about to be terminated. The alternative was to take the train, which was now running only about once a month. The trains and the railroads had been so poorly maintained that what had once been a two-day trip now took a week, even two weeks. Conditions on the overcrowded train were uncomfortable, to say the least. It used to be possible to make the trip by truck or car, but, since the 1970s, many of the roads had become impassable, and the bridges had collapsed. If we made it to Kongolo, there was a very real chance that we'd be stuck there for several weeks. Howell could not afford to be late for work, so he had to return without seeing Papa.

Papa was getting older, his eyesight wasn't that good, and we didn't want him to make the risky trip to the south of Shaba. Besides, communication with Kongolo was so poor that it would have been difficult to arrange such a trip in time. The only way I could see Papa was to head off for Kongolo. I decided that I could not risk Alex's safety on such a trip, so I left him with Josée. I brought with me dozens of photographs, so Papa could see what his grandchild looked like.

After Howell's departure, I lucked out: the flight to Kongolo was still operating, and one was leaving that week. I bought a ticket the day before the plane's scheduled departure. When I arrived the next day at the Lubumbashi airport, I was told that, overnight, the cost of the ticket had more than doubled and that, if I didn't pay the difference immediately, I would lose my seat. Luckily, I had enough money to get on board.

Papa expected me to visit that summer, but he had no idea when I'd be arriving in Kongolo. When the plane landed, I met at the airport a prominent businessman who had known me as a little girl. He volunteered to drive me to the house where Papa now lived, just outside of the downtown area.

"I'm glad to see you turned into a lovely lady," the businessman said as we drove. He laughed and added, "You used to be quite a tomboy, do you remember that? Your sister was much more serious than you were. But look at you now, married with a child. Well, Monsieur Benoit sure knew what he was doing when he sent you to school like boys. I wish I'd done the same with my girls."

Papa wasn't home when I arrived, but *ma* Feza greeted me warmly. She told me he was off tending his fields just outside of town and would be back later in the day. Excited about being back in the town of my childhood, I dropped off my bags and headed out to explore the streets of Kongolo, circa 1991. As I walked, I noticed that many children stopped to stare at me as if I were a white person or some such thing. I stared back, hoping to find something of "me" in them, or at least to understand why they found me so odd a sight. They started pointing at me, and then I understood. They were fascinated by my pants, they obviously hadn't seen many women wearing slacks. After all, Mobutu had outlawed trousers on women for more than a decade-and-a-half and had only recently rescinded his decree. While many women in Kinshasa and Lubumbashi were now wearing

pants, the new fashion hadn't quite reached this far into the interior of
the country yet. I smiled at them and said, *"Hamjambo. Habari gani?*
[Hello! How are you?]" Their faces lit up, as they turned to each other
and said *"Anajua kiswahili, anajua kiswahili* [She knows kiSwahili; she
knows kiSwahili]."

As I continued my walk, I saw that the population of Kongolo
had increased tremendously since my childhood. New houses had
sprung up everywhere. There were barely any trees left where Josée
and I used to roam. All along the Kangoy River, behind our old house
downtown, where once there were banana, cassava, and palm fields,
now I saw row after row of houses. Everything looked, of course, so
much smaller than it had before. Now that I'd scaled the Empire State
Building, how funny it seemed that I used to stand in awe beside our
two-story house in Kongolo.

"Someday, I will show all this to Howell and Alex," I said to
myself. "Maybe one day, one day when things work again and transportation is safe and easier like it was in the sixties."

I re-traced all the paths Josée and I used to take. When I
passed by *kambo* Colette's old house on *Avenue Kindu,* I said a
prayer for the soul of that kind and wise woman. I couldn't resist the
urge to put my ear against the railroad tracks to listen for oncoming
trains, just as Josée, Misère, Benjamin, and I had done so many times
so many years ago.

Of course, the train arrived much less often now than it did in
my childhood. However, outside of the increase in population and
houses, the thing that amazed me the most about Kongolo was how
little it had changed, how little it had developed since Independence.
While the rest of the world surfed the information highway, the people of Kongolo still had no paved roads, no television, and, outside of
a handful of well-to-do businessmen, no telephones and no electricity.
The great majority of homes had no running water either; men were
still sending their women and children to gather water at rivers, wells,
and springs, and then carry the buckets home on their heads. Papa

was one of the lucky ones who had running water in his compound. His neighbors said they were blessed, because they could always rely on getting water from Papa Benoit's faucet.

When I arrived back at Papa's house, he was there waiting for me. I ran to him and gave him a great big hug. He hugged me back shyly and said, "Is it really you *kambo*? I can't believe you are really here. Welcome, *kambo,* welcome."

"He didn't believe me when I told him that you were here," *ma* Feza said with a smile. "He almost got angry at me for making such a bad joke. But then I showed him your bags. Then he believed me. He's been walking back and forth, back and forth, saying, 'When is she coming home? When is she coming home?'"

I pulled out my photographs, and *ma* Feza and Papa invited half the neighborhood in to see Papa Benoit's grandchildren. Then, I really thrilled them by bringing out the camcorder. Papa didn't have a VCR, of course, but I was able to replay some scenes I had taped in Kolwezi for Papa to see through the viewfinder. He couldn't hear them talk, and he could barely see the tiny picture, but he did see his grandchildren move. I then gave Papa some presents from Josée and me.

"You shouldn't bother yourselves like that," he said, as he always said when we gave him gifts. "All I want is to know that you girls are doing well. And when you can come visit, like you are doing now, I am the happiest father on earth."

For a few hours we just enjoyed our reunion, but that night, Papa told me that he had been having some strange dreams recently about my visit. "In my dreams, when you arrived in Kongolo, I saw you but you couldn't see me. I started to wonder if the dreams meant that I would be dead before your arrival." As I listened to his fears, I wanted so much to talk with him about the terror looming over Josée, to get some comfort and wisdom from him. I had asked Josée in Kolwezi whether she wanted me to tell him she has HIV.

"What's the point of it?" she had said. "It will only bring him lots of grief. Why don't we wait and see, maybe some medicine will be invented. Then we wouldn't have worried him for nothing." She had given me a letter for Papa, in which she didn't mention HIV. I didn't tell him either. I had a feeling this was a mistake, but I didn't want to disrespect Josée's wishes.

Papa was working with some Greeks selling farm products. He showed me another house he was building on his compound, so that when we visited him with our families we would have a big enough place to stay. During the days, Misère and her husband and daughter would come to visit, and, at night, Papa and I would stay up late sharing all the news of the years apart. Almost every day that I was there, I got gifts from Papa's "relatives." Almost every one of them told me stories about how Papa had helped them during hard times. How proud I felt of him.

He still looked strong and handsome, but some nights, in the middle of a conversation, he'd fall asleep in his chair. It was then I studied him more closely, to see how the years had caught up with him. His hair was now all white, and, though still lean and strong, his biceps didn't quite bulge as they used to. *Ma* Feza told me that he was not going to visit his beloved farm on the other side of the Lualaba River much any more; the long walk was starting to fatigue him.

I used to take for granted all the things that my father did for us. Sometimes I even resented his rules and regulations, his strict discipline, and his constant exhortations to study harder. As I grew up and saw how many parents lacked discipline, and the harm this did to their children, I came to respect him greatly. But it was when I became a mother that I came to truly cherish him and all that he had done for me. I had no doubt that Papa loved us more than anything in his life. His love was gentle and, at the same time, his discipline was tough. It's a fine line between the two, but he walked it with the greatest of skill.

After eight days, I had to leave Kongolo. There was a plane coming in and, not knowing when the next one might arrive, I couldn't pass this one up. I was anxious to get back to Kolwezi and see Alex. *Ma* Feza smoked some of the chickens their friends had given me to take back to Josée. The airport workers knew Papa well, and they let him take me up the airplane stairs to see me off. Papa, of course, asked me to send his regards to his old friend, *bibi* Thérèse. When it was time for me to go into the plane I couldn't resist giving him a great big hug. In our culture, this was not something that adult women did to their fathers in such a public place. As I put my arms around him and squeezed, he was a little taken aback. There was a brief silence, but when I let go of him, I saw in his wet eyes that he understood my feelings. He looked at me with that smile he used to have when his two little girls would pull off his socks and play with his toes.

I found Alex doing very well in Kolwezi. His Mama Josée and cousin Sandra had taken wonderful care of him. In fact, he was chubbier than he ever had been before, so he must have liked whatever they were feeding him. The rest of our stay in Kolwezi was calm and pleasant. I tried, on several occasions to give Josée an opportunity to talk with me about her health, her fears, her wishes, but it seemed like we never had a chance to be alone.

A few days before we were to leave for Lubumbashi, we heard stories about riots breaking out in Kinshasa. It wasn't the thieves or unemployed masses who were rebelling—it was Mobutu's own soldiers. Apparently, they hadn't been paid for several months, and they couldn't take it any more. There were some television and radio news reports about gangs of soldiers looting Kinshasa stores, but the journalists continued to give the lion's share of coverage to the negotiations for the constitutional convention. Caught up in the emotions of my last few days with Josée, I didn't pay much attention to Kinshasa's troubles.

On my last night in Kolwezi, Josée and I stayed up late. We talked about the war years. We squeezed each other's hands as we recalled the gunfire, the dead bodies and the chaos of everyone fleeing from Kongolo. We raised our glasses and offered a toast to Mama Apoline as we remembered her unbelievable courage in placing her body in front of the rifles soldiers were aiming at us. Josée teased me about how I used to limp from my sores on our trek to Samba. I teased her about how Honoré the Katangese soldier was going to take her home to be his son's fiancée. She tried to capture for me the terror of the moment when she heard the sniper's gun go off and saw Papa fall into the Kangoy River.

I wanted to tell her the terror I was feeling as I saw her forming the bull's-eye for a different type of assassin. I wanted to tell her that, surely, if God had saved us from all the dangers we faced during the wars, surely He had a plan for us and, just as surely, that plan couldn't possibly include taking her away at such a young age. I wanted to tell her that we were strong, hardened by our experience as refugees, and that we could and would overcome this latest crisis. But I didn't tell her these things. She wasn't ready to talk about it. Every time I tried to bring it up, she'd quickly change the subject. As hard as it was to talk openly about AIDS in the United States, it was even harder in Zaire. People in Zaire had all sorts of horrible misconceptions about the disease, and they made life extremely difficult for anyone known to be infected with HIV. Even after people died from AIDS, their relatives would usually say it was something else, anything else that had caused the death.

Josée and her three children came with us to Lubumbashi, where we were scheduled to catch the plane to Kinshasa three days later. From Kinshasa we'd fly to Paris and then New York. In the morning, we left Alex with *da* Louise, and Josée and I headed downtown to re-confirm my flight at the *Air Zaire* office. When we got there, we noticed a great deal of commotion inside. Many people were arguing with each other and with the *Air Zaire* staff. Trying to ignore the hubbub, we made our way to the counter and calmly asked the clerk to confirm that I had a seat on the plane.

With an air of condescension, the clerk responded, "Don't you know that all the flights to Kinshasa have been canceled?"

"What?" Josée asked. "How can all the flights to Kinshasa be canceled?"

"Ndjili Airport has been closed. Haven't you heard the news?

The soldiers in Kinshasa have mutinied. They took over the airport."

Josée and I looked at each other in terror. Had it all gotten out of control so quickly? Could this be the start of another war? Finally, after all these years of suffering, was the great rebellion against Mobutu about to begin? And were we going to get out of it alive? My one thought was my baby boy. He was American, he shouldn't have anything to do with this nightmare. I had to get him out. I spoke to the clerk with the same fury I had seen in the other customers.

"Listen, I've got an *Air Zaire* flight from Kinshasa to Paris that I have to catch."

"The airport is closed, *madame*," he said, with no hint of apology.

"But you've got to get me to Paris. I paid for it. What are you going to do for me?"

"I can get you on a flight to Johannesburg tomorrow. From there we can put you on a flight to Paris."

"Great, that's great. When does the flight leave from Johannesburg?"

"I don't know, *madame*."

"What do you mean, you don't know? Look at the schedule."

"All the regular schedules have been put on hold, *madame*. I have no idea when they'll get to the Paris flight. Maybe the next day, maybe the next week."

"I guess I have no choice. Where will you be putting me up in Johannesburg?

"We won't be putting you up in Johannesburg, *madame*."

"But I have a baby with me. I don't know anyone in Johannesburg. I don't have any money for a hotel."

"That's your problem, *madame*."

Around us, people were talking about the looting and shootings the previous night in Kolwezi. We quickly left the *Air Zaire* office to grab a taxi to the home of a friend of Josée; from there Josée called Lolo in Kolwezi to make sure he was okay. He was home, safe, and he said that it appeared that calm had returned to the city. "Last night was terrible. The soldiers went on a rampage. They were looting and ransacking all of the downtown stores. Once they finished there, they broke into homes and hauled off televisions, radios, jewelry, even furniture."

"They tried to break into our home," he went on, "but the bars on the windows kept them out. I heard them shouting, it sounded like they were all drunk. They broke quite a few of the windows, but they couldn't get in. I stayed up the whole night, expecting them to crash through the doors. But, from what I hear, they're sleeping it off today, and the officers are trying to reassert discipline. I think we've seen the worst of it."

I didn't want to take any chances that the worst of it was yet to come. I took Josée to the nearby American Consulate and asked for their help. The consular officials had already gone into crisis mode and were trying to get all Americans out of town. They were extremely kind and assured me that they would get Alex and me out of Zaire safely. The best bet would be a Zambian Airways flight to Lusaka, Zambia, that was leaving in two days. From there the U.S. Embassy would figure out how to get us to Paris. The consular officials promised that they would arrange for my tickets and travel to the airport. They asked me to return to the Consulate a few hours before the scheduled departure time; if more trouble broke out, however, they would try to come to *da* Louise's house to get me.

From the Consulate, Josée and I decided to head to Rwashi Parish to visit with Father Albert. It seemed like this would be my last opportunity to see him. On the taxi ride to the parish, we saw many merchants hurriedly closing their stores. As we passed a market, early in the day when business should have just started picking up, we saw sellers were closing their stalls and packing up their goods. I began to wonder whether we shouldn't have headed straight home to *da* Louise's.

At the parish, an elderly Zairian man told us that Father Albert had moved to another parish and no longer lived there. "Be careful, ladies," he warned us. "I just heard that the soldiers have arrived down-town. They've already started looting."

We grabbed a taxi, but, unfortunately, we had to pass through the downtown area to get home. A few blocks from the heart of the city, we started hearing loud, popping sounds, first one pop, then two pops, then a whole string of them. We recognized the sound, we'd heard it before: gunfire. The taxi driver put on the brakes, "I'm not going any further."

"Alright," Josée told him. "Turn around and drop us at my friend's house." As she gave the driver the address, I fought back the urge to shout at him to keep going. I wanted him to race through down-town, past the soldiers, so I could get home and make sure my baby was safe. I was not going to let my baby go through a war as I had done.

Then I turned to Josée and realized that she did not have an American passport, she did not have my freedom to get away. Dear Lord, as if what she was going through wasn't enough, now she and her family also had to endure the horrors of war. "How I wish you and the children could flee with Alex and me!"

We got to her friend's house safely and spent the next few hours sitting on the floor, hoping to avoid any bullets that might crash through the windows. Finally we heard no more of the popping sounds. Early that evening, when all seemed calm, Josée's friend's hus-band drove us safely back to *da* Louise's house.

Everyone stayed inside that night and all the next day as well. If this was going to be the next big war, it was going to be quite differ-ent from the wars of the '60s. We watched television scenes of sol-diers in Kinshasa crashing through store windows and exiting with large televisions, stereos, and appliances in their arms. Of course, some people said it was the television coverage of the riots in Kinshasa that inspired the riots in Shaba. The television news also featured appeals by generals and leading opposition politicians, pleading with the soldiers to go back to their barracks for the good of the nation. By the second day, some sense of normalcy had returned to

Lubumbashi. Small stores and markets began to re-open, though they still closed several hours earlier than usual. More people took to the streets.

Despite the seeming calm in the city, on the day of our flight to Lusaka, tension palpable to each breath hung in the air. As Martin drove Josée, Alex, and me to the American Consulate, we passed by the devastated downtown area. Row after row of battered buildings and stores, some charred by fire, most with windows shattered or doors smashed off their hinges lined the streets. There were no goods visible in store windows. I clutched Alex close and was thankful when we made it to the Consulate without running into any trouble. The officers there allowed Josée to come with us to the airport, so she joined me and about fifteen other fleeing Yankees in a mini-van for the ride. It was a quiet trip; everyone was on edge and spoke little. Arriving safely at our destination brought a small measure of relief.

At the airport, as we sat nervously in a waiting room, Josée did her best to keep me from worrying. "Looks like the soldiers have gotten it out of their system," she said. "Things have really calmed down. Now that there's public opposition to Mobutu, people will put their energies into politics. Everyone remembers what the '60s were like, believe me. Nobody wants another war. It won't happen. We'll be fine."

She reached over to pat my hand reassuringly. However, I couldn't keep my mind off the other "war" we were fighting. I looked at her beseechingly. "*Dada*, please don't ever keep anything from me. I'd rather know the worst news than to be left in the dark. Don't hide anything from me."

She looked at my knowingly and nodded. "I won't, I promise. It helps me so much to know that you know, that you are praying for us. And I'm so glad that I had the chance to visit you and meet your family and friends in America. It really helps to know that you are in good hands." She thought for a moment and then added softly, "If anything happens to me, all I ask is that you keep in touch with my children, even if just by mail, so that they know they're not really alone in this world."

I nodded, tears welling up in my eyes. She was holding Alex the whole time. But now it was time to go, and I reached over to take him. She hesitated before turning him over to me.

"I don't know how long it will be before I hold him again," she said with wet eyes. "But don't worry, we'll see each other again. Let's just keep on writing in the meantime."

I tried not to show her the dread I felt deep within. But I couldn't keep it in any longer, as I saw tears flowing down her face. Since I came into this world, she had always been there. I could not imagine life without her. *Dear Lord*, I prayed, *Please send us a miracle. She deserves it.*

"Are you starting to cry, *da* Geolo?" she asked through her own tears. Then she pulled herself together and added, "You know it's bad luck to cry when you're getting on a plane. Come on, let's get ready. I'm sure Howell can't wait to see you two."

She looked at me, kissed Alex, wiped her tears, and said, "It's just that I'll miss you guys so much, I miss you already. But don't you worry about us here, things will get better." We embraced one last time. As we went to board the plane, I turned to see her one last time. I raised my fingers up in the air and crossed them, and she did the same back to me—an old sign we had that things would turn out all right. We smiled through our tears as I disappeared through the plane door.

"Hope," that's what I kept on repeating to myself. What good would it do to be pessimistic, why focus on my pain and fears? Hope was the best weapon Josée had going for her, and it had to be my weapon as well. As the plane began moving down the runway, I thought I could still make out Josée's face leaning against the window of the terminal watching us depart. I trembled with fear for Josée, her children, Papa, Maman, and all who remained in the land I had left behind. Then I felt a tug from my twenty-one-month old boy. He was leaning toward the window, eyeing the land of my birth, waving his hand, and saying, "Bye-bye."

It took us less than an hour to get to the airport in Lusaka, where a mini-van whisked us immediately to the United States Embassy. From there I was able to call Howell to tell him, "We're safe and we're on our way home." He had been worried sick about us. For the past week, he had stayed up all night trying to follow news reports of the rioting in Zaire and spent many hours contacting the U.S. State Department for any information it had. The Embassy loaned me money to pay for a ticket from Lusaka to London and then from London to Paris, where we would be able to catch, after all the turmoil, our regularly scheduled flight home. Physically exhausted and emotionally drained, Alex and I arrived home in New York on September 29.

Josée and the children stayed with *da* Louise in Lubumbashi for two more weeks before heading back to Kolwezi. There, strife still reigned and the looting continued. One night a few weeks later, while Lolo, Josée, and the children slept, burglars—almost certainly soldiers—cut through the metal bars on the windows and entered their home. The thieves made off with just about all of the family valuables, including their television, VCR, clock, and finest tableware. Fortunately, everyone slept through the break-in, and no one was hurt.

It was many months before businesses started re-opening in downtown Kolwezi and Lubumbashi. Some businessmen closed their shops for good. Some couldn't afford to re-stock their inventories; others, particularly foreigners, chose to leave Zaire once and for all, fearing an imminent return of the bloodshed of the 1960's. Even after things had settled somewhat, consumers had to get their goods from impromptu outdoor malls that had sprung up in the military camps. Here, the soldiers openly sold the goods that they had brazenly stolen from honest businessmen and families. Fearing an outbreak of new riots, the military leaders and civil authorities didn't have the courage to shut down the soldiers' tawdry exercise in entrepreneurship.

Meanwhile, the ugly specter of tribalism and ethnic hatred was resurfacing. The Governor of Shaba Province, Kyungu wa Kumwanza, began inciting the population against people from the Luba tribe whose ancestors came from Kasai Province but who had lived in Shaba for generations. "They are the cause of all our problems," he assured the people. And the appeal to the basest of instincts worked: thousands of Lubas were inhumanely kicked out of their jobs and homes, and many died while massed for months at train stations because they couldn't afford a ticket back to a homeland they had never seen.

Josée wrote that her children's school had lost some of its best teachers, who happened to be Luba. "It used to be an excellent school, the best in town," she wrote to me. "Now they don't have enough teachers and many of those who remain are the least competent. They're now putting fifty, sixty, even seventy kids in one class. How can the children learn under such conditions?"

The economic situation, so bleak to begin with, had deteriorated dramatically. Ironically, Papa was much better off in the primitive, underdeveloped countryside, where he could get all the food he needed from his own fields. In the cities and towns, even well-paid professionals like Lolo were now hard pressed to provide their families with adequate food, clothing, and shelter. Even engineers for the mining company were getting their paychecks weeks and often months late.

"We live now by the law of the jungle," Josée wrote. "And it's getting worse every day."

Chaos reigned once more and, this time, it seemed like the 1960's might actually be repeated. The government no longer made a pretense about providing any services to the people. The soldiers were completely out of control. Would my family, my homeland ever find true peace?

CHAPTER 27

THE BRIDGE IS LOVE

Back in New York I had the freedom to pursue my dream of education. I enrolled in Pace University's master of business administration program. This time both Howell and I were studying at the same time. While working full-time as director of a heart health promotion program serving a Latino community in Manhattan, he was studying part-time for his doctoral degree in health education at Teachers College, Columbia University. And, we were raising Alex and getting ready for our second child.

In early April, 1993, during the last days of my pregnancy, I received a letter from Lolo in Kolwezi. As was the case with most of my sister's and his letters, it was postmarked from Belgium and had probably been dropped in a Belgian post office by a colleague of Lolo's on assignment in Europe. We had received letters from Lolo before, but usually they came along with letters from Josée. I was a little concerned about not hearing from her, but I knew that she might have sent a letter around the same time that some absent-minded mining engineer had left in the bottom of his suitcase. Lolo wrote that they were doing well, considering the situation that the country was going through. "Our health is reasonably good and Josée may be going soon to visit my uncle in Geneva for a vacation." I wrote back right away, saying that we wanted Josée to come visit us after her trip to Geneva.

On April 11, 1993, out of my womb and into our lives came a beautiful eight-pound girl who we called Tatiana Jeanne, her second name a tribute to my younger sister who had passed away two years earlier. I quickly sent Josée a letter with the great news and photographs of our precious little girl.

Two months later, on June 21st, Howell was taking his very last course for his doctoral degree. It was a hot, muggy day in New York City. The students were sweating in the classroom, which wasn't air conditioned. But my husband had been a Peace Corps Volunteer in the hottest region in one of the hottest countries on the hottest continent on the planet. He could deal with heat. And, as a public health professional, he knew enough to keep himself hydrated: he sipped constantly on a bottle of water. But suddenly, thirty minutes into the class, he felt cramps in his gut. They started to get stronger and stronger, till it felt like nothing he had ever experienced before. He needed to stretch out, lie down, something. He got up from his chair, took one step to the door, and crumbled to the floor unconscious. By the time the ambulance came, he was revived and the cramps were gone. He felt weak but fine. Medical tests the next day found nothing wrong with him. But I was frightened, Howell had never fainted like that before.

Six days later, on June 27, 1993, we got the call. It was Lolo's uncle from Geneva. I had never spoken with him on the phone before. His voice cracked as he started talking to me.

"Have you had news from Kolwezi lately?" he asked.

"No, not for two months," I said. "Why?"

"My dear," he said softly, "Josée has left us."

"Josée has left us," I repeated in a voice which didn't resemble my own.

My feet started to fail me. Deep inside, I knew what he meant, but outwardly I wanted not to.

"She has left, to go where?" I asked him.

"Dear, Josée has passed away. She died over a week ago on June 17th. I am so sorry, I know how close you two were."

I didn't hear what he said after that. I dropped the phone, fell to the ground, and screamed. The whole world had just turned upside down. Howell, who had been standing beside me, took the phone and asked Lolo's uncle for more information. Alex, three-and-a-half years old, came to my side to cry with me. He had never seen his Maman like this before. When Howell hung up the phone, he joined Alex and me on the kitchen floor; the three of us wrapped our arms around each other and cried and cried and cried.

"Why didn't they tell me when she got sick?" I asked over and over again.

My sister, my oldest, dearest friend had left this world, and I hadn't been by her side. She was just three months past her fortieth birthday. The cause of death was cerebral meningitis, complications from her very first AIDS-related illness, which had begun only in May. That made it all the more shocking and painful. We had expected her to have multiple illnesses, to slowly waste away, to give us time to get used to the pain. "Perhaps it is a blessing she didn't suffer so much," Howell said to me.

Two days later we got a call from my cousin Emérence in Kinshasa and learned that Lolo's uncle had been mistaken. Josée didn't pass away on June 17th. She actually died on June 21st, the very day Howell had fainted so mysteriously.

The days that followed were a blur of tears. Many kind friends and relatives came by to mourn with me. Howell thought I needed some kind of ceremony to help me accept the reality of Josée's death, to bring me some kind of comfort, to ease, in some way, my pain. I thought a memorial Mass would be appropriate, because, to the very end, Josée had remained a devout Catholic; she never seemed to have the same doubts that plagued me. Howell went to the church that I attended in the Bronx and explained the situation. The church secretary asked if I was a member of the parish. Howell said no, but that I came to Mass at the church fairly regularly. "In that case," she said, "you can have a memorial Mass—in six months." I never entered the doors of that church again.

Fortunately, we had a very dear friend, Meryl Perrotta, who was an active member of a small Catholic church, St. Andrew the Apostle, in Brooklyn. She explained our situation to the pastor, Father Danny Murphy, and he quickly arranged for us to have a special Mass there on July 10th. Meryl also arranged a reception at her home for all the friends and relatives who joined us.

Upon entering the church, I walked to the front and sat in the first row. When I saw on a table by the altar a framed photograph of Josée, I burst into tears. Robin, who was sitting beside me after having driven up from Washington, held my hand tight.

"How could this be?" I asked myself, weeping. "What sort of awful nightmare am I having?" Tatiana stirred, then placed her head against my heart as she dozed off in her kangaroo pouch. Alex sat in the row behind us, playing with his cousins, my sister-in-law Barbara's children. They had driven up from Philadelphia to be with us. Howell was everywhere, welcoming friends as they arrived, giving Father Murphy information about Josée's life, checking on me and the children, making sure everything was okay. Soon he came to join us in the front row, but I couldn't stop sobbing. Seeing his Daddy holding me as I cried harder and harder, Alex moved to the front row, looked into my wet eyes, reached for my hand, and held it tight. He had seen me cry so much these past few weeks. Death had entered his vocabulary, inextricably linked with the name of Mama Josée. Tatiana, awakened by my loud sobs, started to fuss. Her Aunt Barbara took her outside to calm her.

I pulled myself together as Father Murphy entered and the Mass began. Father Murphy welcomed us all with great kindness and warmth. After some prayers, he introduced Howell. My husband gave my hand a tight squeeze and smiled warmly at me as he went to the pulpit to read a eulogy he had written in honor of Josée.

These are the words that Howell used to describe my sister's wonderful life.

Kanero Suruba Marie-Josée was born on March 24, 1953, in the town of Kongolo in what was then called the Belgian Congo and now is known as Zaire. She was the first child of her father, Suruba Benoit. Like many eldest children, Josée always seemed to be older and wiser than her years. For her family and friends, she was a pillar of strength and stability—the mature one, the compassionate one, the one you could always rely on, the one who took care of all those in need.

And yet, in many ways, Josée also had the spirit of the youngest child. She had a twinkle in her eyes, a ready laugh, a delightful sense of humor. She could be very mischievous, very silly. She was great fun to be with.

She was so pleasant, so sweet, that you might have found it hard to believe that she had encountered so many extraordinary difficulties in her life, that she had endured so much pain. Like the last years of her life, the early part of her life was a time of chaos and violence in her country. When she was seven years old, Josée experienced things no child should ever have to face.

Fighting broke out suddenly in Kongolo, and Josée and her family were forced to flee their home. With bullets flying all around them they ran past dozens of corpses, including some of people they knew. Josée and her siblings were separated from their father for several months without knowing if he was alive or not. They were arrested by crazed soldiers who aimed rifles at them and came very close to shooting them all. They lived in the forest for months, scavenging for food, sleeping on the hard ground.

Unlike her baby sister, Josée knew this was not a game. She was old enough to be terrified. But she was strong. She helped look after Georgette, my wife, and the other young ones and get the family through this horrifying period.

After the wars finally ended and the country settled down, Josée got a chance to have a peaceful childhood. She went to boarding school with her sister Georgette, or Geolo as they call her in the family. They were both very bright, hardworking students. But Geolo was a troublemaker, a wild tomboy. Josée was the goody goody whose behavior was impeccable; she was adored by the Sisters and usually given positions of responsibility among students.

Ah, but she had that mischievous streak in her. When the lights went out in the dormitory, she would cause a commotion and get everyone laughing, knowing that the Sisters would never blame her for it—they'd probably blame that troublemaker Geolo. Like any siblings, Josée and Geolo would fight from time to time. But everyone at school knew: You did not mess with Geolo when Josée was around because she would never let anyone hurt her baby sister.

Their father instilled in them a great love of learning and a strong capacity for self-discipline. He had this radical idea that girls deserved the exact same opportunity for higher education that boys would get. So Josée worked hard, succeeded on her State Exams, and wound up earning a bachelor's degree in social sciences, no small feat for a woman in Zaire.

Her career reflected her lifelong commitment to helping others. She worked first at the Ministry of Education and later for Catholic Relief Services, where she helped improve the lives of thousands of mothers and children. She supervised

programs that provided food to hungry children, she taught
mothers about health and nutrition, and she managed agricul-
tural and small business development projects.

As an adult, Josée continued to look after her baby sister
Geolo. When she heard that Geolo could no longer go to
school because the government had closed down the university, Josée helped Geolo get a job with Catholic Relief Services
in Kinshasa. There, Geolo worked with and befriended a
friend of Josée's, an American woman named Robin Waite
who later invited her to the United States for her wedding.
And so it was through Josée that Georgette found all of us.

Josée had a boundless love for and devotion to her family.
After having her second child, she became a full-time mother
and homemaker. She and her husband Lolo did a beautiful
job in raising their children. Sandra, Bob, and Rocky are very
sweet kids—extremely bright, friendly, respectful, well-
behaved. They have their mother's kindness and compassion
for others; they help each other as Josée helped her siblings.
And, of course, Josée's children really know how to play, how
to laugh, how to have fun.

Josée's home was open to those in her family and her husband's family who were in need. Her parents and siblings
knew that, if they ever had any problems, Josée would come
to their aid.

There was one time when she did something for herself;
that was when she came here in 1990 for a two-month vacation. We feel so blessed to have had this time with her here.
For the rest of her life, she was filled with joy by the memories
of her visit. What a beautiful smile she would get as she
remembered all the fun we had: those intense Rummikub
games, late night jazz music, fireworks on the 4th of July, that
endless search for Broadway Massapequa, that warm summer
night in which she led a group of us on a march through the

East Village in search of the perfect dessert chanting—in her French accent—"We want Ben & Jerry's ice cream!"

She fell in love with you, our friends, our families. She never forgot the kindness you showed her. I am sure that if she were here, she would offer a prayer of thanksgiving for all you did for her and have done for her sister. And she fell in love with you, her *Bébé* Alex, who, in her best New York patois, she took to calling "Mon Bubela."

She fell in love with our city. She saw all the sights there were to see: monuments, museums, landmarks, skyscrapers. But I'll never forget what she said when I asked her of all the amazing things she had seen in New York, what had most impressed her. She didn't hesitate in replying, "The kindness of the people."

She fell in love with our country. Perhaps my favorite photo from her visit is one of her holding Alex on the ferry boat to Ellis Island. Alex is looking at the camera with a delirious grin and Josée is staring intently at the looming Statue. Josée later told me what her thoughts were: She was saying thank you to the Lady in the Harbor, thank you to this country for the freedom and opportunity it has given her beloved sister and her sister's children.

She so deserved her magical visit here. During her last years, she had to endure unspeakable tragedy. She lost two children—an infant and a four year old—and a younger sister. Since the time we visited her in 1991, living conditions deteriorated drastically as Zaire fell into near anarchy. Her home was broken into and most of her possessions stolen. Everything became dangerous, feeding her children became a challenge. Helping the rest of her family became almost impossible.

Despite all this, Josée persevered, she maintained her buoyant spirit, she continued to love and cherish life. How could she be so strong? She had as profound a faith in God as anyone can. She believed in a compassionate and merciful God, and this gave her solace, it gave her strength. She believed in the future—her children. She knew that, as always, there were loved ones for her to take care of. I am sure that, if she were here, she would be thinking of how she could help us ease our pain. She would want us to work through our grief, our feeling of irreplaceable loss, to carry on with our lives. She would want us to love life as she did: to share jokes, to laugh, to sing, to dance, to enjoy every moment as much as we can. She would want us to be strong and help each other through this and all the challenges to come.

But how do we make sense out of a life in which such a beautiful person is taken from us so soon? Asking this question made me think of a book I read a long time ago, and looking at it this week has helped me. In *The Bridge of San Luis Rey*, Thorton Wilder wrote: "But soon we shall die and all memory of those [we love]. . . will have left the earth, and we ourselves shall be loved for a while and forgotten. But the love will have been enough; all those impulses of love return to the love that made them. Even memory is not necessary for love. There is a land of the living and a land of the dead and the bridge is love, the only survival, the only meaning.

This made me think about the extraordinarily close relationship between Georgette and Josée. The story of their lives reminded me of the lives of another pair of siblings—George and Harry Bailey. You may be familiar with them—they're fictional characters from one of our favorite movies, *It's a Wonderful Life*. George was the older brother. Due to fate and his sense of duty, George wound up spending his whole life in his small hometown, helping his family and all the people of the town to have a better life—even though he himself continued to be poor, even though he had to give up all his personal dreams of travel and adventure. Thanks to George's sacrifices, Harry, the younger brother, did get to travel, to see the world, to have the great adventures George had always dreamed of having. George was very proud of his little brother, he helped him all along the way, but he was quite frustrated with how his own life had turned out. At the end of the movie, however, George finally comes to realize what everyone else has known all along: By helping others, he has had a wonderful, glorious life.

Though she was taken from us much too soon, how grateful we are, how blessed we have been to have shared in the wonderful life of Kanero Suruba Marie-Josée. In one of the last lines of the movie, Harry Bailey raises his glass and makes a toast, saying: "To my big brother, George, the richest man in town." We can make the same toast here today. To Georgette's big sister, Josée, the richest woman in town. For like George Bailey, Josée was fabulously rich in the only currency that really matters—love.

Da Josée, *tokobosana yo mokolo moko te*—we will never forget you. *Bolingo bwa bisu ekoki kosila te*—our love for you will never end. *Lala malamu, da* Josée *wa bisu*—sleep well, our dear Josée."

At one point during Howell's vivid description of my big sister's life and what she meant to me, I gazed at the photograph on the table but saw *dada's* tear-drenched face as we parted from each other at the Lubumbashi airport just two years earlier.

"Did I tell her that I loved her?" I asked myself. "Did I remember to tell her, before Alex and I boarded the plane, did I tell her?"

I was snapped back to the present when I heard people in the church laughing a little. Howell was telling them about how mischievous I was as a child and about all the good times Josée had had on her trip to America.

The memories brought a brief smile to my face, as well. But as Howell began to talk of the end of her life, and the meaning of her life, I began to sob again—but so did, I think, all the people in the church. When the Mass ended, I went to Josée's photograph, kissed my fingers tenderly, and, lightly touched them to her face. "I love you, dear sister, dear friend," I said. "You will always be within my heart."

CHAPTER 28

TO LIVE AGAIN

I was determined to go to Zaire to see Josée's grave and mourn with my family. But the country was still in chaos, practically anarchy. We heard many tales of violent crime and soldiers out of control. My close friends and family advised me not to go; it was just too dangerous and I had a three-month-old baby to worry about. I couldn't be separated from my daughter, but I couldn't risk taking her with me to Zaire. I had no choice but to agree with them. I took Tatiana with me instead on a trip to Canada, so I could be with Josée's best friend, *da* Jacquis.

How comforted I was to arrive in British Columbia and see that *da* Jacquis was dressed in black. She truly loved Josée like a sister; she mourned with me, and she understood the depth of my pain. She organized a memorial Mass for Josée while I was there and circulated a letter to friends Josée had made during her short visit in the summer of 1990. She even raised money to help Josée's children. One evening she and her husband Staf gathered their three boys together, and we all talked about the happy memories we had of Josée.

Da Jacquis saw how devastated I was and she gave me loving advice to live by: "You have to know, even though it might be hard to accept at this time, that every single person in this world has her or his own life to live. Josée has left us. Nobody knows better than I do how much pain you feel. But you have your own life to live, and you must continue to live it. Take all the time you need to mourn, but remember that you have your life to lead, and your husband and two children to take care of."

I arrived in Canada feeling that I could not go on living any longer. I thought, for sure, that at any moment I would simply fall to the ground and die. But two weeks of love from my sister's dearest friend began to lift my spirits. And a giant bouquet of flowers with a tender note from Howell on our wedding anniversary made me remember how lucky I was to have his love and our children. I began to live again.

Once I returned to New York, Howell and I began talking of Josée's three children. We knew that their father, also infected with HIV, was likely to get sick and die in the near future. "With what the country is going through, the children's future looks bleak. There isn't anyone from either family who has the resources or motivation to take proper care of them," I said and Howell agreed. Although our financial situation wasn't very good, we decided that it would be best if the children came to live with us. We offered this to Lolo, and he agreed that this was the best choice for his children.

We hired a New York immigration lawyer to help us figure out the best way to get the children here legally. First, we tried to bring over Sandra, the oldest child. Our efforts were plagued, however, by the miserable state of telephone service and mail delivery in Zaire. Fortunately, Lolo's older brother had recently moved to Zambia, a relatively stable country just south of Shaba, and Sandra was able to go stay with him. After consultations with our lawyer, we realized that the best way to get the children to the U.S. was to adopt them in a court overseas. The U.S. Government recognized such adoptions as legally binding and would then give them immigrant visas. We had little hope for getting any legal action taken in Zaire, particularly with the American Consulate in Lubumbashi closed due to security concerns. In any case, Zaire had become too dangerous for Tatiana and me to visit. Instead, we decided to try to arrange the adoption in a court in peaceful Zambia. We asked Lolo to bring Bob and Rocky to Zambia, and, with help from our families and friends in America, we bought tickets for Tatiana and me to fly there. We had no idea whether the court in Zambia would accept our plea or how long it might take, but we knew for the children's sake we had to do all we could.

It wasn't easy for me to leave four-year-old Alex and Howell for an unknown length of time. It had been a very difficult period for Alex. Since the day we'd received the news of Josée's death, he'd seen my moods of sadness and watched me burst into tears again and again. He'd learned that, with a hug or a joke, he could get me to smile again, so he tried to stick close to me. Every now and then he'd come near me and examine my eyes to see if I had been crying.

Before we left New York, we learned from Robin that Ken Puvak, a colleague of Howell's from his Peace Corps service in Zaire, was living in Lusaka, the Zambian capital, serving as the director of the Peace Corps program in Zambia. Despite tragedy, sometimes the synchronicity of stumbling onto a piece of such good luck in its midst makes you wonder if there isn't a higher Power looking out for you, after all. Not only did Ken put us up at his house, but he helped me find a highly competent, honest Zambian lawyer to guide us through the adoption process. And he and other members of the Peace Corps Zambia staff befriended me and gave me wise advice as I struggled to make the adoption happen.

My first day in Lusaka, I received a call from Lolo in Lubumbashi. We had asked him to bring the two boys to Zambia, and he was calling to say he'd be leaving the next day. Then he put Maman on the phone; I hadn't spoken with her since Josée's death.

"Hello, Georgette, is it really you? How are you? How's Jeanne Tatiana?" Maman said, in a trembling voice.

"Hello, Maman. We're... " I couldn't complete the sentence without breaking down in tears.

"Be strong, my dear. Life is hard. All we can do is just thank the Almighty for Josée's love and life. Your sister is resting in peace with Him."

I had hoped that Maman would be able to come with Lolo, but she said he didn't have enough money to pay for her bus fare and to get her across the border.

"Have *da* Louise borrow the money, Maman," I said. "I'll give it back to her when you get here. But I must see you and *da* Louise here in Lusaka."

"That would make me very happy, my dear," Maman said. "Oh, I can't wait to see baby Jeanne. Thank you so very much for naming her for my Jeanne."

After a difficult, 250-mile bus ride across the border and through northern Zambia, Lolo, Bob, and Rocky arrived in Lusaka. Lolo was just recovering from a severe eye infection, his first AIDS-related illness. The next day I went to the lawyer's office, where our attorney explained the process to me.

"Normally, it would take anywhere from three to six weeks, depending on what else is going on in the court," she said. "There is a chance, however, that this case might take a little more time, because the children are Zairian. However, I think our judges should be sympathetic. They know how bad the situation is in Zaire and, after all, this is a case of a woman taking her sister's children. I'm hopeful that we can resolve it in less than three months."

I was delighted by her optimism but dismayed by the thought of being away from Howell and Alex for three months. Of course, had we been living in Zambia or Zaire or any African country, I wouldn't have needed to go through this whole adoption process. The children would have just moved in with us; all we would have needed to prove was that we were related to their mother. But this adoption had to be done to legal perfection to make sure there were no snags which would lead to problems with the United States Immigration and Naturalization Service. I explained my situation to the attorney and told her how I badly needed to get back home as soon as possible.

"I'll do all that I can," she said. "I've lived in the States, and I know how difficult the immigration agency can be. Having the children's father here documenting his consent will make it a lot easier."

I returned to her office three days later with Lolo. "You're in luck," she said. "According to Zambian family law, a sister should have no difficulty adopting her deceased sister's children, with the father's consent. The only possible problem will be the availability of the judge. But I think we're pretty much on the court calendar for two weeks from today."

Just two weeks—was that another stroke of luck or divine providence? Howell and I had never thought it could be settled so quickly. During those two weeks I worked overtime, marching under the hot Zambian sun on the never-ending circuit between the Zairian embassy to get the children's passports, the Zambian immigration office to arrange the boys' visas for their stay in that country, and the United States embassy to make sure the groundwork was laid for our United States visa applications for the children. Lolo's relatives in Zambia did nothing to help me, even though they must have known that this adoption was in the best interests of the children.

When the big day arrived we all showed up in court, a little nervous, expecting something to come up to complicate matters. The judge, looking austere on his mahogany bench, asked Lolo a couple of questions, "Are you truly the father of these three children? Are you truly willing to renounce your rights as their parent?" To both, Lolo softly replied, "Yes." It must have been terribly difficult for him to part with his children, but he knew that this was the best thing he could do for them. Then the judge asked me some questions. "Are you truly the sister of the children's mother? Are you truly willing to become their lawful parent?" After each question, I said "Yes." "Does your husband concur with your decision to adopt these children?" I presented a packet of documents Howell had prepared in New York, with an affidavit in which he swore that he did, indeed, concur with the decision to adopt, plus a variety of documents attesting to our financial and emotional stability. The documents had been notarized by the office of the United States Secretary of State. The judge had no further questions to ask, and the wheels of Zambian justice moved swiftly. All that remained was to sign the adoption decree. The only remaining obstacle was obtaining United States visas for the children, which we had been told would take several months. In the meantime, they would stay with their uncle in Zambia and wait.

After the court hearing, Lolo and I headed to the Zambian immigration office to renew Sandra's Zambian visa, which was scheduled to expire that night. We expected this to be a mere formality but were stunned to find out that her visa was no longer renewable.

"You must be making a mistake," I said, naïvely, to the Zambian immigration officer.

"No mistake," the immigration officer replied. "She has no right to be on Zambian soil after midnight tonight."

"But how can that be?"

"She entered Zambia on a visitor's visa. She was obliged to renew that visa every month until she obtained an immigrant visa. Her visitor's visa has not been renewed for the past three months, so she must be expelled. If she is in this country tomorrow, she will be arrested."

This was devastating news. Getting someone across the border from Zaire into Zambia was a costly proposition. And the Zambian border officials might not look kindly on a visa application from a young girl who had recently failed to comply with their country's immigration rules. Add to that the uncertainty over whether Lolo's health would permit him to guide her back to Zambia. We weren't sure, if she returned to Zaire, that we'd be able to get her back into Zambia for a flight to the United States. Lolo's brother was supposed to take care of Sandra's legal arrangements for staying in Zambia, but his neglect had put the child's entire future in jeopardy.

I turned to my Zambian attorney for help and asked how much it would cost. "You don't need to pay me for this," she kindly said. "It's a very noble thing that you and your husband are doing. I would be happy to help."

She took me back to the Immigration Office, but, having a lot of important connections, she bypassed the immigration officer I had seen and went straight into the office of the man's boss. She talked small talk for awhile, spent some time flattering him, and then pleaded my case. She talked about all the sacrifices I had made to help my sister's children and how wrong it would be to punish Sandra because someone else had been careless. The official talked about the importance of following government regulations, but my lawyer wore him down with her emotional arguments on behalf of the African family. He signed a new visa for Sandra that would allow her to stay in the country until her American visa came through—though he did make me pay a stiff fine for the service.

This whole experience was terribly nerve-wracking and more was to come. A few days later I returned to the immigration office to make sure the boys' visas were in order. The official who handled my case came up with one reason after another for why the children should not have their visas extended, even though I explained that their stay would be temporary and they'd be leaving for the United States in a few months. I turned to the United States Embassy for help, and a kind consular officer wrote a letter asking the Zambian immigration authorities to extend the children's visas, while he waited for Washington to approve their U.S. visas. That only seemed to make the immigration officer angrier. He wrote me a letter saying I had to leave Zambia in two weeks, even though my visa was good for another five months! He said I had become "undesirable."

"For what reason?" exclaimed my Zambian lawyer. "For trying to do everything legally? This is intolerable." She saved me once again by going to higher authorities, who, without hesitation, extended the children's' visas and let me stay.

Fortunately, telephone service between Zambia and the United States was pretty good, so I was able to keep Howell informed of my progress. And I got to speak with my four-year-old son, who always asked when Maman and "Tatinana" were coming home. "Very soon, *Bubbe*," I told him, "because I miss you and Daddy very much."

Sandra, Bob, and Rocky stayed with their uncle in Mumbwa, which was a couple of hours north of Lusaka. Ken invited them to come stay at his house for my last few weeks in Zambia. There I played them a tape recorded message of Alex sending his wishes to them, telling stories, and singing songs. That helped re-acquaint them with their cousin, who had grown up so much since our visit to Zaire. They each took turns holding and playing with Tatiana.

One day later, Maman and *da* Louise arrived in Lusaka, and Ken said they could stay at the small guest house that adjoined his main house, where the children and I were staying. After hugging me, Maman immediately asked, "Where is Jeanne Tatiana?" Tatiana was sleeping, but we picked her up from her bed and put her right in her grandmother's arms.

"Thank the Lord," Maman said through her tears, "that I have lived to see and to hold the namesake of my Jeanne."

Over the next few days I talked with Maman and *da* Louise about everything. They hadn't known that I knew what had caused Josée's death.

"Our biggest concern was the children," Maman said. "Now that they will be with you and *baba* Howell, we just thank the Almighty for everything. It's a huge load to take all three of them beside your own, but with God's help, you'll pull through. We're all proud of what you're doing for your sister."

Maman told me all about Josée's last days. Maman's absence

had caused Josée so much pain early in her life, but she was by Josée's side throughout her illness until the very end.

"She talked so much about her trip to America," Maman said. "And, in the end, when she was delirious, she called out your name, '*Da* Geolo, *da* Geolo, where are you?'"

I began to sob. Maman looked away and said softly, "She was really like your mother, I know that."

I asked "Has anyone received word yet from Papa? I haven't received any responses from him to my letters after Josée's death." *Da* Louise told me that Lolo had sent several messages for Papa through the shortwave radio to the Archbishop of Kongolo, but he never got a reply. But they had learned that one of our cousins who was living in Kongolo had broken the news to Papa.

"It sounds like he had a hard time accepting the news," *da* Louise said. "He was angry at everyone in Kolwezi and Lubumbashi for not finding some way to let him know that she was sick. They say that he then went and spent a week on his farm alone. When he came back to town, he sat in mourning for another week."

After a two-week visit, Maman and *da* Louise headed back to Lubumbashi, and the children returned to Mumbwa. I gave the children English-As-A-Second-Language books and tapes that Howell had sent from New York so that when they would arrive in the United States, they would know at least a little English.

"Don't forget to write," Maman repeated over and over again as she and *da* Louise boarded the bus. As we hugged goodbye, she blessed me in her native language, kiTabwa: "May God put you and all of yours under His protection."

And it seemed that God was protecting us, for He provided us with the extraordinarily dependable Ken Puvak to look after the remaining legal paperwork for Sandra, Bob, and Rocky. I was able to leave at peace, feeling that I had done my best and that Josée's children would soon be safe in the United States under our care. Six weeks after my departure, Tatiana and I arrived home in New York, back in the loving arms of Howell and Alex.

The children's visas were issued by the United States Immigration and Naturalization Service in May 1994, and they arrived in New York just before Memorial Day. Alex and Tatiana considered them their brothers and sister right from the start. We put them immediately to work learning English, knowing that mastery of the language would be critical to their academic and social success. Howell had taught English as a Second Language, so he was able to prepare lessons for them. I worked with them several hours during the day and he conducted review sessions in the evenings after returning home from work. Of course, Alex and the television set helped teach them a great deal of English as well.

Life was complicated by the fact that we lived in a two-bedroom apartment with only one bathroom and seven people. We had to prepare a schedule, giving everyone their own time slots for taking showers. Howell and I also typed up and discussed with the children "house rules," so that everyone was clear about what was expected of them.

It was not and still is not an easy situation. I had never anticipated having more than three children and now, in the blink of an eye, there were five. Our finances were drained by the adoption process, and our living expenses soared with three more mouths to feed. Fortunately, we also had help from our families and friends, and Sandra, Bob, and Rocky adapted well to life in the United States of America. They learned English in no time and have done remarkably well in school.

A few months after their arrival, we moved to Atlanta, where Howell had obtained a position as a behavioral scientist with the Centers for Disease Control and Prevention's (CDC) Division of Adolescent and School Health. He wasn't going to start at CDC until January 1995—he had to complete his doctoral dissertation in New York in the Fall—but we thought it would be good to get the children enrolled in Atlanta area schools for the entire school year to avoid the disruption that a mid-year move would cause. And we were desperate to find a larger apartment that we could afford, a next-to-impossible task in New York City.

In August, we moved to Atlanta, where housing costs were much more reasonable. Howell helped get the children started at school and then headed back to New York; he would fly down to visit us a couple of times a month. Sandra started eighth grade, Bob sixth grade, Rocky fifth grade, and Alex began his last year of preschool.

The four months when Howell was primarily in New York was an extremely stressful period, with a large house to manage, two little children to nurture, and three older ones to acclimate to life in an American school and homework. Things got much easier when Howell completed his doctorate in health education and settled in with us full-time in January. With his formal schooling completed, it was now time for me to return for the graduate education I had abandoned at the time of Josée's death. I enrolled in Mercer University's Master of Business Administration program.

In the meantime, Lolo continued to write to his children and Howell and me. The rebellion that everyone was anticipating for Zaire hadn't occurred yet. The infrastructure, the economy, the quality of life continued to deteriorate. There had been several more riots of soldiers, and the menace of such violence was always looming. The constitutional convention had been a farce; Mobutu never had any intention of sharing power, and he continued to brilliantly play off his rivals, one against the other. There was no real order in the country, but life went on.

In late 1994, Lolo wrote that he would be going to Johannesburg, South Africa, for medical treatment. His eye infections had recurred, and there was little the Zairian physicians could do for him. While in Johannesburg, he was able to reach us by telephone and speak to his children. He was amazed by their progress in English. He told us that he had heard that Papa was planning to come to Kolwezi to visit Josée's grave. Lolo returned to Kolwezi by the end of November.

While he was in Johannesburg, we received a letter from him with a Belgian postmark. When I opened the envelope I saw, to my astonishment, that the letter had been written in June 1993, more than a year earlier. Apparently, he had given it to a colleague to mail while on a trip to Europe and the colleague had misplaced it for a year. In the letter, Lolo congratulated us on the great news of Tatiana's birth. And he told me that Josée was sick, very sick, and that she had been hospitalized. He had no idea what would happen next.

In August 1995, we received the next call that we dreaded. After a series of illnesses, Lolo had passed away.

CHAPTER 29

WHAT I HAVE BEEN, WHAT I AM

After telling me that Lolo had died, Lolo's friend turned the telephone over to someone else.

"*Kambo*, is that you?" said a male voice.

"Yes, it's me," I said, breaking into tears as I realized I was talking with Papa for the first time in four years, for the first time since Josée's death. It was, in fact, the first time I had ever spoken with him by telephone.

"It's all right, *kambo*, don't you cry. It's all right," Papa said.

Papa told me, "I've been in Kolwezi for almost two weeks. I have come to visit Josée's grave and, strangely, I arrived just as Lolo had begun to lose his struggle for life." Before that, Papa had spent a few days in Lubumbashi, where he visited his old friend, *bibi* Thérèse. It had been twenty-five years since Papa had made a trip so far from Kongolo.

"How are you feeling, Papa? And how is *ma* Feza?" I asked.

"We're okay. I have some problems with my eyes, but that will pass."

He thanked me for taking care of Josée's children. "Please put

317

everything in God's hands; that's all we can do," he said. "Please take good care of yourselves. And keep on writing to me, I love to hear from you."

He spoke a little with Howell in Lingala. When I took back the receiver, I didn't want to let my father go, I wanted to keep him on the line forever. But Lolo's friend said that our time was up, and so we had to say goodbye.

After the call, memories and visions of the past swept through my mind. From our early childhood on, Papa had always stressed the importance of education. Nothing in his life had made him prouder than the secondary school and university degrees that Josée and I earned. Every time I struggled with a course, every time I doubted my capabilities, I heard his voice saying, "My girls can do anything boys can do. If they want to succeed at school, they will succeed." Every time I hesitated before enrolling for night courses, on top of all my other family and household responsibilities, every time I questioned whether all this work was worth it, I heard Papa's voice saying, "Remember what is important in life. Education is the key to your future. Don't let anything stop you from getting the education you deserve." Papa's words made me feel proud.

In December 1996, this little tomboy from that tiny, isolated country town in the middle of Africa earned a Master of Business Administration degree from Mercer University in one of the fastest growing cities in the greatest country in the world. And what a wonderful world it could be!

As we settled into life in Atlanta, we began to think seriously of our children's religious education. We wanted Sandra, Bob, and Rocky to have what their parents would have given them, so we had them join and participate regularly in Mass at Holy Cross Roman Catholic Church near our suburban Atlanta home. We enrolled Bob and Rocky in Confirmation class; Bob was confirmed in 1997 and

Rocky in 1998. Sandra, who had been confirmed in Zaire, marched beside each of them in their Confirmation ceremonies.

Howell explored some synagogues in Atlanta and decided to join Ahavath Achim Congregation, which belongs to the Conservative branch of Judaism. He enrolled Alex in the Congregation's Hebrew school and took both Alex and Tatiana with him to synagogue every Saturday morning. Sometimes I went along with them. As the lone black woman in the synagogue, I certainly stood out, and people tended to remember me. But they all treated me kindly, and I was happy that Howell had found such a comforting place for himself and our children.

It seemed that only I had no spiritual home. I had tried hard to connect with the Catholic Church, but it just didn't work for me. After my return from Zambia in 1994, I started asking myself why it was that the Church couldn't bring me the peace that I felt when praying in a Jewish synagogue or at home during a Jewish holiday celebration. And then it occurred to me: I had found a spiritual connection, after all. It wasn't just that I found more peace in Judaism than in Catholicism, it was that I had found peace in Judaism. I had found my connection to the One, the loving, caring God, and it was the God of Abraham, Isaac, and Jacob. This wasn't a game of comparisons, it was a game of yes or no, and, for the first time in my life, I realized that the answer was most definitely YES!

But was I sure? Conversion was an awfully big commitment. Inside I knew, but I proceeded cautiously. The turning point that tipped me over the edge was the religious conversion of our children, Alex and Tatiana. According to Conservative Judaism, Alex and Tatiana were not officially Jewish since their mother was not Jewish. To participate in a Conservative synagogue's educational program, they would have to be formally converted to Judaism. Now, all they had known since their births was that they were Jews. The Reform and Reconstructionist branches of Judaism have come to accept the children of Jewish fathers as Jews, but Conservative Judaism maintains the traditional, matrilineal definition of Jewish identity. Howell wasn't too happy about this at first, but he wanted to join Ahavath Achim and he came to think that we could make a meaningful, religious experience out of the children's conversion.

As we prepared for Alex and Tatiana's conversion ceremony, I started to ask myself, "What are you afraid of? You know you belong there with them; you know that in your heart you are already Jewish. Why don't you do it?" I couldn't think of any reasons not to do it. I wanted to make clear that this was coming from me, for me, so I didn't even discuss it with Howell. I called Rabbi Stephen Weiss at Ahavath Achim and asked if I could be converted at the same time as Alex and Tatiana. He told me that it wouldn't be possible for an adult to get converted so quickly.

"Usually people need to take classes for a year or two to make sure they understand Judaism, then we can discuss the possibility of conversion," Rabbi Weiss explained. Of course, he wasn't aware then of my more than ten years of involvement in Judaism. When I met with Rabbi Weiss several times and he got to know me, he said it probably wouldn't take me very long to be ready. He told me to take some time to prepare myself and gave me some books to study.

Meanwhile, the children's conversion ceremony in December 1996 went beautifully. The ceremony consisted of saying some prayers and being completely immersed in a *mikvah*, a bath of pure water. Marilyn and Herb flew in from Florida to participate, and Alex's godfather, Jon Brooks, flew in from New York for the occasion. The children took off their clothes and showered, then Howell took them down the steps into the rectangular-shaped *mikvah*. Marilyn, Herb, two Rabbis, and I stood by the water, while our friends gathered in a room next door from which we could hear their blessings. Alex and Tatiana dove under the water with no hesitation; they thought the whole experience was great fun.

Afterwards, we went to the sanctuary, where Rabbi Weiss led us in prayer and song. We read some stories from the Bible and Jewish folk tradition, and Alex and Tatiana said in Hebrew the *Sh'ma*, the great Jewish declaration of faith in one God. At the end, per the tradition for joyous occasions, we threw candy at the two celebrants, who quickly gathered it all up with many squeals of delight. It was an extraordinarily moving and joyous ceremony, and I couldn't wait to do it myself.

In the weeks since my meeting with Rabbi Weiss, I read the books he had given me and studied the Hebrew *alefbet* [alphabet]. In mid-February, he told me it was time to schedule my conversion ceremony, and the great event was finally scheduled for April 1st, no kidding. Howell and his family were thrilled with my decision, of course.

As an adult, I had to meet with a panel of wise Jews who would question me before letting me proceed to the *mikvah*. Three distinguished rabbis, including Rabbi Weiss, comprised the panel. They asked me some basic questions about Judaism to test my knowledge and probed my motivations for wanting to convert. Then they asked me to leave the room while they deliberated. Soon Rabbi Weiss emerged to call me back into the room, where they told me that it was the opinion of the panel that I was ready for conversion.

I went into the shower to prepare for entering the *mikvah*. Since I was a woman and I had to go in naked, the three male rabbis couldn't be in the *mikvah* room with me; they waited in the anteroom next door with Howell, the children, and our friends. There were holes high in the wall between the two rooms so that one could easily have a conversation from one room to the other. My good friend Kathy Feldman, who is Jewish, came into the *mikvah* room to be the witness who would tell the rabbis that I was completely immersed. The whole experience came naturally, perhaps because only four months earlier we had been there with Alex and Tatiana, so I knew exactly what to expect.

When I felt ready to go in the *mikvah*, I let Rabbi Weiss know it was time. I removed my towel and stepped, naked, into the soft, warm, perfectly clear water. With just my head above the water, I said in Hebrew two prayers, as instructed by Rabbi Weiss. The voices of the rabbis and my loved ones, unseen from the other room, saying "Amen" in unison sounded like the voices of angels from above. I stooped a little, and let myself drop down, down, down until I was fully immersed in the sweet water of life. I felt like a baby in the womb, getting ready to face the world, my whole life ahead of me.

"Yes, she is completely under," I heard Kathy say. After hanging limp in the delicious water for a few, long seconds, I pulled myself up to the surface and saw Kathy's smiling face. And that was it. I was officially converted.

After I dressed, we entered the sanctuary while a beautiful song about Ruth, the Bible's most famous convert to Judaism, played on a tape recorder. Rabbi Weiss led us in prayers and blessings, while Alex, Howell, and Kathy read the stories and poems we had put together for the occasion. Howell then talked about the role my family in Zaire, particularly Papa, had played in helping me reach this moment in my life.

> The Bible's great exemplar of a Jew by choice is, of course, Ruth. The Book of Ruth tells the beautiful story of Ruth's devotion to her mother-in-law Naomi and her full-hearted commitment to joining the Jewish people. The Book of Ruth tells us clearly what Ruth did, but it doesn't really tell us why she did it. She could have gone back to her family as Orpah, Naomi's other daughter-in-law, did. Instead, she left all that she had ever known, all who had ever been dear to her, to embrace this foreign land, this foreign people, this foreign faith. Why did she do it?
>
> Well, a cynic—or a television movie producer—might come up with a *midrash* [a story that expands upon stories told in the Bible] in which Ruth's departure to Israel was actually a flight from Moab. They might spin a tale in which she refused to return to her family because her family was dysfunctional,

maybe even abusive. But that's not Suruba's midrash for Ruth. In Suruba's heart, Ruth's kindness and devotion to Naomi sprang from the kindness and devotion she received from her family as a child; and Ruth's tolerance for and interest in a different people and faith sprang from a family that taught her to respect those who are different. A family that gave her the strength to sacrifice for others. A family that loved her dearly, but did not suffocate her with jealousy or possessiveness. A family that nurtured her, believed in her, and gave her the freedom to follow her dreams. A family that taught her what family is all about.

And that's how Suruba's *midrash* would explain Ruth's embrace of Judaism. It's only natural that she would come up with such an interpretation, because it so closely parallels how Suruba has reached this point of her spiritual journey. Knowing the man her father is, both Suruba and I are very sure that were he here today he would be completely supportive of her decision. He would ask his beloved daughter, "Does this make you happy? Does this make your family happy?" When he would hear her strong answer, "Yes," and look into her eyes, he would most certainly give his blessing. And Suruba would tell him that it was he who planted the seeds of much of her Judaism. For it was he who gave her her deep faith in one God, it was he who taught her how to live a life of loving one's neighbor as oneself, it was he who gave her a passionate commitment to learning, it was he who encouraged Suruba to follow that most Jewish of pastimes: asking questions, tough questions, on any and all topics, even those for which there could be no answers.

Then, it was my turn to speak.

In the tenth year of my marriage to a Jewish man and the eighth year of our regular celebration of *Shabbat*, I have decided to formally convert to Judaism. My love affair with Judaism has not been a wild-eyed, love-at-first-sight, infatuation. It has been a different type of love, a more gradual and perhaps more genuine passion.

I was raised Christian and followed that spiritual path with my family. It was a beautiful journey that gave me my basic values and decency. The legacy from my Christian upbringing that has always meant the most to me is the fundamental teaching Christianity absorbed from Judaism: Love thy neighbor as you love thyself.

A great part of me has long wanted to become one with the Jewish people and God. But until this past year, I wasn't ever quite able to acknowledge it. My inner debate reminds me of that scene in *Fiddler on the Roof* when Tevye asks his wife Goldie, "Do you love me?" Like Tevye, that part of me which was long ago ready to be Jewish was asking the rest of me, "Do you love me? Do you love Judaism enough to commit yourself to it?"

And, like Goldie, the rest of me wasn't ready to hear the question, let alone answer it. Judaism asked me, "Do you love me?" And I replied, "I'm Christian." But I could not hide from my doubts and disbelief in basic Christian theology. Judaism asked me again, "Do you love me?" And I replied, "Excuse me, I've got to go to church." But I found no inner peace in church and disagreed all too often with what I heard there.

Judaism asked me again, "Do you love me?" And I replied, "For years, I've been observing *Shabbat* and the Jewish holidays and enjoying them very much." With rising frustration, Judaism asked me again, "But do you love me?" And I replied, "For ten years I have helped my husband re-embrace his faith and it has brought me great joy. I have without reservation raised my children as Jews and helped them learn of their traditions, and it has brought me great joy."

Almost exasperated, Judaism asked me again, "But do YOU love me?" And I replied, "I find beauty for myself in having a Jewish home. I find peace for myself in Jewish prayers and synagogue worship. If that's not love, what is?"

And Judaism heaved a great sigh of relief and said, "So you do love me."

And I said what I say now before you, dear friends and family, "Yes, I do. I do love you. And I am proud to become what I have been, what I am—a Jew."

In 1994, we watched in horror as the genocide against the Tutsi people in Rwanda played itself out on our television screen. Little did we know that this catastrophe, in that tiny country on Zaire's eastern border, would lead to unbelievable changes for my own native land.

News reports indicated that President Mobutu was being treated in Europe for prostate cancer. Well, we'd heard those kinds of rumors before. But could it be true this time? Could he finally be on the way out? In 1996, Mobutu's support of the Hutu extremists who had tried to exterminate their Tutsi rivals backfired. An anti-Mobutu rebellion sprang up in eastern Zaire, and the victorious Rwandan Tutsis helped it along. One more time, Mobutu's army folded and ran in the face of trouble. Who could blame them? What sane person would risk his or her life to defend the most corrupt government on the planet?

The rebels started to capture towns in eastern Zaire, and more and more frustrated Zairians joined their side. Soon, governments of neighboring countries, fed up with Mobutu meddling in their affairs and supporting rebellions against them, sent support to the rebels. Every week another city fell. This was no longer a rebellion located in just one province, it was sweeping the nation. Once again, Mobutu turned to his European and Moroccan friends for help, but he was no longer geopolitically relevant. The gig was up; this time he was not going to get any help. He swore that his army would defend the Republic, but instead his soldiers looted and pillaged the towns they were fleeing, rather than defending. As we followed news reports about the rebels advancing on Kongolo and Lubumbashi, we worried desperately about the safety of Papa and Maman. But Mobutu's army was so dispirited that the rebels were able to capture these cities with little fighting and hardly any civilian casualties.

On the 17th of May, 1997, the rebels captured Kinshasa and had the entire country under their control. Was it just a dream? Could the dictator really be gone after thirty-two years of tyranny? Yes, indeed, it was true. We watched it with our own eyes on all the television news shows, we read about it in *The New York Times*. Mobutu fled with his family and entourage to beg for sanctuary in Europe, but soon realized that his old friends had no use for a dying dictator. Only, King Hassan of Morocco, offered him refuge. And it was there in Morocco, so far from the land he despoiled, that the great dictator succumbed four months later to the cancer that had ravaged him.

Thank God, Maman and Papa survived the revolution that toppled Mobutu. They felt safer with Mobutu's soldier bandits stripped of their guns. However, prices continued to mount, and getting the necessities of daily life remained a challenge.

Communication with our loved ones in the new Congo remains difficult, and we haven't had the means to visit. Papa, of course, doesn't have the means to travel to the United States. He has started writing more regularly, however; we're now getting a couple of letters a year. He had some health problems in 1997, but said he and *ma* Feza are in good health.

I imagine he still writes to *bibi* Thérèse. After all this time, they are still friends. And yet, the only time they have seen each other in the past twenty-five years was when Papa went to visit Josée's grave. How I wish they could have been with us for joyous occasions, like the birth of our children. Maybe, God willing, they will make it to our son's bar mitzvah!

With the rebel victory, the name of Zaire was relegated to the dustbin of history. The country became known again as the Democratic Republic of Congo. Mobutu's flag and national anthem were changed. The devastated economy was not so easy to change for the better. And though the new government showed some immediate signs of changing Mobutu's legacy of corruption, it has lingered.

There was only an interim period of peace. In the end, fighting again broke out and another war has been waged. However, in the hearts of all of us who care about the future of Africa, hope has not died—hope that we can one day tap the great resources of the Congo and the Congolese people.

The current leaders may not be the ones who will finally bring real peace and progress to Zaire. Some say they already have reverted to Mobutu-style tyranny. However, the legacy of corruption, incompetence, and cruelty that have become synonymous with Zaire must be eradicated. As we pray in synagogue: *May God instruct them to administer all affairs of state in justice and equity, that peace and security, happiness and prosperity, right and freedom, may forever abide among the people.*

EPILOGUE

The story is now up to date, and I see that towering above it all has been one man. An ordinary man of extraordinary kindness, wisdom, and bravery. I need to tell you, Papa, how much you have meant to me; how lucky I have been to have had such a man as my father.

Dear Papa, you have given me the foundation necessary to live my life fully, no matter what obstacles life throws in my way. You have shown me time and time again that it is always possible to find a way to do the right thing for yourself and for those you love.

We don't say "I love you" much in our culture. That's just the way it is. But you and I know that we have a bond, a tie that nothing can break. Forgive me, Papa, for being my wild, impetuous self, but I must say it, I must shout it out loud so the whole world can hear: "I love you, Papa; I love you very much."

THE END

GLOSSARY

A
anajua (kiSwahili): he or she knows

B
ba___ (kiSwahili): prefix indicating plural (e.g., one person from the Luba tribe is a *muLuba*, two persons from the Luba tribe are *baLuba*)

baba or *ba* (kiSwahili): father; also used as a title of respect for a man who has children; also used with a child's name as a nickname for a father (e.g., Marie's father can be called *baba* Marie)

balozi (kiSwahili): witches

ba-mukwe (kiSwahili): father-in-law

beignets (French): sweet, fried pastry, usually round

bi-mukubwa (kiSwahili): first wife in a polygamous family

bibi or *bi* (kiSwahili): Madame, used as a title of respect for a woman

bikelekele (kiSwahili): joyful noise made by flipping the tongue quickly up and down while moving one or two hands over the mouth *bubela* (Yiddish): pet name for child

bukari (kiSwahili): doughy starch made from cassava and/or corn flour that is dipped into vegetables or meat with sauce and eaten with fingers

bwana (kiSwahili): Mister; sir

C

cachot (French): prison

colon (French): colonist

D

dada or *da* (kiSwahili): sister; female cousin; also used as a title of respect before the name of a sister or female cousin

diamba (kiSwahili): marijuana; hashish

E

(les) évolués (French): the evolved, a colonial and early post-independence era term to describe Congolese who were educated and typically had white collar jobs

G

gendarmes (French): police officers

H

habari (kiSwahili): news; used to ask "What's new?" or "How are you?"

hamjambo (kiSwahili): hello

hodi uku (kiSwahili): a polite way of asking if anyone is at home when knocking at a door

huppah (Hebrew): wedding canopy

J

jambo (kiSwahili): hello

K

kaka or *ka* (kiSwahili): brother; male cousin; also used as a title of
    respect before the name of a brother or male cousin

kalani (kiSwahili): person with a white collar job

kambo (kiSwahili): grandmother or grandfather

kampulumayamba (kiSwahili): the restless one who is always full of
    energy and on the move

kange (kiSwahili): children's game that involves singing and jumping
    up and down

karibu (kiSwahili): welcome

kartel (kiSwahili): Katangese paramilitary thugs during the civil wars
    of the 1960s

L

lenga-lenga (kiSwahili): green vegetable similar to turnip greens

leo (kiSwahili): today

liberté (French): freedom

lipanda (kiSwahili): independence

M

mama or *ma* (kiSwahili): mother; also used as a title of respect for
    older women; also used with a child's name as a nickname for
    a mother (e.g., Marie's mother can be called *mama* Marie)

mambo (kiSwahili): problem; situation

ma-mukwe (kiSwahili): mother-in-law

matembele (kiSwahili): sweet potato leaves that are usually fried after
    being sun-dried

mbaya (kiSwahili): bad; ugly; naughty

mondele (liNgala): white person

mtwangio (kiSwahili): wooden stick about two to three feet long and
    five to ten inches thick that is used for pounding cassava and
    green vegetables in a mortar

mukwe (kiSwahili): son-in-law or daughter-in-law

mulozi (kiSwahili): witch

mutokachini (kiSwahili): someone from the northeastern region of Congo

muyomba (kiSwahili): maternal uncle

muzungu (kiSwahili): white person

N

ndakala or *ndagaa* (kiSwahili): small, sun-dried fish

ngai-ngai (kiSwahili): green vegetable with a bitter taste

P

pagne (French): cloth wrap, approximately 2½ yards long, that Congolese women wear around the lower half of their bodies

S

semeki (liNgala): brother-in-law or sister-in-law

Shabbat (Hebrew): Jewish Sabbath, which lasts from Friday evening until nightfall on Saturday

shangwe (kiSwahili): party; feast

simba (kiSwahili): lion

simbiliki (kiSwahili): a huge rodent that resembles a guinea pig but is twice as big

sombe (kiSwahili): cassava leaves, the most commonly eaten vegetable in Congo

U

uhuru (kiSwahili): Freedom

W

wakambo (kiSwahili): grandparents; senior citizens; ancestors

wake-wenzake (kiSwahili): co-wives in a polygamous family

Y

yaya or *ya* (liNgala): sibling or cousin; also used as a title of respect
   before the name of a sibling or cousin